# Absolute Beginner's Guide

## to

# Home Automation

Mark Edward Soper

800 East 96th Street,
Indianapolis, Indiana 46240

# Absolute Beginner's Guide to Home Automation

## Copyright © 2005 by Que Publishing

International Standard Book Number: 0-7897-3207-6

Library of Congress Catalog Card Number: 2004107076

Printed in the United States of America

First Printing: June 2005

08  07  06  05          4  3  2  1

## Trademarks

All terms mentioned in this book that are known to be trademarks or service marks have been appropriately capitalized. Que Publishing cannot attest to the accuracy of this information. Use of a term in this book should not be regarded as affecting the validity of any trademark or service mark.

## Warning and Disclaimer

Every effort has been made to make this book as complete and as accurate as possible, but no warranty or fitness is implied. The information provided is on an "as is" basis. The author and the publisher shall have neither liability nor responsibility to any person or entity with respect to any loss or damages arising from the information contained in this book.

## Bulk Sales

Que Publishing offers excellent discounts on this book when ordered in quantity for bulk purchases or special sales. For more information, please contact

**U.S. Corporate and Government Sales**
**1-800-382-3419**
**corpsales@pearsontechgroup.com**

For sales outside the United States, please contact

**International Sales**
**international@pearsoned.com**

**Associate Publisher**
Greg Wiegand

**Executive Editor**
Rick Kughen

**Acquisitions Editor**
Todd Green

**Development Editor**
Kevin Howard

**Managing Editor**
Charlotte Clapp

**Project Editor**
Mandie Frank

**Copy Editor**
Mike Henry

**Indexer**
Ken Johnson

**Proofreader**
Kathy Bidwell

**Technical Editor**
Dave Rye
Snr. Vice President/Technical Manager,
X10 (USA) Inc.

**Publishing Coordinator**
Sharry Gregory

**Designer**
Anne Jones

**Page Layout**
Susan Geiselman

# Contents at a Glance

# Table of Contents

# About the Author

**Mark Edward Soper** is president of Select Systems and Associates, Inc., a technical writing and training organization.

Mark is a 22-year veteran of the technology industry. His previous experience in photography, creative writing, and journalism has helped him make high technology useful to everyone.

Mark has taught computer troubleshooting and other technical subjects to thousands of students from Maine to Hawaii since 1992. He is an A+ Certified hardware technician and a Microsoft Certified Professional. Mark's previous books on home technology subjects for Que include *The Complete Idiot's Guide to High-Speed Internet Connections*, *Absolute Beginner's Guide to Cable Internet Connections*, *Easy Digital Cameras*, and *Absolute Beginner's Guide to Home Networking*. Mark is also the author of TechTV's *Upgrading Your PC, Second Edition*, published by another Pearson Technology imprint, Peachpit Press.

Mark coauthored both the first and second editions of *Upgrading and Repairing PCs, Technician's Portable Reference, Upgrading and Repairing PCs Field Guide* (which has been translated into several languages) and *Upgrading and Repairing PCs: A+ Study Certification Guide, Second Edition* with Scott Mueller, one of the world's leading PC hardware experts. Mark also co-authored the original edition of TechTV's *Upgrading Your PC* with Patrick Norton. Mark has been writing technical documents since the mid-1980s and has contributed to many other Que books, including *Upgrading and Repairing PCs* (starting with the 11th edition through the current 16th edition); *Upgrading and Repairing Laptops; Upgrading and Repairing Networks, Second Edition; Special Edition Using Microsoft Windows Millennium Edition; Special Edition Using Microsoft Windows XP Home Edition* (all editions); *Special Edition Using Microsoft Windows XP Professional Edition* (all editions); *Platinum Edition Using Microsoft Windows XP*. Mark has also contributed to *MaximumPC Ultimate PC Performance Guide* and *MaximumPC Guide to Building a Dream PC*.

Mark has been writing for major computer magazines since 1990, with more than 140 articles in publications such as *SmartComputing, PCNovice, PCNovice Guides*, the *PCNovice Learning Series*, and *MaximumPC*. His early work was published in *WordPerfect Magazine, The WordPerfectionist*, and *PCToday*. Many of Mark's articles are available in back issues or electronically via the World Wide Web at www.smartcomputing.com. Mark welcomes comments at mesoper@selectsystems.com.

# Dedication

*This book is dedicated to the memory of Tom Wood (1943–2001). A true home technology enthusiast, he introduced me to the joys of X10 home automation. This book is also dedicated to his wife of many years, Diane Wood, who has encouraged me in my writing career and passed on Tom's home automation hardware and enthusiasm to a new generation.*

# Acknowledgments

First of all, I thank God for the opportunity to write about technology and make it understandable to the average reader.

I thank Cheryl, as always, for putting up with the long hours I spent at the keyboard and for her patience with me as lights turned on and off mysteriously around our house as I experimented with X10 modules.

This book was a new subject for me, and I'm grateful to my first grandson, Jarvis, for reminding me about how exciting it is to discover new worlds of technology. At age two, he's already mastered the art of saying "yight" (his pronunciation of "light"), picking up the X10 remote, and smiling when he finds the right button. He's also good at losing the remote, but that's okay with Grandpa. I'm also thankful that Jarvis, his mother Kate, and father Hugh live nearby so that Jarvis can help me experiment more often.

I want to thank X10 Home Technology, Inc., whose enthusiasm for this project, constructive feedback and hardware helped make this book possible.

I also want to thank Smarthome, whose technical advice and hardware also helped make this book possible.

My association with Que Publishing as a reader goes back more than 20 years to the very beginning of the personal computer age, and as a writer for over 7 years. Now that the PC Age is rapidly being succeeded by the Home Technology Age, I'm delighted to have the opportunity to bring their terrific team with me as we explore making technology useful where you live. In particular, big thanks go to the following folks:

Greg Wiegand, who keeps the Que team pointed in the right direction and fields your questions.

Rick Kughen, who first suggested this subject and kept the dream alive until the right moment.

Todd Green, who helped me bring the topic into sharp focus and kept the project rolling from start to finish.

Kevin Howard, for his excellent suggestions and feedback through the editing process.

Dave Rye, for bringing an insider's expertise to this topic and patiently correcting my early mistakes.

Mike Henry, for editing the copy.

Mandie Frank, for riding herd on those pesky author reviews.

Ken Johnson, for making sure that the index helps you find what you need right away.

Susan Geiselman, for making this book attractive and easy-to-read.

Sharry Gregory, who keeps those payments on track.

The design, illustration, and layout team, who turn my rough sketches into finished artwork and incorporate them into a coherent design. The proofreaders, who extermi-nate any spelling errors that survived my edits.

# We Want to Hear from You!

As the reader of this book, *you* are our most important critic and commentator. We value your opinion and want to know what we're doing right, what we could do better, what areas you'd like to see us publish in, and any other words of wisdom you're willing to pass our way.

As an associate publisher for Que Publishing, I welcome your comments. You can email or write me directly to let me know what you did or didn't like about this book—as well as what we can do to make our books better.

*Please note that I cannot help you with technical problems related to the topic of this book. We do have a User Services group, however, where I will forward specific technical questions related to the book.*

When you write, please be sure to include this book's title and author as well as your name, email address, and phone number. I will carefully review your comments and share them with the author and editors who worked on the book.

feedback@quepublishing.com

Mail:    Greg Wiegand
           Associate Publisher
           Que Publishing
           800 East 96th Street
           Indianapolis, IN 46240 USA

For more information about this book or another Que Publishing title, visit our website at www.quepublishing.com. Type the ISBN (excluding hyphens) or the title of a book in the Search field to find the page you're looking for.

# INTRODUCTION

## Smart Homes for Everyone

Ever since I was a kid growing up in the 1960s watching TV shows like Hanna-Barbera's *The Jetsons* and reading stories such as Ray Bradbury's "There Will Come Soft Rains," the idea of a "smart house" has fascinated me. In some ways, the smart house of the future is already here for many of us:

- TV screens are getting larger and larger.
- Home theater systems combine digital surround sound and better-than-broadcast video.
- Internet access enables us to work from home remotely.

However, in other ways, today's homes are often stuck in the past. In my youth I saw older homes with rotary light switches, relics of a retrofit from gaslight to electricity. Today's homes use toggle or decorator paddle switches, but you still have to walk across the room to turn off a lamp or an overhead light fixture.

Now, just as then, if you're not around to turn off the lights when your kids leave the room, the lights stay on, ripping a hole in the family utility budget. If you forget to turn down the thermostat when you head out for the day or go on vacation, you'll make your utility company very happy. If you're away from home and you don't have somebody keeping an eye on things for you, your vacation or business trip might be frittered away with worry about what might be happening while you're away.

If you're building a brand-new luxury home, many home builders can build-in "smart house" features that provide remote control of lights and appliances, remote control of heating and cooling, and security. But you don't need to be a millionaire to make your home a smart home.

Whether you want to reduce the drudgery of turning off the lights at bedtime, make your home look lived in when you're away, provide extra security for your home and family, or use your home PC as the PC that runs your home, this book is for you. This book shows you how to turn the dream of home automation into a practical reality at minimal cost. From controlling your lights with a wireless remote to equipping your home to call you when there's a problem, this book provides practical advice on buying, installing, and using the most popular home automation standard on the market today, X10. We chose to focus on X10 because of its popularity, low cost, and versatility. However, if you are using another home automation standard such as Z-Wave, UPB, or others, the home automation software programs discussed in Chapters 11 and 12 can be used to create a home automation solution that combines X10, X10-compatible, and non-X10 home automation products.

I have spent many hours in my own home experimenting with many of the products described in this book and countless time researching other products. My goal in writing this book is to make sure that you have a fast track to transforming your home into the smart home you want...today.

Although X10-compatible products have been on the market since 1978, the continued development of new features, new types of home automation products, and the ability to interconnect X10 with other types of whole-house or do-it-yourself home automation standards through computer control make X10 an evergreen technology.

As you'll learn in the following pages, the X10 standard offers a huge universe of home automation possibilities. But the X10 standard often hides behind various brand names. This book shows you how to choose the right home automation products from leading vendors to accomplish practical tasks. If you're looking for Rube Goldberg contraptions, this is not the book for you. But if you're looking for practical advice about how to make your home smarter, friendlier, more economical to run, and even more secure, keep reading!

# How This Book Is Organized

This book contains 12 chapters and two appendices. You don't need to read it cover to cover, but to make the most of it, take a moment and review its basic plan:

- In Part I, "Home Technology Basics," you will learn about major uses for home automation and home automation standards (Chapter 1); the basics of X10, the world's most popular home automation standard (Chapter 2); and how to plan your future home automation projects (Chapter 3).

- In Part II, "Using X10 for Basic Home Automation," you will learn how to use X10 to control home lighting (Chapter 4), appliances (Chapter 5), and how to upgrade your X10 home automation projects with more powerful controllers and timers (Chapter 6).

- In Part III, "Using X10 for Advanced Home Control," you will learn how to use X10 to control central heating and cooling systems and portable fans, heaters, and window air conditioners in your home (Chapter 7); how to control exterior lights, garage lights and outlets, and other landscaping and exterior features (Chapter 8); and how to use X10 to provide home security through motion detectors, video cameras, and alarm systems (Chapter 9).

- In Part IV, "Remote Access to Your X10 Home Control System," you'll learn how to control your home by telephone (Chapter 10), with your home computer (Chapter 11), and remotely via your home network or the Internet (Chapter 12).

To make sure that you're fully equipped to enter the wide (and sometimes wild) world of the X10 home automation standard, I've added two appendices:

■ In Appendix A, "Integrating X10 with Other Home Control Systems," you'll discover which whole-house and non-X10 systems can be added to an X10 installation. You'll also learn the many brand names used for X10-compatible hardware over the years.

■ In Appendix B, "Troubleshooting X10," you'll learn how to bridge X10 signals between different phases of your home wiring, how to boost X10 signal strength, and how to test your X10 installation.

# How to Use This Book

You can read this book in two ways:

■ If you're truly an absolute beginner to home automation, start with the first chapter and keep reading. The early chapters provide essential grounding in home automation concepts, terms, and technology you'll need as you progress.

■ If you've already dipped your feet into the ocean of home automation, feel free to go straight to the chapters that interest you most. I've added a lot of cross-references when they're needed to make sure that you have the help you need when you need it.

Either way, I know you'll have as much fun using this book to help you create a smarter home as I had writing it.

# Conventions Used in This Book

Commands, directions, and explanations in this book are presented in the clearest format possible. The following items are some of the features that make this book easier for you to use:

■ Shortcut to Success—I use this feature to provide tips that make a task easier to complete.

■ Cautions and Warnings—I use this feature to keep you out of trouble when you're performing potentially dangerous or tricky tasks.

■ On the Web—I use this feature to guide you to useful websites that provide more information on the topic or product being discussed.

■ The Big Picture—I use this feature to bring you up to speed on major home automation concepts.

# PART I

# HOME TECHNOLOGY BASICS

1

# UNDERSTANDING HOME TECHNOLOGIES

Home automation technologies bridge the gap between the pushbutton house of the future and the homes we live in today. By adapting the technologies already in your home, home automation enables you to create a more comfortable and more controllable home at the level of expense and sophistication you're comfortable with. If you're unfamiliar with home automation concepts, this chapter is the perfect place to start exploring what you can do.

# Ways to Automate Your Home

The dream of home automation has been with us for at least a century. It has inspired innumerable science-fiction stories, animated cartoons, and "homes of the future" at world's fairs and expositions. Now, home automation is no longer a dream, nor is it restricted to the very rich. Whatever your budget, it's possible to control your home at the push of a button and keep an eye on your home from far away. The following sections introduce you to the many ways you can automate your home—today.

## Lighting Systems

Although electric home lighting has been around for more than 120 years, most homes are still lit using inefficient incandescent light bulbs that differ little from Thomas Edison's pioneering design of 1879(!). Incandescent lighting is inefficient, putting out only 15% of the energy it uses as light and the remaining 85% as heat. This inefficiency hits your wallet every time you pay your electric bill.

Turning off the lights in an unoccupied room is an easy way to reduce the cost of lighting, but if you've ever needed to walk through a couple of rooms to turn off a light, you'll appreciate an easier way. Controlling floor and table lamps remotely is the easiest and cheapest way to try home control. You can also add remote control to built-in lighting if you're comfortable replacing light switches (see Figure 1.1).

**FIGURE 1.1**
You can control table and floor lamps with starter kits for most home automation solutions.

For romance and glamour in your living room, den, or bedroom, you can add dimmer-enabled remote lighting controls or switches if you use incandescent lights. Make room lighting even more controllable by using modules or switches that can store preset dimming levels (scenes) or by using your PC to store macros that can adjust lights to different levels with a single command.

You can also control exterior lights such as accent lighting, garage, or floodlights with a remote control or photocell. Therefore, whether you're concerned about energy savings, mood lighting, safety, or security, home control of lighting should be high on your list of home automation projects to consider.

Learn more about basic and advanced lighting control in Chapter 4, "Using X10 to Control Home Lighting." To learn more about using interior and exterior lighting to enhance home security, see Chapter 9, "Using X10 to Provide Security."

## Appliance Control

Appliances, from air conditioners and fans to radios and TVs, surround us. Some of them have remote controls, but many don't. And even those that have remote controls usually require an unrestricted line-of-sight between you and the appliance. If you're in another room and you want to turn on or turn off your appliance, you have two choices:

- Take a walk
- Add appliance control to your home automation system

You can turn on and turn off appliances remotely by using simple appliance adapters and radio-frequency home control remotes or tabletop controllers, saving steps and making your home more efficient. You can shut off a noisy radio so that you can make a phone call, turn it on when you're done, and much more.

By using temperature sensors, you can automatically turn on a fan or window air conditioner when a room gets too warm, and automatically turn off the same device when the room reaches the desired temperature.

Learn more about adding appliance control to your home automation system in Chapter 5, "Using X10 to Control Appliances," and Chapter 7, "Using X10 to Control HVAC Systems."

## Alarm and Security Systems

When you combine lighting modules with a timer (see Chapter 6, "Using Timers and Advanced Remotes for X10," you can give your home a lived-in look, even when you're away. However, a home automation system can do more than turn lights and appliances on and off: It can provide active security against intruders.

Door and window sensors can alert you to burglars trying to break into your home or kids who are trying to sneak out for after-hours mischief. Motion detectors can keep you informed of trouble in the garage or other normally unoccupied spaces. Compact wireless cameras can show you who's at the door, what's going on in your home office, and whether the motion detector in the garage has spotted a small animal that's running for cover or a car thief driving away with your new SUV. Security devices can also turn on interior or exterior lights when triggered.

To learn more about adding security features to your home automation system, see Chapter 9.

## HVAC Systems

A home automation system can also control your heating, ventilation, and air conditioning (HVAC) systems. By adding temperature sensors around your home and replacing your conventional thermostat with a home automation-compatible model, you can

- Detect problems with heating and cooling
- Adjust home temperature in response to actual weather conditions
- Check and adjust home temperature with a keychain remote control
- Turn on the furnace earlier than usual if you get up early some mornings

Learn more about adding HVAC control to your home automation system in Chapter 7. To learn how to be alerted to heating, flood, or other problems at home via telephone, see Chapter 10, "Accessing X10 Home Control via Telephone."

## Window Control Systems

Home automation systems can also be used to control window and drapery systems. Instead of racing from room to room to let the sunshine in, you can push a button to open draperies and blinds, or to close them before leaving your home or at night.

Window and drapery systems can also be coordinated with room lighting: When you open the draperies or blinds, you can turn off lights in the same room. When you close the blinds, on come the lights. You can even coordinate window blind and lighting control to work on a timed schedule.

## Remote Access

Most home automation systems can be connected to your PC through a serial or USB port. To name only a few possibilities, PC control of home automation enables you to

- Control multiple devices from a single centralized location
- Control multiple devices with a single command (a macro), such as a "breakfast time" macro that starts the coffeemaker, turns off porch lights, turns on the computer, and turns on the radio

- See current home temperature information
- View security cameras and see other security information in your home or remotely via the Internet

Many home automation systems can be connected to your telephone, which enables you to

- Activate devices with a few touch-tone pushbuttons
- Hear current HVAC information and activate heating or cooling if necessary
- Receive security information

By connecting the PC used to control your home automation system to an always-on broadband Internet connection, you can control your home and check its condition from any web browser in the world. If you choose a home automation system that supports touch-tone telephone or voice commands, you can control your home from any telephone.

Learn more about remote access to your X10 system in Part IV, "Remote Access to Your X10 Home Control System," of this book.

# Major Home Automation Standards

There are several current and forthcoming home automation standards. When you purchase home automation products, you need to make sure that the products you purchase are compatible with the home automation products you already use. Some of the major standards are discussed in the following sections.

## X10

X10 is the original home automation system. It uses the AC electric wires in your home to carry signals between remote controls and devices. X10 can be used for virtually any home automation task you want to perform. And because X10 lamp and appliance automation modules (see Figure 1.2) plug between the AC wall socket and the lamp or appliance they control, X10 is easy for almost anyone to install.

---

**X10 AND X10 COMPATIBLE**

Because X10 uses power line signaling, it is sometimes referred to as *PLC (power line control)*. However, it is not the only power line–based home automation standard. Therefore, this book uses the term *X10* to refer to the X10 PLC standard or to hardware made by one of the X10 family of companies. *X10-compatible* is used in this book to refer to products that work with X10 standards, but are made by third-party vendors.

---

**FIGURE 1.2**
A typical X10
lamp module
used with a
table lamp.

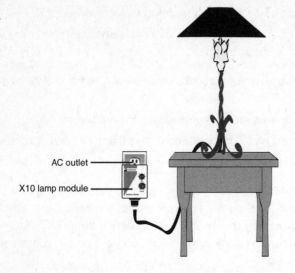

AC outlet

X10 lamp module

However, don't let the apparent simplicity of X10 fool you. If you don't mind changing a few wall outlets or light switches, you can extend X10 control to places and devices where plug-in modules don't work. You can also control heating, cooling, ventilation, and even security features with X10.

Although X10 is a relatively simple system to start with, it has become extremely popular. Most current home automation products, including elaborate whole-house systems that require professional installation, are based on X10 or can be interconnected with X10 through adapters. For more information about third-party systems compatible with X10 and for more about the many brand names X10-compatible products are sold under, see Appendix A, "Integrating X10 with Other Home Control Systems."

Classic X10 is a one-way system, but bidirectional versions of X10, enabling status messages to be sent back to the user, and wireless versions of X10, enabling wireless remote controls and security cameras, are also popular. Although most X10 starter kits include a wireless transceiver and remote control, you can also use a plug-in tabletop controller.

The body of this book covers the use of X10 home automation products.

## Universal Powerline Bus

Universal Powerline Bus (UPB) was developed in 1999 by Powerline Control Systems as a native two-way power line control system. It supports 250 devices per home and uses onboard memory to store configuration information. UPB and X10 can coexist on the same power line. See www.smarthome.com/upb.html, www.webmtn.com/, and www.webmtn.com/ for more information.

Currently available UPB modules include plug-in lamp and appliance-control modules, wall switches, contact closure modules, phase couplers, and desktop controllers. UPB interfaces to PCs via serial (RS-232) and USB ports. Some whole-house controllers such as HomeVision/Home Vision Pro, ELK-M1 Cross Platform Control, and HAI OmniPro II also support UPB.

---

**CHECKING OUT THE WORLD OF UPB**
To learn more about UPB technology and vendors, visit Powerline Control Systems' Pulseworx website at www.pulseworx.com/.

---

## Z-Wave

Z-Wave uses radio frequency (wireless) signals exclusively to communicate between devices and remotes. Z-Wave natively supports two-way signaling, and Z-Wave modules transmit data between modules and the signaling device.

Although Z-Wave devices are not compatible with X10, some PC software used with X10, such as Homeseer (www.homeseer.com) and HALdeluxe (www.automatedliving.com), can also be used to control Z-Wave devices. Although Z-Wave technology was developed by Zensys, Z-Wave devices are sold by Sylvania and HomePro.

---

**CHECKING OUT Z-WAVE**
Learn more about Z-Wave by stopping by the Zensys website: www.zen-sys.com.

---

## Ethernet/Wi-Fi Home Automation Systems

With the increasing popularity of ethernet networking, particularly wireless ethernet (known popularly as *Wi-Fi*), some automation vendors are using ethernet or Wi-Fi as the basis for home automation systems. An ethernet-based system requires you to wire your home with CAT (short for *category*) 5/5e/6 *unshielded-twisted-pair (UTP)* cable—the same cable used for ethernet home and business networks.

If you live in a home built with structured wiring (network/telephone/audio-video cable built into the home at original construction), an ethernet-based home automation system as well as an ethernet-based home network will cost very little to install. However, if you need to run cable through your home, you will need to consider the costs of hiding the cable, running it through walls, and managing it.

A home network can also be used to connect X10-based or other types of home automation systems to a broadband Internet access connection for remote access if the dedicated module or PC-based home automation system includes a web server. A web server provides access to the host's program via a client PC's web browser.

A web browser can be accessed via the Internet or from other computers on the home network. For example, you can enter the IP address of the PC running the home automation program's web server into the web browser of a PC in another room of your home or at a remote site and control your home automation. To learn more about using a web server–enabled home automation program with remote access, see Chapter 12, "Accessing X10 Home Control via Your Home Network and the Internet."

---

**ETHERNET-BASED HOME AUTOMATION ONLINE**

Learn more about Global Cache's GG-100 ethernet-based home automation controller at www.globalcache.com.

Discover the HomeSeer PRO-100 automation controller at www.homeseer.com/products/hardware/pro_series.htm.

Check out Smarthome's PowerLinc IP X10-compatible automation controller at www.smarthome.com/1132IP.html.

---

**MORE ABOUT HOME NETWORKING**

To learn more about both wired and wireless ethernet (Wi-Fi) home networks, see my book *Absolute Beginner's Guide to Home Networks* (Que, 2004).

---

Because of the high cost of wired ethernet home networks, some vendors who offer ethernet-based home automation now support Wi-Fi wireless ethernet. Wi-Fi home automation, like Wi-Fi home networks, can be configured to provide high security and use the 2.4GHz or 5GHz radio frequencies. You can add Wi-Fi support to a device designed for wired ethernet with a Wi-Fi/ethernet bridge.

Unlike X10 and Z-Wave, ethernet-and Wi-Fi–based home automation systems are primarily designed for professional installation. However, you can easily connect most home automation systems to a PC on your home network. For details, see Chapter 11, "Accessing X10 Home Control via Your Home Computer."

## Proprietary Home Automation Products

Home improvement and electronics stores are full of various types of home automation products. However, if you're serious about building a true home automation system, ask yourself these questions:

- Can the home automation product be used as part of a larger system? Many products fail this test.
- Can the home automation product be used with different brands of products? X10-based products and products that include X10 support pass this test with flying colors, but few other types of home automation systems do. In many cases, you might be limited to buying products from a single manufacturer.

If the home automation product you're considering locks you into a single vendor and isn't compatible with standards such as X10, think twice about purchasing it.

# Methods for Controlling Your Home

Home automation systems often offer a wide variety of methods for controlling your home. As you build your home automation system, you can move from the simplest methods (listed first) to more powerful and more costly methods whenever you decide that the additional features are worthwhile.

## Interactive Home Control

The simplest home automation setup, naturally enough, is found in the starter kits sold by many home automation vendors. A typical X10-based home automation kit, for example, consists of a radio frequency remote control, a transceiver that plugs into an AC wall outlet, and some lamp and appliance control modules. Such a starter kit enables you to turn lamps and appliances on and off at the touch of a button (see Figure 1.3).

**FIGURE 1.3**

A typical home automation starter kit for X10 includes a transceiver that can control any X10 module, a remote control, and a lamp module.

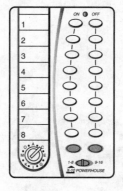

There are limitations to this approach, including these:

- You must control each device individually. For example, if you want to turn on all the lights, you must send the "on" command to each light individually.

- You are limited in the types of devices you can control. For example, the appliance control modules in typical starter kits don't work with three-prong (grounded) appliances or with high-amperage (over 15-amp) appliances.

- Entry-level appliance and lamp modules don't provide feedback. If you can't see whether the lamp or appliance received the command, you don't know for certain that it turned on or turned off as requested.

For more information about setting up a home automation starter kit, see Chapter 2, "Getting Started with X10 Home Automation."

## All Lights On/All Units Off Controllers

The next step you can take in popular home automation systems is to automate a simple operation, such as turning all the lights in the system on with a single command. This feature is common in plug-in X10 remote controls. It works because lamp modules and light switches are designed to respond to an All Lights On command, whereas modules for appliances ignore this command. Even low-cost X10 plug-in remotes usually have this feature, enabling you to improve your home automation for less than $20.

Many controllers with the All Lights On feature also support an All Units Off setting. This feature can turn off appliances as well as lights. Figure 1.4 shows a typical tabletop controller that features All Lights On/All Units Off.

**FIGURE 1.4**

A typical X10 tabletop controller (Maxi Controller) can be used to control groups of modules and supports All Lights On/All Units Off commands.

For more information about the benefits of adding more powerful remote controls to your home automation system, see Chapter 6.

## Timer-Based Control

You can add timers to many home automation systems. A timer enables you to trigger specified devices at a particular time. For example, a timer could automatically turn off the porch lights at bedtime. The next morning, the timer could turn on the coffee maker and, a few minutes later, turn on the lamps in your bedroom as a supplement to, or replacement for, a conventional alarm clock (see Figure 1.5).

**FIGURE 1.5**

Using an X10 timer to trigger devices at a set time for the morning wakeup routine.

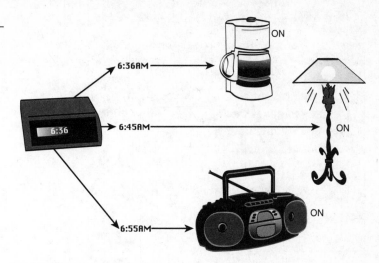

6:36AM → ON

6:36

6:45AM → ON

6:55AM → ON

Some timers also feature a randomization feature that can be used to give an unoccupied home a lived-in look. Some timers double as plug-in remotes with All Lights On and All Units Off features.

For more information about using timers as part of your home automation system, see Chapter 6.

## Photocell-Based Lighting Control

Instead of adding a photocell-based lamp to your home, you can add a photocell detector to some home automation systems and use it to turn on your porch or other lights after dark. Such systems don't interfere with your ability to control the lights by other means, but help you further automate safety and security for your guests. A motion detector that can also be used as a photocell detector is shown in Figure 1.6.

For more information about adding photocell controllers to your home automation system, see Chapter 8, "Using X10 to Control Exterior Landscaping," and Chapter 9.

## Sensor-Based Controls

Photocells aren't the only types of sensors you can use to control your home. Sensors on doorframes and windows can be used to detect motion and trigger security cameras and lights. Temperature sensors can trigger heating or air conditioning, and send an alert to your office phone or email indicating the house or vacation home has a problem.

**FIGURE 1.6**
This motion
detector can also
trigger lights at
dusk.

For more information about using sensors to improve home security, see Chapter 9.
For more information about using sensors to improve home heating, ventilation,
and cooling, see Chapter 7.

## Programmable Devices and Remote Controls

Although you can manually dim any incandescent light connected to even the simplest X10 module, simple modules don't have the capability to store different lighting levels that can be triggered by commands from a remote or tabletop controller.
Scene-capable modules enable you to send a single command to dim or brighten a
lamp to a preset level. By using a PC-based X10 interface and home automation
software, you can create scenes using any X10 module.

To get the most out of programmable devices, you need a remote control capable of
sending X10 codes without sending an on/off signal. Typical wireless remotes send
on/off/dim codes, but more powerful plug-in remote controls such as the one shown
in Figure 1.4 can send codes without sending an On or Off command, enabling you
to program devices that accept, or require, multiple codes.

## Remote Control by Telephone

You can add remote access by telephone to X10 and many other types of home
automation systems. You connect your telephone to a special receiver that connects
to your home automation system, and when you call in, you can use your touch-
tone keypad to send commands just as if you were home with your normal home
automation controller.

Figure 1.7 shows a typical telephone transponder, the X10 Touch Tone Controller.

**FIGURE 1.7**

The X10 Touch Tone Controller can control up to 10 modules remotely or up to 8 modules when used as a tabletop controller.

Some types of telephone access don't require a touch-tone telephone. Instead, they can respond to voice commands. This is useful if you're using a rotary phone or if you're not in a situation where using the keypad is convenient.

For more information about enabling telephone control of your home automation system, see Chapter 10.

## Computer Control

By using timers and scene-capable modules, you can provide a lived-in appearance to your home while you're away by triggering lamps and appliances at specified times. For full control, however, nothing beats using your home PC to control your home automation system. Most home automation systems provide a computer-controlled option in which you connect your computer to an interface module and use software to send commands to your home automation system. Figure 1.8 shows devices and commands created with the Smarthome Manager program.

Commands can be interactive or can be set to run later. Some computer programs even enable you create a home plan that displays your home layout onscreen.

The simplest computer interface modules require that you leave your computer on all the time to control your home. However, more powerful interface modules contain nonvolatile memory and a built-in timer. These devices, such as the Smarthome PowerLinc controller shown in Figure 1.9, can store and run programs when your PC is shut down.

**FIGURE 1.8**

The Smarthome
Manager pro-
gram can down-
load event and
time-triggered
actions such as
those shown
here to a USB or
serial-port con-
troller.

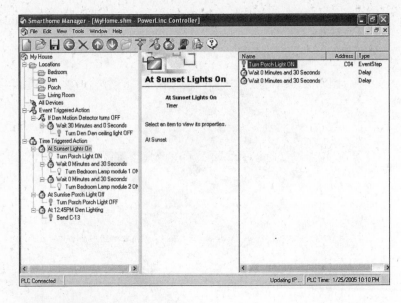

**FIGURE 1.9**

The Smarthome
PowerLinc con-
troller can store
and run pro-
grams created
by Smarthome
Manager or
other home
automation pro-
grams.

For more information about enabling computer control of your home automation
system, see Chapter 11.

# Home Network Control

If you have a home network, you can control your home from any PC on the network. Most home-control software uses a web-browser interface: Open Internet

Explorer, Mozilla Firefox, or any other web browser, enter the IP address of the computer running the home automation program, and check your home's status or make adjustments from any PC in your home (see Figure 1.10).

**FIGURE 1.10**

Using the HomeSeer web server to control bedroom lamps.

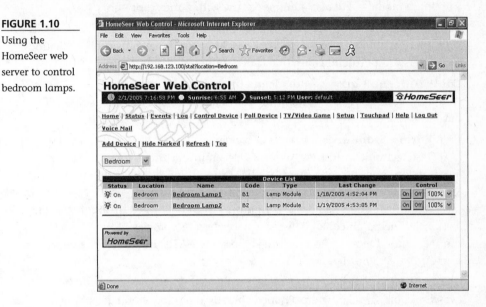

For more information about enabling computer control of your home automation system via your home network, see Chapter 12.

## Remote Control via the Internet

If you have an always-on Internet connection such as DSL or cable, you can use it to provide remote access to many types of home automation systems. The same web-based interface you use at your PC (refer to Figure 1.10) can be used remotely to configure or check the status of your home automation system. Some vendors provide a proprietary client instead of a web server. Note that not all home automation computer programs support remote access.

For more information about enabling computer control of your home automation system via the Internet, see Chapter 12.

# Home Technology Glossary

Home automation and technology can be a little overwhelming if you're an absolute beginner. The terms in this section appear frequently in this book, so use this section as a cheat sheet to get up to speed.

**AC**—Alternating current. X10 and other PLC-based home automation standards use the AC wiring in your home to send and receive commands.

**Appliance module**—A module for X10, Z-wave, and other home automation systems that supports appliances. An appliance module differs from a lamp module in its capability to handle an electrical load and its inability to support dimming. Appliance modules are also suitable for use with fluorescent lights.

**Broadband Internet access**—Internet access that provides download speeds over 200Kbps and upload speeds over 100Kbps. Most forms, such as cable, DSL, and recent versions of satellite, don't tie up your phone line.

**Cable (Internet) access**—Broadband Internet access provided by your cable TV company. Most services provide peak download rates of over 2Mbps (2,000Kbps), but the speed varies with number of users.

**CAT Wiring Standards**—A series of copper wiring grades specified by the EIA/TIA (Electronic Industries Alliance/Telecommunications Industry Association) 568 standard and the equivalent ISO/IEC (International Organization for Standardization/International Electrotechnical Commission) 11801 standard. To meet a particular CAT standard, wiring runs must be limited to 100 meters (328 feet) including patch cables between devices and receptacles. Wiring, patch cables, connectors, and receptacles must meet the same CAT standard for the network to support that standard.

**CAT1**—Short for *Category 1 UTP cable*. Unshielded untwisted-pair or twisted-pair two-wire cable, also known as Phone cable. Used in older home telephone installations. Also called *Grade 1*. Obsolete.

**CAT2**—Short for *Category 2 UTP cable*. Two-pair (four-wire) unshielded twisted-pair cable based on IBM's Type 3 specification for Token-Ring 4Mbps networking, but also used for ARCNET networks and some phone systems. Also called *Grade 2*. Obsolete.

**CAT3**—Short for *Category 3 UTP cable*. Two-pair (four-wire) unshielded twisted-pair cable supporting maximum speeds of 16Mbps. Supports 10Base-T, 100Base-T4, and 100Base-T2 Ethernet networks. Obsolete.

**CAT4**—Short for *Category 4 UTP cable*. Two-pair (four-wire) unshielded twisted-pair cable supporting maximum speeds of 20Mbps. Supports 10Base-T, 100Base-T4, and 100Base-T2 Ethernet networks. Obsolete.

**CAT5**—Short for *Category 5 UTP cable*. Four-pair (eight-wire) unshielded twisted-pair cable supporting transmission at frequencies up to 100MHz. May be used with 10Base-T, 100Base-T4, 100Base-T2, and 100Base-TX Ethernet (Fast Ethernet). May support 1000Base-T (Gigabit Ethernet), but cable should be tested for compliance. Superseded by Cat5e.

**CAT5e**—Enhanced version of CAT5 exceeds CAT5 performance. May be used with 10Base-T, 100Base-T4, 100Base-T2, 100Base-TX Ethernet (Fast Ethernet), and 1000Base-T (Gigabit Ethernet). Features improved specifications to reduce power loss, interference, and crosstalk between wires. CAT5e can be used in place of CAT5. CAT5e is the minimum standard for new construction.

**CAT6**—Enhanced version of CAT5e supporting signal speeds up to 200MHz. Supports same networks as CAT5e and can be used in place of CAT5e. Designed to support proposed 1000-BaseTX network standard.

**Controller**—Device that sends commands to receivers in a home automation system.

**Dimmer**—A switch or control that can dim lights. Incandescent and similar types of lighting can be dimmed when controlled by a lamp module. Some light switches support local as well as remote dimming.

**DSL**—*Digital subscriber line*. DSL is a form of broadband Internet that uses your telephone line. Download speeds generally reach 384Kbps to 1500Kbps or higher, depending upon service level, but are more consistent than cable.

**Ethernet**—A form of home and small-business networking that uses CAT3 (10Mbps) or CAT5/5e/6 (100Mbps and faster) to carry data.

**Fluorescent light**—A form of household lighting that uses glowing gas in a tube. Use appliance modules or appliance-rated light switches to control this type of lighting.

**Gateway**—A device or computer that provides Internet access on a home network. The most common type of gateway is a router.

**Ground wire**—The wire (often bare) used to connect an electrical outlet's third prong to a ground source (such as the earth).

**Grounded outlet**—A three-prong outlet; the third outlet is tied to ground (earth) for better electrical quality. Some three-prong outlets in older homes might not be connected to ground. Use an outlet tester to verify ground and proper wiring.

**Group**—Two or more X10 or other PLC modules that are set to the same house and unit code so that they can be triggered by the same command. You might want to group front and back porch lights together, for example.

**HomePlug**—A home networking standard that sends data at up to 14Mbps between computers and routers or other devices. The HomePlug standard can coexist with DSL and X10.

**House code**—A code from A–P on an X10 module, transceiver, or remote control. All devices using the same house code can be controlled by a remote set to that house code.

**Hub (ethernet)**—A simple device for connecting computers or other devices on an ethernet network. A hub has an RJ-45 port for each device connected to it with CAT3, CAT, or better cable types. Hubs have been largely replaced by switches.

**HVAC**—*Heating, ventilation, and air conditioning*; your home heating and cooling system.

**Incandescent light**—Light source that uses a glowing wire within a vacuum-sealed glass bulb. Incandescent lights can be controlled and dimmed with a lamp module.

**IR**—*Infrared*. Also a remote control standard used by TVs and other home entertainment systems. Some X10 remote controls also support IR functions so that a single remote can be used to run home entertainment and X10 functions.

**ISP**—*Internet service provider*. An ISP is an organization that connects subscribers to the Internet via dial-up or broadband service.

**Kbps**—Kilobits per second. Used to rate transmission speed of Internet and network signals. 1000Kbps = 1Mbps.

**Keypad**—A type of controller used with X10 and other types of home automation systems. Keypads can be connected to your home wiring or use RF signaling. Some keypads can be programmed, whereas others provide simple on/off/dim commands.

**Lamp module**—A type of home automation module that supports incandescent lighting, including dimming. Not designed for use with motors, appliances, fluorescent lights, or other types of electrical devices.

**LAN**—*Local area network*. A LAN is any two or more computers that share an Internet connection or other resources (printer, disk drive, and so on). A home network is one example of a LAN.

**Line**—The wire that carries voltage through an AC outlet. The line wire is also called the *hot* wire or live wire.

**Load**—The wire that does not carry voltage through an AC outlet. The load wire is also called the *switched hot* wire. To determine line and load wires, use a voltage sensor as described in Chapter 4.

**Local control**—The ability to turn on a lamp or appliance connected to an X10 appliance module or outlet. If you want to prevent a user from controlling the lamp or appliance without using an X10 controller or remote, use a module or outlet that does not support local control.

**Macro**—A single command that triggers a series of commands. For example, a home automation macro called "movies" might turn off the lights in the den, dim the lights in adjoining rooms, turn on the TV and DVD player, and turn on the coffeemaker in the kitchen for refreshments. Use a programmable controller or a PC interface with home-control software to create macros.

**Mbps**—Megabits per second. Mbps is used as a measurement of broadband Internet access and home network performance. 1Mbps = 1,000Kbps.

**Neutral**—The wire (usually white) in light-switch wiring standards. The neutral wire is required for switches used to control appliances, fluorescent lights, low-voltage lights, and ceiling fans. Some two-way X10-compatible dimmer switches also require the neutral wire. Some switch boxes do not have a neutral wire, but it is present in all electrical outlets.

**One-way module**—An X10 lamp or appliance module that can receive, but not send, signals.

**Outlet tester (AC)**—A device that plugs into an AC outlet to determine whether the outlet has power and whether it is wired correctly.

**PLC technology**—A general term for any automation system that uses power line control, such as X10 and others.

**Power-over-Ethernet (PoE) technology**—A technology that enables CAT5/5e/6 cable to carry power to an ethernet device such as a router or switch that does not have a nearby AC power source.

**Programmable controller**—Any controller that can store a sequence of commands (macros) or timed events for later playback. The term is also used to refer to remote controls used to program macros.

**Receiver**—An X10 device that receives signals, such as an appliance or lamp module, light switch, or outlet.

**Relay**—The type of switching mechanism used in X10 appliance modules or outlets. Relays make a loud noise when the device connected to the module or outlet is turned on or off. Some modules and outlets use quieter-than-normal relays.

**RF**—*Radio frequency*. RF also refers to any device that uses radio waves to receive signals. RF is often referred to as *wireless*.

**Router**—A network device that connects one network (such as a LAN) to another network (such as the Internet).

**RS-232**—A serial interface standard supported by older types of home automation computer interfaces.

**RS-485**—A different serial interface standard that's well-suited to use in home automation for carrying signals between controlled devices connected to a centralized control module. Uses CAT5/5e/6 cable. RS-485 interfacing for thermostats and other types of devices is supported by whole-house controllers such as JDS Stargate, ELK Magic Module, and RCS CommStar among others.

**Scene lighting**—A type of lighting in which lamp control modules and switches dim at different rates depending upon the scene. Modules must support stored programs or be controlled by a PC.

**Switch (ethernet)**—A device that has an RJ-45 port for each ethernet device connected to it. A switch provides faster performance than a hub. Switches are often built into routers.

**Three-prong**—A grounded outlet. An appliance module that supports grounded devices uses a three-prong outlet.

**Transceiver**—A home automation device that sends and receives signals.

**Transmitter**—A home automation device, such as a remote control, that sends signals.

**Triac**—Type of control used in lamp modules and switches that support dimming.

**Two-phase wiring**—Common type of wiring used in homes. Signals travel from one phase to the other through the transformer servicing the home, which can cause reliability problems with X10 and similar PLC systems.

**Two-prong**—Ungrounded outlet. Most low-cost lamp and appliance modules don't support grounded devices.

**Two-way**—A lamp or appliance module or switch that can send and receive information. All Z-wave modules are two-way and act to relay information to each other. However, most X10 modules are one-way devices.

**Unit code**—Codes from 1–16 used on X10 modules, switches, and outlets. All unit codes that use the same house code can be controlled by the same remote.

**UTP**—*Unshielded twisted-pair* cabling. UTP cable is used for telephone and Ethernet networks.

**Voice recognition**—A type of home automation control that recognizes key phrases uttered by the user through a remote telephone, a local telephone, or a microphone connected to the computer running the home automation program.

**WAP**—*Wireless access point*; a device on a Wi-Fi network that connects stations to each other. A Wi-Fi network must use a WAP (which can be integrated with a router) to obtain Internet access.

**Wi-Fi**—Wireless ethernet; specifically applied to devices that have passed tests by the Wi-Fi Alliance for operability with other brands of devices.

**Wireless**—Any type of signaling that does not use a wire, such as radio frequency (RF).

**X10 coupler**—A device that plugs into a 220-volt outlet or an electrical panel to provide a direct signal path for X10 signals. An X10 coupler improves the reliability of signal transmission between wiring phases.

**X10 filter**—A device that helps prevent interference with X10 signals.

**X10 signal bridge**—Refer to **X10 coupler**.

**X10 standard**—The standard for PLC control supported by X10.com and many other companies. X10 devices use house and unit codes.

**Z-wave**—A wireless rival to X10 offering fewer device options.

# THE ABSOLUTE MINIMUM

- Home automation can be used to control lighting systems for energy savings, convenience, and safety.

- Appliance control provides more convenient operation of noisy appliances and the ability to pause some operations.

- Home automation enables alarm and security systems to interact with home lighting or other features to enhance security.

- HVAC monitoring and control enables you to override normal furnace operation from your bedside and monitor and control temperature remotely if desired.

- Window control systems can control draperies interactively or on a time-delay or program basis.

- Remote access solutions for home automation systems include telephone, home computer with Internet access, and home networking.

- X10 is the oldest, one of the simplest, and one of the most complete home automation systems.

- UPB is another power line control system that is not as widely supported as X10, but can coexist with it.

- Z-wave is an all-wireless home automation system that does not support as wide a range of equipment.

- Home networks based on standards such as ethernet, Wi-Fi wireless ethernet, and others can also support home automation.

- To be assured of satisfaction in your home automation quest, look for standards with wide support, especially from multiple vendors.

- Simple home control uses a handheld or tabletop remote to directly interact with lights and appliances.

- Timer-based controls automate operation of devices at set times.

- Photocell and sensors can control devices based on lighting conditions, temperature, and other factors.

- Some home automation modules can store programs for later operation, but most must be controlled by an external device.

2

# GETTING STARTED WITH X10 HOME AUTOMATION

The de facto home-automation standard for do-it-yourself home control is X10. More than 5 million homes have X10 devices installed, and more than 100 million X10 devices have been shipped—numbers that far exceed any other home automation technology. As discussed in Appendix A, "Integrating X10 with Other Home Control Systems," X10 hardware is sold under many brand names. This chapter introduces you to the wide-ranging world of X10 home automation and shows you how easy it is to start automating your home with a typical X10 starter kit.

# What X10 Can Control

Although X10 is a simple system to install (as you'll learn later in this chapter), it can be used to control most electrical appliances in your home, such as the following:

- Interior and exterior lighting
- Heating and cooling (HVAC) systems
- Electrical appliances of all types
- Portable heating and cooling devices
- Hot tubs and spas

X10 devices can also work with security systems, which include

- Alarms
- Motion detectors
- Security cameras

Using X10 home automation has many benefits:

- Control lights anywhere in your home at the touch of a button
- Dim and brighten lights on command for an elegant mood when entertaining
- Provide safety and security outdoors and indoors with motion-triggered or timed lights and security cameras
- Turn on and turn off lights and appliances at random times when you're out of the house to give your home a lived-in look
- Control lights, appliances, and other electrical devices remotely via touch-tone telephone, home network, or broadband Internet connections

Whether you need to improve safety and security, reduce the cost of heating and cooling, put in elegant lighting, or just add convenience, X10 home automation can do it.

# Why Use X10 for Home Control?

As compared to other systems, X10 offers quite a few advantages for home control:

- You can install many parts of the X10 system by yourself. You don't need an electrician to install X10 control for floor or table lamps or for small home appliances.
- X10 products are inexpensive: You can purchase an X10 starter kit for less than $30. Control modules for lamps start at less than $15, and modules for use with many other appliances and devices are also reasonably priced.

- X10 is a modular system: You can buy what you need when you need it. You can add additional control modules when you want to control additional devices. Although you can save money by purchasing kits from some vendors, you can also buy individual components to customize your home-automation system to meet your exact needs.

- X10 can be controlled on a time basis. You can use a Mini Timer to trigger individual devices at specified or random times—wake up to bright room lights instead of a blaring alarm clock.

- X10 can be operated remotely. You can control X10 appliances through your telephone by installing a touch-tone controller that connects to your telephone line and your X10 system. You can also control X10 remotely through your home computer if you have a broadband Internet connection.

- X10 can be programmed. By using a home computer to interface with your X10 system, you can create macros that can trigger multiple events.

---

**X10 AND YOUR ELECTRICAL SYSTEM**

X10 uses signals transmitted via your home's AC wiring. So, anywhere you have an AC wall socket, you can add an X10-controlled device. If your garage or workshop connects to the same electrical service as your home, you can use the same X10 system to activate lights and other options there as you use in your home.

---

# How X10 Systems Work

An X10 system has two basic components:

- A **module** that receives signals from the X10 transceiver through your home's AC wiring and controls the device connected to it. Figure 2.1 illustrates a typical lamp module used with incandescent table or floor lamps. Modules can also be wired into the AC wiring (switches or outlets) or built into a device. Because X10 signals are transmitted through AC wiring, X10 is also sometimes referred to as *power line control (PLC)*.

- A **controller** that sends X10 signals to the module.

There are three major types of controllers. Many X10 starter kits include a **transceiver** that plugs into an AC outlet (see Figure 2.2), receives signals from a wireless **remote control** (see Figure 2.3), and sends X10 commands to the modules.

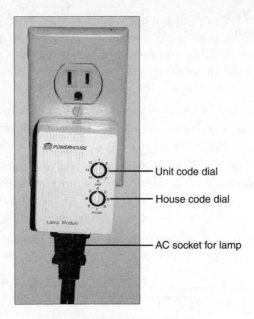

Unit code dial

House code dial

AC socket for lamp

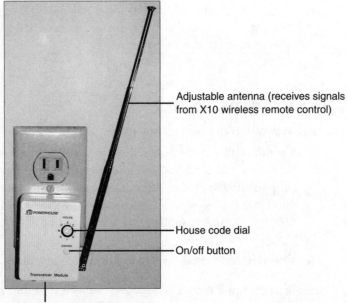

Adjustable antenna (receives signals
from X10 wireless remote control)

House code dial

On/off button

AC socket for lamp or appliance

You can also purchase various types of **tabletop controllers** that plug directly
into an AC outlet (see Figure 2.4). Both types of controllers can be used in an X10
system. You can also use a universal remote control, which sends infrared (IR) and
X10 wireless signals. This type of controller can be used with home entertainment
devices and X10 home automation systems (again see Figure 2.4).

**FIGURE 2.3**

Typical X10 wireless remote controls. The smaller unit can control two devices.

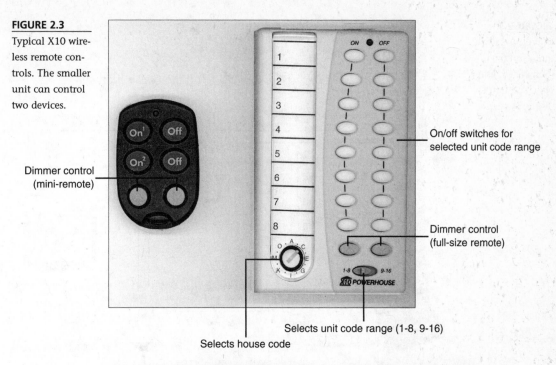

Dimmer control (mini-remote)

On/off switches for selected unit code range

Dimmer control (full-size remote)

Selects unit code range (1-8, 9-16)

Selects house code

**FIGURE 2.4**

A typical X10 tabletop Maxi Controller (left) and a universal X10 wireless/IR remote control (right).

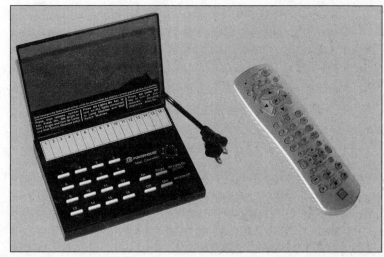

Figure 2.5 shows how wired and wireless X10 controllers can be used to control X10 modules.

**FIGURE 2.5**

A typical X10 home automation system using wired and wireless controllers.

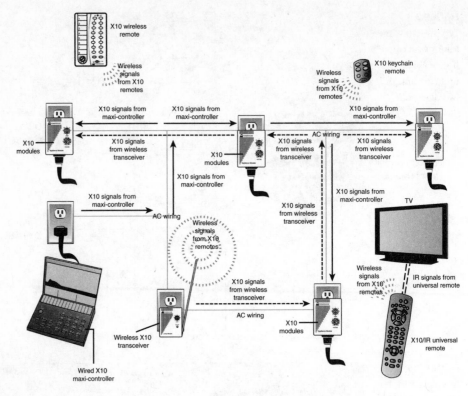

## LAMP AND APPLIANCE MODULES

X10 lamp modules are designed for use with incandescent lamps only. They can be used to dim incandescent lamps, but lack the capability to handle electrical loads caused by appliances, fluorescent, or other types of lamps. Use appliance modules for devices other than incandescent lamps (they also work with incandescent lamps, but don't support dimming). X10 wireless transceivers incorporate an appliance module.

A **module** has two settings: a house code and a unit code (refer to Figure 2.6). Each module in an X10 network must have a unique unit code, whereas all devices and the controller must have the same house code. When you install X10 modules and a controller, you select the house code you want to use for the system, and select a unique unit for each module.

## YOUR TRANSCEIVER IS ALSO AN APPLIANCE MODULE

Transceivers can also act as appliance modules. The TM751 illustrated in Figure 2.2 has a fixed unit code of 1, whereas the RR501 has a sliding switch used to select unit code 1 or 9. To control a device with a transceiver, plug the device into the AC outlet on the bottom of the transceiver.

Appliance modules can also be used with lamps, but don't support dimming.

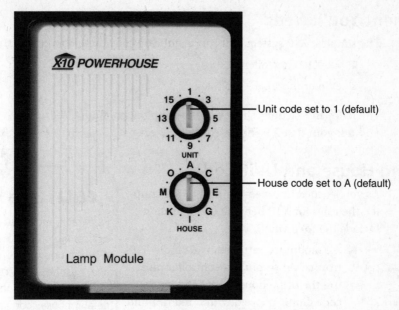

## A Technical Look at What Makes X10 Work

X10 works over your home AC power lines. In North America, alternating current (AC) current works by fluctuating 60 times a second between 120V+ and 120V-. In other parts of the world, the voltage (240V) and cycle times (50 times a second) are different, but the principle is the same. During the cycle, voltage periodically reaches zero. This *zero crossing point* is the time window (200 milliseconds long) at which X10 signals are sent and received. An X10 signal is a 5V, 120kHz pulse sent during the zero crossing point. The pulse is coded to carry house and unit codes and commands (on, off, dim, bright).

Surge suppressors interfere with this signal, which is why X10 modules, transceivers, and tabletop controllers should not be plugged into a surge suppressor.

Now that you understand the basic elements of an X10 home-control system and what makes it work, it's time to show you how to set up a simple X10 system.

# Setting Up a Simple X10 System

Although X10 can be used to control most electrical devices in your home, you can begin your exploration of what X10 can do very simply. I suggest that you start by automating a floor or table lamp and a portable appliance such as a fan. The components in a typical X10 starter kit work with these devices, and you have instant feedback: You'll see the lights and fan turn on and off at the touch of a button.

## Equipment You'll Need

The simplest X10 system you can install contains these components:

■ An X10 controller

■ One or more X10 modules

The following sections show you how to plan, configure, set up, and test your first X10 home-control project.

## Selecting House and Unit Codes

As you learned in an earlier part of the chapter, the rules for X10 network configuration include the following:

■ All modules controlled by a single X10 transceiver or plug-in controller must use the same house code. The house code dial is marked with a red rim and has positions from A–P.

■ The transceiver or plug-in controller must be configured to use the same house code as the modules that it controls.

■ The remote control must be configured to use the same house code as the transceiver and modules.

■ Each module you want to control independently must use a unique unit code. These unit codes need not be

> **caution**
>
> By default, most X10 devices are preset to use A as the house code and 1 as the device code. You should change the default house code to make it more difficult for another user to control your devices. For example, you wouldn't want a nosy neighbor to turn all your lights on at midnight. (X10, unlike computer-based home networks, doesn't offer any signal encryption.) Don't put more than one device on the same device code unless you want them turned on or turned off at the same time.

sequential. The unit code dial is marked with a black rim and has positions from 1–16. If you want two or more devices to work with a single command, you can assign each of them the same unit code. Even if you are starting out with just a lamp module or two in your X10 configuration, you should record your X10 configuration using a simple chart like this:

House code B

Lamp module unit code 2

Appliance module unit code 3

Transceiver unit code 1

Most wireless remote controls and tabletop controllers have a space for recording unit codes and module descriptions, or you can put your notes on removable tape.

# Configuring the Components

To configure your X10 devices, follow this procedure:

1. After you've decided what house code and unit codes to use, use a coin or small straight-blade screwdriver to set the house code and unit codes on each device.

2. Make sure that the lamp or other device you want to use is turned on.

3. Plug a lamp into a lamp module; plug a lamp or other device into an appliance module.

4. Plug the lamp or appliance module into an AC wall outlet.

5. If you use a transceiver and you want it to control another lamp or an appliance, plug the lamp or appliance into the transceiver. Check the transceiver's amperage rating (see rear of module) to determine what you can plug into the transceiver. Check the documentation to determine what unit code(s) it supports.

6. Set the house code (and unit codes, if necessary) on your remote control or tabletop controller. Some remote controls, such as the larger one shown in Figure 2.3, use a round dial for house codes and have preset buttons for unit codes. Other remote controls, such as the small keychain remote also shown in Figure 2.3, store house and unit codes in battery-backed memory. Keep in mind that you must reprogram the house and unit codes when you replace the battery in a keychain remote. A tabletop controller also has preset buttons for unit codes.

Figure 2.7 illustrates correctly and incorrectly configured devices.

**FIGURE 2.7**

The remote control can control the transceiver and one lamp module because all three are set to house code C. The tabletop plug-in controller can control the other lamp module because both are set to house code A.

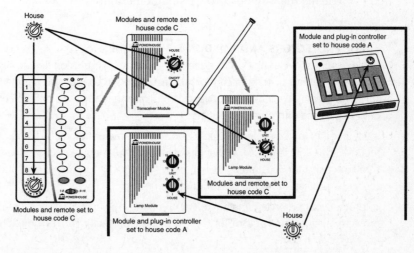

---

**LOCAL CONTROL AND X10**

Most X10 modules support a feature called local control. Local control enables you to turn on and turn off a device plugged into an X10 module without using the remote. Keep in mind that if you use the device's own on/off switch to turn off the device, you can't turn it on again with X10. You will need to turn on the device, use X10 to turn off the device, and then turn it on again with X10.

---

# Testing the System

To test your first X10 installation, do the following:

1. Make sure that the lamp or appliance plugged into each X10 module or transceiver has its on/off switch turned on.

2. Make sure that the transceiver or tabletop controller is securely plugged into an AC outlet.

3. Press the On button corresponding with the unit code of the device to turn it on. If you use a tabletop controller that utilizes separate unit codes and On/Off buttons, press the unit code button and then the On button to turn on the device.

4. If the device doesn't come on, make sure that the switch on the device is set properly. For example, a three-way lamp might be turned off, or on low, medium, or high. If the device is turned off, refer to the "Local Control and X10" sidebar earlier in this chapter.

   When the lamp or other device comes on, congratulate yourself. You've entered the world of X10 home automation!

---

**SURGE PROTECTORS AND X10 DON'T ALWAYS MIX**

Surge suppressors can block X10 signals. If you plug an X10 module into a surge suppressor, you might not be able to control it unless a plug-in controller is plugged into the same surge suppressor. A plug-in controller or transceiver might not be able to control other devices plugged into other AC outlets.

If you need to employ a surge suppressor on the same outlet you're using for an X10 module, avail yourself of an X10 appliance (not lamp) module with a three-prong pass-through connector (illustrated in Chapter 5, "Using X10 to Control Appliances") and plug the surge protector into the pass-through connector.

To protect your home and maintain X10 compatibility, you can get a panel-mount surge protector such as the Leviton 51120-1. This surge protector is X10 compatible. Learn more at www.leviton.com.

---

# Troubleshooting Your First X10 Installation

If you're having problems with your first X10 installation, check the following:

- Make sure that you are using the same house code on all modules and controllers (tabletop, transceiver, remote) in your system.

- Make sure that you know which module is set to a particular unit code.

- Make sure that the house and unit code dials are turned to the desired position. For example, a dial set partway between house codes A and B, or between unit codes 1 and 2 isn't going to work.

- If you use a keychain remote, make sure that you follow the directions for configuring it. Instead of using house and unit code dials, you must push buttons in particular sequences to store the house and unit codes you want the keychain remote to control. If you have problems, remove and replace the batteries to purge onboard memory and start over again.

- Make sure that the transceiver or plug-in controller is plugged securely into the AC outlet (*not* a surge suppressor).

- Try a different outlet for the transceiver or plug-in controller if you can't control some or all of your modules.

- If one particular device won't turn on when commanded, it might be turned off with its own on/off switch. Refer to the "Local Control and X10" sidebar earlier in this chapter for help.

# THE ABSOLUTE MINIMUM

- X10 can control lighting, security, appliances, HVAC, and most other electrical devices.

- X10 systems can be builtup gradually with additional components.

- X10 uses your home's AC house wiring to control devices by sending coded pulses.

- A basic X10 system includes one or more device modules and a controller. This can be a plug-in tabletop controller or a transceiver to pass commands to device modules, and a remote control to control device modules.

- X10 systems are configured with two settings: a house code and a unit code.

- Each device using the same house code can be controlled by a remote control set to the same house code.

- House codes range from A–P.

- Unit codes range from 1–16.

- Problems with X10 can be caused by incorrect house and unit code settings, loose or disconnected transceivers or plug-in controllers, and interference from surge suppressors.

# 3

# STRATEGIES FOR ADDING HOME TECHNOLOGY FEATURES

Because do-it-yourself home automation standards such as X10 are so easy to build up, it's all too easy to start buying X10 equipment and find yourself sitting on a pile of equipment with no clear idea of what to do with it; or, worse, a pile of equipment that might not be the best choice for your home. This chapter helps you harness your enthusiasm by showing you how to plan your automation projects, budget for them, and it points you in the right directions to get started.

# Determining Your Home Automation Budget

Budgets are an important part of any project, but let's face it: It's easier to develop a budget for a task you're already familiar with. If you're an experienced wood-worker, for example, you probably won't worry about making a budget for your next cabinet or table. However, if you're new to home automation (and you proba-bly are!), building a home automation budget might strike you as a bit more diffi-cult than building a budget for a more familiar subject.

If you want to get the most bang for your buck, I suggest this strategy for your home automation budget:

1. Decide what you want to automate.

2. Decide how much you want to spend.

3. Decide how you want to control it.

4. Decide what features you must have, what features you'd like to have, and what features don't matter.

5. Look for versatile components that can do more than one job if your needs change over time.

6. Consider add-ons and accessories that will help you get the job done right.

7. Don't forget to budget the time needed for each task. Although some X10 automation devices are as easy to install as plugging them into the wall, others require rewiring or programming.

8. If the answer to step 1 is "automate my whole house" or "automate my life," break down your project by room or task and create a budget for each project.

Let's look at each of these steps in order.

## Selecting Where to Start

Automating your entire home is a big project. It's easy to be overwhelmed by the sheer size of controlling the lights, adding security devices, HVAC (heating, ventila-tion, and air conditioning) controls, and so forth. Instead, turn your dream of home automation into a reality by dividing your master plan into sections. You can do this by

■ Automating room by room
■ Automating task by task

## Automating on a Room-by-Room Basis

If you decide that you want to automate a particular room, you first need to decide what to automate. Some possible answers might include

- Lights
- Appliances
- Draperies
- Fans
- Security

The list of possible automation subjects for even a single room can be a long and somewhat complex one. To automate every possible task in a single room would involve a lot of different types of X10 modules, some specialized devices, a fair amount of expense, and some potential for problems. It might be better, especially if you plan to do the entire project yourself and have a limited budget, to automate particular tasks. This, in fact, is the approach I took in automating my home.

## Automating on a Task-by-Task Basis

If you decide to automate on a task-by-task basis, your list of potential starting points might look like this one:

- Lighting control
- Appliance control
- HVAC
- Security
- Outdoor lighting
- Outdoor devices

The lists are similar, but by focusing on a single type of automation throughout your home, every part of your home can enjoy automation, and you might find the installation and setup process to be easier as well.

For many home automation beginners, lighting is the most obvious first project to tackle. But, no matter what you decide to tackle first, you have a few more decisions to make.

## Evaluating Products and Price Ranges

As with many other home improvement and electronics endeavors, X10 has a low entry cost: You can pick up a basic home automation kit for less than $30. However, it's also true that the sky's the limit. If you decide to go with top-of-the line two-way dimmer switches, for example, you can spend hundreds of dollars just to control lighting in your home. Consequently, as you decide *what* to automate, decide *how much to spend* on automation.

Before you specify a particular dollar figure, spend a few minutes looking over some of the premier X10 online stores such as X10.com and Smarthome.com. Take a look at starter kits, individual components, and bundles. If you're considering lighting for your first project, you'll probably develop a list of possibilities that looks something like Table 3.1. The prices in Table 3.1 are in U.S. dollars.

**TABLE 3.1**  Price Ranges for Typical X10 Lighting Projects

| Price Range | Components | Limitations | Upgrades |
|---|---|---|---|
| Less than $50 | Basic one-room automation (lamp, appliance, remote) | Most modules don't include two-way features or scene storage; check wattage ratings carefully for large fixtures | Scene-enabled modules; three-prong modules; additional remote controls |
| $50–$100 | Two-way automation for two lamps, dimmer switches for one or two lamps; timer or Maxi Controller | Check wattage ratings carefully for large fixtures | X10 computer module and msoftware; scene lighting option for modules |
| $100–$250 | Scene lighting for several lamps, computer control | — | |

Table 3.2 is a similar table, but it's blank. Use it as a model for building your own price-range estimator for your preferred X10 home automation solution. You might want to leave this form alone until you've finished this chapter, or even the entire book, but don't worry: Whenever you want to use it, it'll be waiting right here for you.

**TABLE 3.2**  Blank Template for an X10 Home Automation Project

| Price Range (A) | Components (B) | Vendors (C) | Limitations (D) | Upgrades (E) |
|---|---|---|---|---|
| | | | | |

Project Goal: _____

_____

Location: _____

In column A (Price Range), put down a range of prices for your project from low to high. In column B (Components), list the components you'd need for the job you want to do. In column C, Vendors, jot down the vendor name and contact information (website, phone). In column D (Limitations), write down the real-world limitations of the devices in this row. In column E (Upgrades), record what types of devices or what features you'd prefer to get if possible. Why use Column E? You might find a deal on a discontinued, open-box, overstock, or auction device that has the upgrade features you want for less money than your original selection!

---

**LIMITATIONS IN THE REAL WORLD**

If you use Table 3.2 as a planning sheet for your X10 project, keep in mind that Limitations (column D) isn't meant for listing all the features that device X doesn't have, but rather only a feature that device X would need *to meet your needs* that it doesn't have. For example, when I installed X10 light switches to control my porch lights, I chose low-cost nondimming switches. Although they don't dim or support other advanced features, it's not a limitation in this case because all I want them to do is turn on and turn off on command. However, I chose a two-way dimmer switch for my bedroom because I want dimming and scene features there.

---

## Deciding on a Control Method

After you've decided on what you want to control and how much you want to spend, you should decide on a control method or methods. X10 was originally 100% electric-wire-controlled; the wireless remotes popular in many starter kits were introduced later. Table 3.3 compares the prices and features of some typical X10 controllers; see Figure 3.1 for a visual comparison.

### **TABLE 3.3**   Sample X10 Controller Features and Price Ranges

| Controller Type | Sample Product | Price Range | Features | Limitations | Alternatives |
|---|---|---|---|---|---|
| Wired Mini Controller | Smarthome Mini Controller | $11 | All lights on/all devices off; dim/bright; 8 devices | Can't send house/unit codes for programming some types of modules | Wireless remote; Maxi Controller |
| Basic wireless remote | X10 Palm Pad controller | $20 | Controls 16 devices; dim/bright | Lacks all lights on/all devices off; can't send macros | Maxi Controller |

**TABLE 3.3** (continued)

| Controller Type | Sample Product | Price Range | Features | Limitations | Alternatives |
|---|---|---|---|---|---|
| Wired Maxi Controller | X10 Maxi Control Console | $16 | Controls 16 devices; all lights on/all devices off; dim/bright; programmable codes and macros | — | — |
| Learning remote | Five-in-One remote | $35 | Controls TV, VCR, and other devices as well as X10 | Might not control all functions of a DVD player; requires separate IR/X10 interface or X10 wireless transceiver | More powerful learning remotes with greater DVD and home theater capabilities |
| Timer | X10 Mini Timer | $34 | Controls X10 devices by time or random (security), all lights on/all devices off, sleep | Can't send macros | Computer interface module |
| Telephone | X10 telephone responder | $70 | Controls X10 remotely via touch-tone | Controls 10 devices via phone (8 via touchpad); not compatible with some answering machines or voice mail services | HAL Deluxe (voice activation) |
| Computer Interface | CM11A | $50 | Controls X10 via RS-232 serial port interface | Some PCs don't have serial ports | USB interface; with onboard memory/timer |

**TABLE 3.3** (continued)

| Controller Type | Sample Product | Price Range | Features | Limitations | Alternatives |
|---|---|---|---|---|---|
| | CM15A | $50 | Controls X10 via USB port interface; also includes all-house-code transceiver | — | |

If your major concern in starting out with X10 is saving a few steps, a basic wired or wireless remote will be sufficient. However, if you want more powerful automation, you need to consider more powerful control systems like those listed in Table 3.3.

**FIGURE 3.1**

X10 wireless, wired, and computer-based controllers.

Maxi Controller

Mini Timer

IR Controller for X10/universal remote

Keychain remote

Eight-device remote

USB computer interface

X10/5-in-1 universal remote

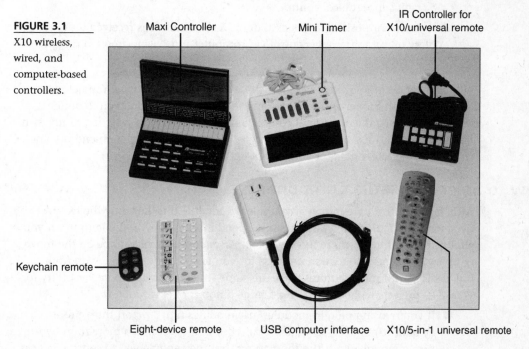

**NEW LIFE FOR OLD X10 REMOTES**

If you find that you're ready to upgrade to a more powerful remote, you can still use your old X10 remote elsewhere. For example, if you put a wired Mini Controller in your home office so that you can turn on all the lights if you hear a prowler, move surplus wireless remotes to family cars: I use one to turn on the porch lights when I arrive or off when I leave.

## Choosing the Most Important Features

No matter which X10 home automation job you decide to tackle, you can spend almost any amount of money on it. You can buy a basic on/off switch with remote dimming support for about $12, but a deluxe dimmer switch with two-way and scene support is about $70. You can always spend more, but should you?

My rule of thumb is to spend more *only* if it buys me more useful features. As I mentioned in the sidebar called "Limitations in the Real World" earlier in this chapter, a low-end device isn't a compromise if it does what you need it to do. In other situations, you should spend more money to get a better solution. For example

- If you don't want nosy visitors to know the details of your X10 setup, choose modules that are programmed through a remote or have a cover over the dials instead of modules with visible dials. Units without visible code dials also look better.

- If you want an electrical outlet that can't be overridden by someone's flipping the on/off switch on the lamp or appliance, choose an outlet that doesn't support local control.

- If you want positive feedback that an X10 module has received a signal (very useful for remote control via computer interface), choose a module with two-way support.

I'll point out additional examples like these in following chapters. You get more capabilities with higher-end modules and remotes, but it's up to you to decide whether you need the additional costs of deluxe modules and switches. In my own X10 installation, I use a mixture of entry-level, mid-range, and high-end modules. I choose the module, outlet, or switch that fits the situation.

## How to Select Versatile Components

Although you can save money if you select a module that has only the features you need for a particular job, you could also spend more money in the long run if you change your mind. If you're the type of experimenter that likes to be on the move with devices, it might make more sense for you to spend more money up front to buy devices with more features. Here are some ways to provide more versatility for your X10 projects without spending a huge amount of extra money:

- If you're using plug-in modules, use modules that support three-prong (grounded) outlets (see Figure 3.2). They don't cost much more than two-prong modules with similar features, but they enable you to control devices that can't be connected to two-prong modules.

- If you're always short of electrical outlets, use three-prong modules that have pass-through connectors. The pass-through connector supplies regular uncontrolled power for one device while the X10 outlet controls another device. Figure 3.2 illustrates a three-prong outlet with a pass-through connector.

■ If you're planning to set up programmable lighting scenes later, get a controller that can send the additional codes necessary to program modules and switches (such as the Maxi Controller shown in Figure 3.1) instead of an entry-level Mini Controller.

**FIGURE 3.2**
An X10-compatible three-prong (grounded) module with pass-through outlet.

## Vital and Useful Accessories

What do you really need to implement X10 home automation? Use this checklist to remind you of items you might forget about as you create your first project or move to another project:

☐ Voltage sensor (see Figure 3.3); if you're going to install X10 light switches or outlets, this device can save your life! Learn how to use this in Chapter 4, "Using X10 to Control Home Lighting."

☐ Spare batteries for your remotes; a dead remote can prevent you from controlling your X10 installation.

☐ Straight-edge and Phillips-head screwdrivers; if you're working on wall outlets or light switches, you might encounter both types of screws.

**FIGURE 3.3**
A typical AC (alternating current) voltage sensor.

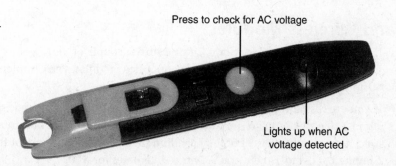

Press to check for AC voltage

Lights up when AC voltage detected

## Selecting Your Next Goal

As you work on your first X10 project, consider your next project. If you're automating your lighting, ask yourself, "Which room would best benefit from automation?" You might want to tackle a bedroom, den, or other room that could benefit from scene lighting and dimming after you've worked on an easier area such as the living room or porch.

## Budgeting Your Time

How much time should you budget for an X10 project? Table 3.4 lists typical suggestions for some simple projects that you might try. Allow more time for complex projects.

**TABLE 3.4**   Estimated Time for Typical X10 Tasks

| Task | Total |
| --- | --- |
| Install and configure plug-in lamp/appliance module (dial controlled) | 5–10 minutes |
| Configure dial/button remote control for house code | 5–10 minutes |
| Install, configure, and test dial-set light switch | 30–45 minutes |
| Install, configure, and test wall outlet | 30–45 minutes |
| Configure X10 timer | 15–45 minutes |

As you can see from Table 3.4, it doesn't take long to perform basic automation tasks. However, if a project involves rewiring more than one outlet or light switch or several outlets, you could easily spend several hours in the process.

# Skills Checklist

What do you need to know to install X10 home automation? You don't need to know a whole lot to install a basic plug-in system, but more elaborate setups require additional skills. Compare your experience and your willingness to learn to the skills listed in the following sections.

## Plug-in and Wireless Modules

If you can plug in a toaster or a TV and turn a couple of dials, you can install a wireless receiver and basic lamp and appliance modules. See Chapters 4 and 5, "Using X10 to Control Appliances."

If you are installing programmable lamp modules, you need to read and understand X10 code charts to send the appropriate commands for dimming and scenes (and have a controller capable of sending them). Learn more about that process in Chapter 6, "Using Timers and Advanced Remotes for X10."

## Electrical Outlets and Switches

If you want to avoid hanging a module on an outlet, or if you want to add X10 control to a built-in light or appliance, you're looking at replacing an outlet or a switch. To replace an electrical outlet or a switch without frying yourself or your home, you need to know how to

- Follow a wiring diagram
- Shut off power to the correct circuit
- Use a voltage sensor
- Determine the correct wiring to use for each connection

Figure 3.4 shows a typical high-end X10 two-way dimming and scene-capable light switch. The wires are color-coded to help you install the switch correctly.

**FIGURE 3.4**

A typical X10 dimming, scene-capable light switch and its color-coded connections.

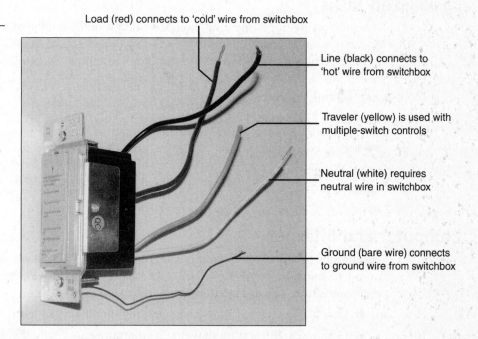

Load (red) connects to 'cold' wire from switchbox

Line (black) connects to 'hot' wire from switchbox

Traveler (yellow) is used with multiple-switch controls

Neutral (white) requires neutral wire in switchbox

Ground (bare wire) connects to ground wire from switchbox

If some of this seems like a foreign language, don't panic! See the clear diagrams, photos, and technical help in Chapters 4 and 5.

## HVAC Controls

X10 can be used to control your home's furnace and air conditioning remotely, but this is a tougher installation job, requiring configuration and wiring of the thermostat and the X10 controller that connects your HVAC system to your X10 system (see Figure 3.5). I'll explain how it works in Chapter 7, "Using X10 to Control HVAC Systems," but this is a task you might consider calling in a professional to handle for you.

**FIGURE 3.5**

Wiring diagram
for a typical X10
HVAC control
system.

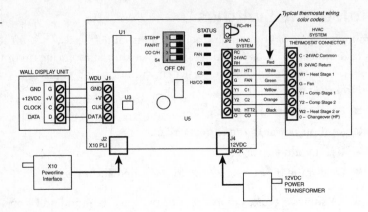

# Specialized Tasks

X10 can control almost anything, from low-voltage outdoor lighting to draperies.
As a consequence, the challenge of a particular project can be as simple as plugging in a couple of controllers or as difficult as decoding a logic circuit.

**READ BEFORE YOU BUY**

How can you find out how difficult (or how easy) an X10 product will be? Do what I do!
Read the product manual *first*. Many X10 vendors, such as X10.com and Smarthome.com,
offer links to their product manuals at their websites, usually on the same page as the
product description. All you need is a free copy of Adobe Reader (the latest version of
what was formerly called *Abobe Acrobat Reader*). Get it from www.adobe.com.

# Computer and Internet

The ultimate in home automation is computer control—especially if you can control your home from your office via the Internet. If you're considering moving up to
computer control, you need to understand the following items:

- How to connect devices to your computer's serial or USB ports
- How to use X10 control software to program your automation system to run
  when you're not at home

**X10 SOFTWARE YOU CAN TRY BEFORE YOU BUY**

If you're wondering whether X10 automation via your PC is right for you, you don't need
to spend a penny to learn about it. Set your browser to one of these websites to see
screen shots, videos, and more information (some also offer free trial downloads):

- HomeSeer: www.homeseer.com
- Smarthome Design, ActiveHome, HomeVision, others
  www.smarthome.com/DEMOS.HTML

# Deciding When to Call in the Pros

As you plan your home automation project, you might be wondering "Can *I* do this?" In most cases, the answer is "Yes!" However, if you're looking at a whole-house automation project or HVAC control, it might be time to get in touch with a professional. These systems can be tricky to set up, might require many outlet or switch replacements, and have the potential to foul up your HVAC system if they're not installed correctly.

## Selecting a Contractor

Installing a large-scale or complex X10 system isn't for everyone. If you've decided that you need help with your next X10 installation, here are some sources for contractors experienced with X10 installation:

- X10.com has an installer finder at its website. Go to www.x10.com/pro/installer_home.htm.

- Smarthome.com's installer finder enables you to specify the approximate cost of your project and the type of project. Go to www.smarthome.com/asp/projref.asp.

When you interview a contractor, be sure to ask these questions:

- *How experienced are you with X10?*—Get specifics: number of installations, number of years, types of installations.

- *Can I contact two or three of your recent clients?*—You want recent referrals (within the last 12 months), and preferably for the type of project you're considering. Older referrals might not be valid because of personnel or management changes.

- *What type of training and support do you offer after the sale?*—You want to make sure that the installer can help you with problems that might crop up later.

Be sure to get a written quotation that specifies types of equipment that will be used, installation schedule, and a firm price.

# Just Do It!

The following pages provide examples of some simple home automation projects you want to try. For each project, I provide a checklist of materials and chapter references for more information.

## Controlling Seasonal Lighting

Merry Christmas! Happy Holidays! Happy Halloween! Happy _____! Whatever holidays your family celebrates, X10 can make controlling the lights you use to celebrate easier for you.

_Interior Lights (Christmas Tree, Window Decorations) for Remote Control_

- ☐ An X10 lamp module (see Figure 3.6) for each separate display. If you have lights in two rooms, you need a module for each display.
- ☐ An X10 plug-in controller (see Figure 3.6) or a wireless controller with remote.

**FIGURE 3.6**

An X10 plug-in controller (left) and an X10 lamp module (right).

Use the wireless remote or plug-in controller to trigger the lights. If you want to trigger all lights at the same time, use the same X10 house/unit code on all modules. To enable you to turn on some lights independent of others, configure the lamp modules with different unit codes and the same house code (use a different house code than other lights in the house). Set a Maxi Controller to that house code and use the All Lights On button to turn on all the seasonal lights at once.

For more information, see Chapters 4 and 6.

_Exterior Lights (Porch, Landscaping) for Dusk-to-Dawn Automatic Holiday Lighting_

- ☐ An X10 outlet with a weatherproof cover (see Figure 3.7).
- ☐ An X10 photocell sensor (see Figure 3.8 later in this chapter).

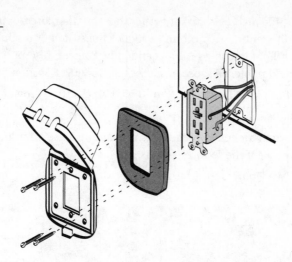

Set the photocell sensor to send signals to the X10 house/unit code used by the outlet.
For more information, see Chapter 8, "Using X10 to Control Exterior Landscaping."

## Turning On Porch Lights at Night

It's wonderful to drive up to your home and see the porch lights are on. It gives your
home a feeling of "come in, we've been waiting for you." Automating porch lights also
makes your home look lived in while you're away. X10 makes it easy to make your
home a more welcoming (and safer!) place after dark.

*Dusk-to-Dawn Automatic Lighting*

☐  X10 light switch for each porch light. You can also use an inline module or a
    screw-in module if the fixture permits it.

☐  X10 photocell sensor (see Figure 3.8).

To trigger all exterior lights at the same time, set them to use the same X10 house/unit
code and set the photocell sensor to send signals to the same X10 house/unit code.

If one porch or outside area gets darker earlier than another, use a separate photocell sensor and a different house and unit code for the switch or module. This enables each porch light to come on independently. You can also purchase floodlights with integrated photocell sensors, such as X10's PR511 Motion Monitor.

For more information, see Chapters 4, 8, and 9, "Using X10 to Provide Security."

*Timer-Based Automatic Lighting*

☐ X10 light switch for each porch light. You can also use an inline module or a screw-in module if the fixture permits it.

☐ X10 timer (see Figure 3.9).

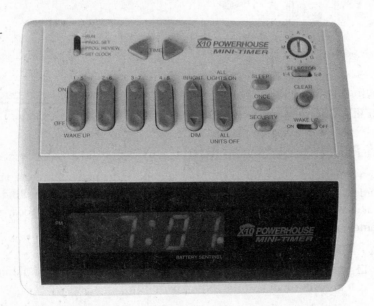

**FIGURE 3.9**

A typical X10 Mini Timer.

Program the timer to turn on porch lights and turn them off at specified times. To trigger all porch lights at the same time, use the same house/unit codes in each module or switch.

For more information, see Chapters 4 and 6.

## Creating a Lived-In Look When You're Away

An empty house can be an open door to thieves and vandals—*if* they know it's empty. Keep the bad guys guessing by using X10 to control lighting and appliances.

*Randomized Lighting Control*

☐ X10 plug-in, light switch, or screw-in module for each light that you want to control.

☐ X10 timer (refer to Figure 3.9).

Set each module or switch to a different unit code. Configure the X10 timer to control the house and unit codes. Set the timer to run in Security mode, which uses random times to turn lighting on and off.

For more information, see Chapters 4 and 6.

*Randomized Lighting and Appliance Control*

☐ X10 plug-in, light switch, or screw-in module for each light that you want to control.

☐ X10 appliance module for each TV, radio, or other appliance that you want to control.

☐ X10 timer.

Set each module to a different unit code. Configure the X10 timer to control the house and unit codes. Set the timer to run in Security mode, which uses random times to turn lighting and modules on and off.

For more information, see Chapters 4, 5, and 6.

## Keeping an Eye on Your Home

Whether you're in your home office, just a few miles away from home at work, or hundreds of miles from home on vacation, you can use X10 to keep an eye on what's happening.

*X10 Home Security Warning of Break-In*

☐ One or more X10 security sensors (see Figure 3.10).

☐ X10 telephone interface.

**FIGURE 3.10**
A typical X10 motion detector.

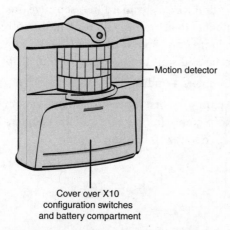

Motion detector

Cover over X10 configuration switches and battery compartment

Place an X10 sensor in each sensitive area of your home. You can use a motion sensor, a door or window sensor, or a breaking glass sensor, depending on the exact location you want to protect. Set the X10 telephone interface to call your office or vacation location if the sensor is triggered.

For more information, see Chapter 9 and Chapter 10, "Accessing X10 Home Control via Telephone."

*X10 Security Camera*

☐ X10 security sensor (motion, door, window).

☐ X10 wireless camera (see Figure 3.11).

☐ X10 lamp module or other module.

**FIGURE 3.11**
A typical X10
wireless video
camera (left)
and receiver
(right).

Place the X10 security sensor and wireless camera in a sensitive area of your home. Use the appropriate lamp module to control the lighting in that area. Set the X10 motion sensor to trigger the lamp and wireless camera (use the same unit code, if necessary) to light up the scene and start broadcasting to your TV or VCR.

For more information, see Chapters 4 and 9.

Now that you know how to plan your first (or next) X10 automation project and you have some ideas, let's keep going! Jump directly to the chapters listed, or move on to Chapter 4 to learn more about X10 lighting control.

# THE ABSOLUTE MINIMUM

■ To build a realistic strategy for your home automation project, you should decide what you want to automate, how much you want to spend, the best ways to control it, what features you need, and determine how much time you need to finish the job.

■ Automating a particular task (such as lighting or security) is a more cost-effective approach than automating on a room-by-room basis.

■ You can purchase a basic X10 starter kit for less than $50, but you can spend much more, depending on what you want to automate and what features you need or want.

■ More powerful remote controls enable you to do more with your X10 system, even if you use entry-level modules.

■ Select lamp and appliance modules, switches, and outlets based on the actual features you need.

■ Add versatility to your X10 installation by specifying modules with pass-through connectors and grounded plugs.

■ Projects involving plug-in modules take very little time, but if you need to program modules or replace electrical outlets or switches, you need more time for those projects.

■ You can use a computer to control your X10 installation, and you can try most X10 computer programs before you buy.

■ If you want to use X10 to control your entire house or HVAC system, consider using an experienced X10 installer.

■ By using different types of controllers and triggers, you can use standard X10 lamp and appliance modules to help provide automatic dusk-to-dawn lighting, security, and other automation projects.

# PART

# Using X10 for Basic Home Automation

4

# USING X10 TO CONTROL HOME LIGHTING

In Chapter 2, "Getting Started with X10 Home Automation," you learned how to set up your first X10 system, using plug-in lamp modules to turn on and turn off table and floor lamps at the touch of a button. However, the typical home has many other light sources, including built-in ceiling light fixtures, accent and track lighting, fluorescent fixtures, three-way and dimmer lights, porch lights, floodlights, and others. Fortunately, X10 can handle virtually any interior or exterior lighting situation, as this chapter demonstrates.

# Understanding X10 Lamp and Appliance Control Modules

Although you can control ordinary incandescent table and floor lamps with lamp control modules, lamp control modules are not suitable for some types of plug-in interior lighting. If you want to connect a fluorescent light or a very high wattage incandescent light to an X10 wall socket module, you need to use an appliance module instead of a lamp module.

Even though the two-prong appliance module strongly resembles the lamp module from the outside, it is designed to handle higher wattage, electric motors, and other devices with a resistive load (such as fluorescent lights) as the label indicates. Appliance modules, unlike lamp modules, do not support dimming and often support higher wattage ratings than lamp modules.

Figure 4.1 compares the labeling on an X10 appliance module to a typical X10 lamp module's labeling.

**FIGURE 4.1**

Labels from a typical appliance module (left) and a typical lamp module (right). Modules courtesy of X10 (USA) Inc.

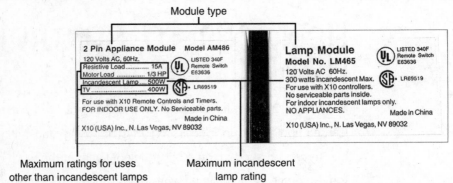

Module type

2 Pin Appliance Module Model AM486
120 Volts AC, 60Hz.
Resistive Load.............. 15A
Motor Load ................. 1/3 HP
Incandescent Lamp.... 500W
TV ............................... 400W
For use with X10 Remote Controls and Timers.
FOR INDOOR USE ONLY. No Serviceable parts.
Made in China
X10 (USA) Inc., N. Las Vegas, NV 89032
LISTED 340F
Remote Switch
E63636
LR69519

Lamp Module
Model No. LM465
120 Volts AC 60Hz.
300 watts incandescent Max.
For use with X10 controllers.
No serviceable parts inside.
For indoor incandescent lamps only.
NO APPLIANCES.
Made in China
X10 (USA) Inc., N. Las Vegas, NV 89032
LISTED 340F
Remote Switch
E63636
LR69519

Maximum ratings for uses
other than incandescent lamps

Maximum incandescent
lamp rating

## X10-COMPATIBLE PRODUCTS MADE BY MANY VENDORS

Although many vendors of X10-compatible hardware resell modules and other hardware made by X10 (USA), products made by other vendors such as Leviton DHC (Decora Home Controls), Smarthome, and others also work with X10. This book uses the term *X10 compatible* to identify X10-compatible hardware made by third-party companies. X10-compatible hardware frequently differs in features from standard X10 hardware.

If you need support for three-prong (grounded and polarized) devices, both lamp and appliance modules are available in three-prong as well as the normal two-prong connector shown in Figure 4.1. Major vendors of three-prong X10-compatible plug-in modules include Smarthome (www.smarthome.com) and Leviton DHC (www.leviton.com/dhc).

# Selecting the Correct Module for Your Lighting Type

All lamp control modules, unlike appliance modules, support dimming via the push-buttons on the remote control (see Figure 4.2) or plug-in controller, enabling you to adjust room light to the perfect level for watching TV, playing board games, or napping.

**FIGURE 4.2**

After you've selected a lamp with the X10 remote, push and hold the down-arrow button on the remote to dim the lamp to the desired level; push and hold the up-arrow button to brighten the lamp to the desired level.

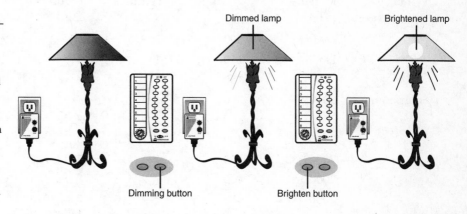

Dimmed lamp

Brightened lamp

Dimming button

Brighten button

Even though basic X10 lamp modules support dimming, you might want to consider more sophisticated lamp modules made by X10 or third-party vendors if you want these features:

- Adjustable dimming (ramp) rate
- Adjustable brightness (on) level
- Support for resuming dim level (memory dim)
- Soft start (ramps from 0% to full brightness when turned on); note that modules that support adjustable ramp rates use this feature to provide soft start
- Pass-through AC connector (enables you to plug in an uncontrolled lamp or other device)
- Status light
- Burnt bulb detection
- Support for preset dimming
- Support for scenes
- Capability to send X10 signals to other devices (two-way X10)
- Support for grounded (three-wire) lamps

Support for advanced features such as these enables you to create moods and provide additional security for your family. Table 4.1 provides a comparison chart listing major X10 and X10-compatible plug-in lamp modules and major features. Consult the vendors' websites for additional features.

**Table 4.1** X10 and X10-Compatible Lamp Modules and Features

| Vendor | Model # | Max. Wattage | Dim Features | Special Features | How Programmed |
|--------|---------|--------------|--------------|------------------|----------------|
| X10 (USA) | LM465 | 300 | 1 | — | Wheels |
| | LM14A | 300 | 1, 2, 3 | 10 | Wheels |
| | LM15A | 150 | 1 | 4 | Controller |
| | SL575 | 150 | 1 | 4 | Wheels |
| Smarthome | 2000SC | 300 | 1 | — | Controller |
| | 2000SHL3 | 400 | 1, 2, 5, 6 | 7, 12 | Controller |
| | 2000SHL | 400 | 1, 2, 5, 6 | 8, 12 | Controller |
| | 2000SLS3 | 400 | 1, 2, 5, 6 | 7, 11, 12 | Controller |
| | 2000SLS | 400 | 1, 2, 5, 6 | 8, 11, 12 | Controller |
| | 2000STW3 | 400 | 1, 2, 5, 6 | 7, 9, 10, 11, 12 | Controller |
| | 2000STW | 400 | 1, 2, 5, 6 | 8, 9, 10, 11, 12 | Controller |
| Leviton DHC | HCP03-1SW | 300 | 1, 2 | — | Controller |
| Radio Shack | 61-3002 | 300 | 1 | 13 | Wheels |

**Table Legend:**

1 Standard dim

2 Memory dim (resume dim)

3 Soft start

4 Screws into lamp base

5 Preset dim

6 Adjustable fade (ramp)

7 Three-prong pass-through outlet

8 Two-prong pass-through outlet

9 Burnt bulb detection

10 Two-way operation

11 Scene support

12 Adjustable on level

13 Control wheels located behind hinged door

To learn more about each feature, read through the following sections.

## Higher Wattage Rating

You need to compute the total wattage rating of the incandescent lamp you want to connect to an X10 lamp module to make certain you don't exceed the lamp's wattage rating. This is especially important if you use X10 to control a halogen lamp or a multiple-lamp incandescent light array. X10 lamp modules support up to 300 watts, whereas most X10-compatible lamp modules support up to 400 watts.

> **caution**
>
> If you need more than 400 watts for a lamp, use an X10 or X10-compatible appliance module. Most appliance modules support up to 480–500 watts for incandescent lighting (depending on the module). However, keep in mind that appliance modules don't support dimming.

## Adjustable Dimming Rate

Low-end lamp modules support only one fixed dimming rate. If you want more precise control over how fast or slow you can dim your lights, look for modules that enable you to adjust the dimming rate. Some modules might refer to this feature as *adjustable fade* or *ramp rate*.

## Adjustable Brightness Level

Some lamp modules enable you to control the brightness level of the lamp when you turn it on, instead of dimming the lamp after you've turned it on at full brightness. This is a useful feature if you want to use your X10 system to establish lighting scenes.

## Support for Resuming Dim Level (Memory Dim)

If the power goes out, some X10 lamp modules can restart at the same dim level in use before power was interrupted. If you live in an area that experiences power outages fairly often and you want to use the dimmer function that's built into X10, this is an important feature to look for.

## Pass-Through AC Connector

As the illustrations in this chapter indicate, conventional X10 lamp modules take over the AC outlet they're plugged into. If you want the option of using an AC outlet for another (non-X10–controlled) lamp or other device while maintaining X10 control of a lamp, specify X10-compatible lamp modules with a pass-through two-pin or three-pin connector, such as the one shown in Figure 4.3.

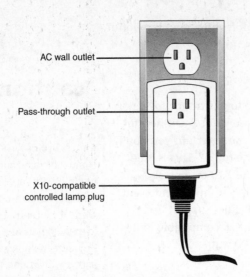

**FIGURE 4.3**

This Smarthome LampLinc X10-compatible lamp module has a pass-through three-pin outlet that can be used by any 115V AC device.

AC wall outlet

Pass-through outlet

X10-compatible controlled lamp plug

---

**ADVANCED X10 PROGRAMMING—LET THE REMOTE DO IT!**

Some X10 and X10-compatible lamp modules, such as the one shown in Figure 4.3, are programmed through an X10 or X10-compatible remote control or tabletop controller rather than with house and unit code wheels. To program such a module, consult the instructions provided with the module.

---

## Three-Prong Plug Support

If you decide to use X10-compatible lamp modules that support pass-through connectors, choose modules that have three-wire connectors (refer to Figure 4.3). Three-wire connectors enable the module to provide standard power to any household device, including computers, surge protectors, and appliances that use grounded outlets.

## Status Light

Some X10-compatible modules feature a status light, usually an LED, which indicates when the module is receiving or sending X10 signals. If you're having problems getting your X10 installation to work, status lights can be very useful for troubleshooting.

## Burnt Bulb Detection

If you use X10 to control lights that aren't easily visible from your location, such as garage or attic lights, or you use a PC control module to control your home via an Internet connection, it would be handy to know whether the light is working properly or has burned out. Some X10-compatible modules detect changes in the electrical load being handled by the module, alerting you to a burned-out lamp.

## Support for Preset Dimming

Some X10-compatible lamp modules are designed to support preset dimming levels. This feature enables you to turn on a light and have it start at the dimming level you want, instead of coming on at full brightness and requiring you to dim it to the desired level. This is useful for scenes, home theater lighting, using a lamp as a visual alarm clock, and other functions.

## Support for Scenes

Any X10 or X10-compatible lamp module can be incorporated into a scene (multiple lights triggered by a single command) command sent from a controller connected to a home computer (consult Chapter 11, "Accessing X10 Home Control via Your Home Computer," for details). However, only a few modules are designed to store scene commands such as "brighten to 50% over a 30-second time period" or "dim to 25% over a 3-minute time period" in addition to the standard house and unit code commands. This type of module assigns a separate house and unit code to each scene stored in memory. For more details, see Chapter 6, "Using Timers and Advanced Remotes for X10."

## Two-Way X10 Support

X10 was originally a one-way system: The controller sent a command, and you hoped the receiver accepted the command and turned on the light, dimmed it, or shut it off. However, if a problem prevented the receiver from accepting the signal or the receiver malfunctioned, you might not know it.

Two-way X10 or X10-compatible lamp modules enable you to get status messages from the module, and they also enable the module to send X10 messages to other devices. If you want to use a PC-based X10 controller to manage your X10 system, two-way modules can be useful because they provide feedback, but they also cost significantly more than one-way modules.

# Programming an X10 Remote to Control Lighting

You program individual lamp modules like this:

1. Select the same house code for all lamp modules and the remote.
2. Select a unique unit code for each lamp module that you want to control individually, or use the same unit code for two or more lamps that you want to control as a group.
3. Press the key on the remote control to turn on or turn off each lamp.

Some X10 and X10-compatible lamp modules, such as the pass-through module shown in Figure 4.3, don't use the usual house code and unit code wheels for configuration. Instead, these modules contain a nonvolatile memory chip that stores house and unit codes transmitted from a remote control. Regardless of how the module is programmed, it responds whenever a remote control activates it.

## Controlling Multiple Lamps with X10

Remote controls and plug-in controllers that use separate unit code and On/Off buttons enable you to control groups of lights. For example, to dim two or more lamps at the same time:

1. Press the unit code button for each lamp you want to control (for example, 4, 5, and 6).
2. Press and hold the appropriate dim or bright button.
3. All selected lamps dim or brighten at the same time (see Figure 4.4).

**FIGURE 4.4**

Dimming a group of lamps at the same time using X10.

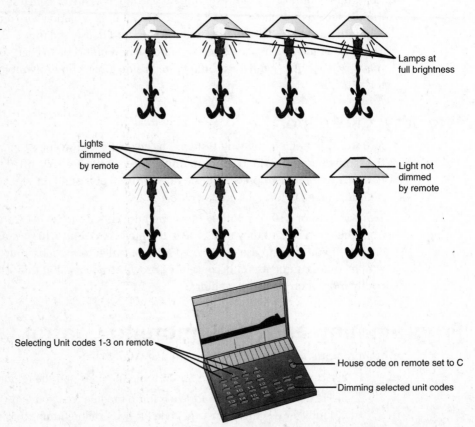

Lamps at full brightness

Lights dimmed by remote

Light not dimmed by remote

Selecting Unit codes 1-3 on remote

House code on remote set to C

Dimming selected unit codes

---

**HOW POWERFUL IS YOUR X10 SYSTEM? ASK YOUR REMOTE CONTROL**

Much of the power of X10 resides in the remote control you use. Basic remote controls can control individual lights or appliances, but more sophisticated remotes can control groups of lights or appliances. You can control groups of lights with a single command by creating macros (groups of commands) with X10-compatible software and a controller connected to your PC (see Chapter 11). If you want to trigger different brightness levels and fade rates without using a PC, use an X10-compatible lamp module that can store scenes in memory (see Chapter 6).

---

Two-way X10 lamp control modules also can be programmed to send messages to other lamp control modules. This enables you to create scenes in which one module tells others to dim or shut off.

# Black & Decker freewire Lighting Control

Black & Decker's freewire system is an X10-compatible home control system for lighting and appliances. freewire differs in some important ways from standard X10 and X10-compatible lighting control systems discussed in this and earlier chapters:

- freewire remote controls are synchronized with the Messenger Hub wireless transceiver to minimize the chances of your system being controlled by an outside party.
- freewire offers outdoor-rated as well as indoor-rated lamp modules.
- freewire is compatible with the HomeLink home-control system built into many recent automobiles (see www.homelink.com for more information).

## Elements of the freewire System

freewire uses a wireless transceiver known as the *Messenger Hub* (see Figure 4.5) to relay signals from wireless remotes to lamp and appliance modules. Unlike conventional X10 and X10-compatible wireless remote controls, the Messenger Hub transceiver and matching remotes feature a Learn switch that synchronizes freewire wireless remote controls to the Messenger Hub. This provides for added security. Also, the Messenger Hub's built-in outlet acts as a high wattage (500 watts maximum) lamp module rather than an appliance module as with conventional X10 wireless transceivers.

The Messenger Hub can be set to any unit code as well as any house code. However, Black & Decker recommends you use unit code 1.

The Indoor Remote (shown in Figure 4.6), like conventional X10 wireless remote controls, features a unit code dial. Instead of using a house code dial, however, it is synchronized to the Messenger Hub during setup.

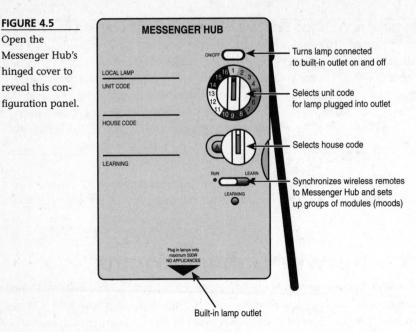

**FIGURE 4.5**

Open the
Messenger Hub's
hinged cover to
reveal this con-
figuration panel.

The unit code dial on the remote and on all freewire dial-configured devices is
divided up into color-coded sections. To make working with your home automation
system easier, you can select unit codes in the same color section for the modules in
a single room. For example, unit codes 14, 15, and 16 are in the black zone. If you
decided to use this zone for a bedroom, you should assign these unit codes to the
modules located in the bedroom.

Note that the remote control has three On/Off toggles and that most sections of the
unit code dial have three positions. To control devices assigned to a particular color,
turn the dial until that color appears at the bottom of the dial, and then use the
On/Off toggle that lines up with each position as shown in Figure 4.6.

The Lamp Receiver (shown in Figure 4.6 inset) has a matching color-coded unit
code dial and a house code dial that is normally hidden behind a hinged cover. As
with conventional X10 lamp modules, the Lamp Receiver's house code dial must be
set to the same house code used by the Messenger Hub transceiver in order for the
transceiver to control it. Select the desired unit code from the unit code dial.

In addition to the Lamp Receiver, freewire lighting control modules are available in
two other varieties:

- Bulb Receiver—This is similar to the X10 Socket Rocket, and is programmed
  through the Messenger Hub and Indoor Remote rather than with unit and
  house code dials.

- Outdoor Lamp Receiver—This is a weather-resistant unit resembling a short
  extension cord (see Figure 4.7). It is programmed through the Messenger Hub

and Indoor Remote, rather than with unit and house code dials. Plug it into an outlet that includes ground fault interrupter (GFI) circuitry, which is standard on most recent home construction for outdoor AC outlets. It is rated for up to 500-watt lamps.

**FIGURE 4.6**

The freewire Indoor Remote (left) and detail of the house code wheel and color control buttons (top right), compared to the control panel of the Indoor Lamp Receiver (bottom right inset).

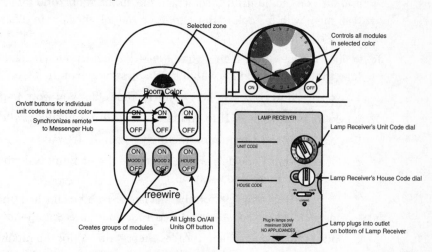

### TAKE YOUR MESSENGER HUB WITH YOU FOR PROGRAMMING SUCCESS

When you program the Bulb or Outdoor Lamp Receiver, you need to plug the lamp with the Bulb Receiver or the Outdoor Lamp Receiver unit into the same outlet as the Messenger Hub. You might find it easier to move the Messenger Hub to the outlet you use for the lamp with the Bulb Receiver or the Outdoor Lamp Receiver.

**FIGURE 4.7**

The freewire Outdoor Lamp Receiver is programmed with the Messenger Hub and Indoor Remote.

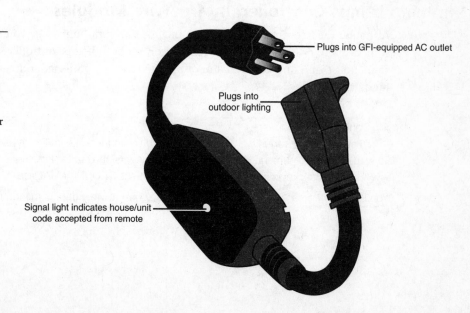

## Controlling Groups of Lights with the Mood Button

After you've installed freewire modules in your home, you might want to control lamp modules in different parts of your home as a group. For example, you might want to turn on the lights in the kitchen, the dining room, and the hallway between them with a single command, even though they are in different color zones.

To do this, use the Indoor Remote and the Messenger Hub to create a group of lamp modules that you can control with a single press of one of the Mood buttons:

1. Note the unit code numbers of the modules that you want to group together.

2. Go to the Messenger Hub and move the Learn/Run slider switch to Learn.

3. Press the Mood 1 button on the Indoor Remote.

4. Turn the Unit Code dial on the remote to the first unit code that you want to add to the group and press On.

5. After the indicator light on the Messenger Hub has flashed (indicating that it has received the code), repeat step 4 for up to three additional modules.

6. After you've stored the unit codes (steps 4 and 5) for the modules you want to include in Group 1, slide the Learn/Run slider on the Messenger Hub back to Run. The Mood 1 On/Off button will turn on or off all modules in Group 1.

To store a group of modules for a second group, repeat the preceding sequence, but use the Mood 2 button in step 3.

## Dimming Lamps Controlled by freewire Modules

Although the freewire remotes do not include dimming functions, you can use any standard X10 or X10-compatible remote control or tabletop controller set to the same house and unit codes to dim or brighten lamps connected to freewire lamp modules.

**FREEWIRE ONLINE**

Visit Black & Decker's freewire website at www.blackanddecker.com/FreeWire/default.aspx. To read or download manuals for freewire components and starter kits, visit www.blackanddecker.com/freewire/HelpCenter/INSTRUCTIONMANUAL.aspx.

You'll need the free Adobe Reader (www.adobe.com) to view the instruction manuals.

# Using X10 with Built-in Light Fixtures

X10 can be used to control built-in light fixtures as
well as plug-in lamps. There are three
approaches you can use to add X10 control to
built-in fixtures:

- Use a screw-in X10 lamp module to retrofit the fixture itself.

- Replace the On/Off switch with an X10-
  compatible On/Off switch.

- Install an inline X10 relay between the
  lamp fixture and the wiring.

Which one is right for you and how do you
install them? The following sections discuss these
issues.

> **caution**
>
> To avoid problems in
> using a screw-in X10
> lamp module, find out
> the height and width of
> the module you're consid-
> ering and make sure that the lamp
> module assembly won't interfere
> with the lampshade or other parts
> of the lamp fixture.

## Installing and Using Screw-in X10 Lamp Modules

A screw-in X10 lamp module is a good choice for single-bulb incandescent lamps if
there's sufficient room for the shade when the module is screwed into the lamp base.
As Figure 4.8 shows, the screw-in module increases the total height of the fixture.

**FIGURE 4.8**

Retrofitting a
lamp with a
screw-in X10
lamp module.

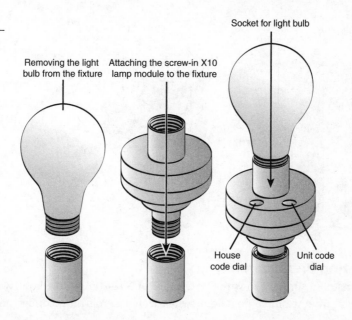

Removing the light    Attaching the screw-in X10
bulb from the fixture   lamp module to the fixture

Socket for light bulb

House
code dial

Unit code
dial

Most screw-in X10 lamp modules support dimming via remote control, just as plug-in lamp modules do. However, some low-profile screw-in lamp modules do not support dimming.

A screw-in X10 lamp module is also a good choice for floor or table lamps if you don't want to use a plug-in module.

Some screw-in lamp modules use house and unit code wheels, but others, such as the X10 Socket Rocket and the Black & Decker freewire Bulb Receiver, store house and unit codes transmitted from a remote or tabletop controller in memory. Consult the documentation for a particular screw-in lamp module for details.

## caution

If you want to add X10 control to a built-in lamp but there's not enough room in your fixture for a full-size X10 screw-in module, check the dimensions for a low-profile module. You might have to give up the ability to dim the light, but if the lamp is used in an entryway or hallway, you might not need or want to dim it anyway.

## Installing and Using X10 Light Switches

If you want to control built-in lighting with X10 but a screw-in module isn't suitable, you need to replace conventional light switches with X10 light switches. You don't need to rewire your home, but you will need some understanding of electricity, its dangers, and how light switches work.

**FIGURE 4.9**
Testing a light switch with a voltage tester.

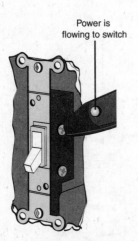
Power is flowing to switch

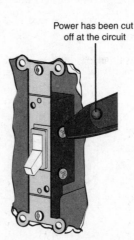
Power has been cut off at the circuit

## Installation Preparations
You can install a simple two-wire On/Off X10 or X10-compatible light switch as a replacement for any single-pole light switch that controls an incandescent light.

Although the switch does not include a dimmer, you can dim the light through a tabletop remote, wireless remote, or computer interface.

If you need to replace a light switch that controls fluorescent, low-voltage lights or appliances, you need to use a three-wire switch made for appliances (see Chapter 5, "Using X10 to Control Appliances").

If you want to use an X10-compatible light switch as a dimmer, you need to determine whether your home wiring includes a neutral line. If it doesn't, you must purchase dimmable X10 or X10-compatible light switches that don't require the neutral line, such as the X10 WS12A or the Smarthome LampLinc RX.

### CHECK YOUR WIRING AND LAMP TYPE BEFORE YOU BUY A LIGHT SWITCH

If the existing light switch you are replacing uses a neutral wire (white wire), make sure to buy a light switch that supports this wire *and* supports the lamp type controlled by the switch. If you are replacing a light switch that controls fluorescent lights, make sure that you use a switch designed to support fluorescent lights (see Chapter 5 for installation details). Some two-way scene-compatible dimmer switches require a neutral (white) wire, so if you want to install this type of switch, make sure that the existing wall box has a neutral wire available, even if it isn't used by your current switch.

## caution

Keep in mind that light switches work with the same 115-volt AC power that AC wall sockets use. **It can kill you** *if* you don't take suitable precautions, including

- Shut off the power to the circuit containing the light switch you are working on.

- Tag the circuit breaker that is shut off as "out of service" to ensure that nobody turns it on while you are working on the light switch.

- Use a voltage tester to check the wiring into the light switch to ensure that power is off (see Figure 4.9).

If you are not comfortable working with electricity, work with a friend who is experienced with AC wiring, or hire a licensed electrician to install your light switches.

### LIGHT SWITCH COMPARISONS AND SHOPPING GUIDES

See these websites for helpful comparisons of X10 and X10-compatible light switches:

ActiveHome Professional: X10 Switches page at www.activehomepro.com/switches.html

Smarthome's X10 Smart Switches: Part 1 at www.smarthome.com/x10_smart_switches1.html (go to www.smarthome.com/x10_smart_switches2.html for a helpful glossary of features)

Figure 4.10 shows typical switchbox wiring that includes the neutral line. The neutral line normally uses white wire as shown here.

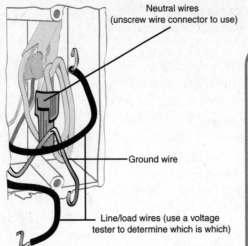

**FIGURE 4.10**

Typical switch-box wiring showing line/load wires, neutral wires, and ground wire.

Neutral wires (unscrew wire connector to use)

Ground wire

Line/load wires (use a voltage tester to determine which is which)

**caution**

If you don't test your wiring to determine which wire is actually hot, you could be injured or killed when you replace your light switch. Use a voltage sensor as demonstrated later in this chapter on both wires going into your light switch to determine which one is hot.

## Selecting the Right Light Switch for Your Needs

If you decide that X10 or X10-compatible light switches are the best way to automate your home lighting, you can choose from switches with a variety of features, including the following:

- Capability to be dimmed by wall switch or X10 control
- Support for high-wattage incandescent lighting, fluorescent lighting, or lights integrated with ceiling fans
- Various maximum wattage ratings
- One-way or two-way X10 control
- Support for three-way or higher numbers of light switches for a single light fixture
- Preset dim levels
- Adjustable *soft start* or *soft on* (turns light fixture on gradually)
- Scene support
- Adjustable dimming rates
- Unit/house code setting by remote control

For more information about most of these features, refer to the "Selecting the Correct Module for Your Lighting Type" section earlier in this chapter.

If you are installing X10 switches in a three-way or higher configuration (two or more switches control the same light), be sure to order

- One master switch; use this switch in the wall box where electricity comes into the circuit
- A slave (companion) switch for each additional switch on the same circuit

Always buy master and companion switches that are designed to work together.

---

**DON'T FORGET THE WALL PLATE!**

Pushbutton X10 and X10-compatible switches, such as the two-wire X10 switch installed in this chapter, use the standard toggle switch plate.

However, many X10-compatible wall switches, particularly those made by Leviton and Smarthome (SwitchLinc), use paddle-type switches rather than the classic toggle switch. Therefore, you cannot reuse your existing wall plate. If possible, order a matching switch plate when you order your switch. However, if you are installing a Smarthome SwitchLinc, Leviton, or other switch that uses a Leviton Decora-style wall switch plate, you can purchase these from many home improvement stores such as Home Depot (www.homedepot.com). However, keep in mind that these stores might require you to buy a bulk quantity rather than a single switch plate.

---

## Preparing to Remove the Old Light Switch

Before you can install an X10 or X10-compatible light switch, you need to remove the old switch. Follow this process:

1. Disconnect power to the switch by turning off the appropriate circuit breaker off or removing the appropriate fuse in the electrical panel (see Figure 4.11).

**FIGURE 4.11**

Shutting off the circuit before replacing a light switch.

Circuit breaker set to off

2. Remove the light switch wall plate.

3. Remove the screws holding in the light switch (see Figure 4.12).

**FIGURE 4.12**

Removing the wall plate and the light switch.

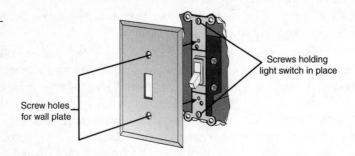

Screws holding light switch in place

Screw holes for wall plate

If you are installing a light switch that uses a neutral wire, such as a switch that can store scene commands, supports two-way operation, or works with fluorescent lights, it is *essential* that you determine which wire is the *load* wire (carries current at all times; also called the *hot* wire) and which is the *line* wire (carries current only when the switch is off; also called the *switched-hot* wire). Even if you are installing a two-wire switch, many vendors recommend this procedure for the most reliable operation.

---

**LINE AND LOAD WIRES: PRACTICE MAKES SAFE—AND PERFECT**

While writing this chapter, I received conflicting opinions from different experts about whether it's really necessary to test for line and load wires when you're installing a two-wire switch. As you can see from the final result, I decided to recommend the test for all switch installations. It might seem like extra bother, but here's my reasoning:

- Sooner or later, you're probably going to install a three-wire (line, neutral, load) switch. You *must* determine which wire is the line (hot) and which is the load (switched-hot) wire to properly install this type of switch.

- If you don't install a three-wire switch correctly, it won't work correctly and it could create a fire hazard.

- If you're not accustomed to checking for line and load wires, it's likely that you'll forget the first time you install a three-wire switch.

My conclusion? It makes sense to be consistent in installation. If you test for line and load wires every time you install a light switch, you won't forget to do it when it's vital to proper switch operation and your safety.

---

## Testing for Line and Load Wires

To perform this task, follow these instructions:

1. Make sure that the light switch is turned off.

2. Reconnect power to the switch circuit.

3. Use a voltage sensor to determine which wire carries current and which wire does not (see Figure 4.13).

4. Turn off power after noting which wire is the line (hot) wire and which wire is the load (switched-hot) wire.

**caution**

A voltage sensor can detect AC voltage up to several inches away from a wire carrying AC current or a device using AC current. It's not necessary to touch the sensor to the wire to get a reading; just push the button on the sensor. It will glow steadily in the presence of AC current, and flash on briefly and then stay off when AC current is not present.

**FIGURE 4.13**

Checking the wires to determine which is hot.

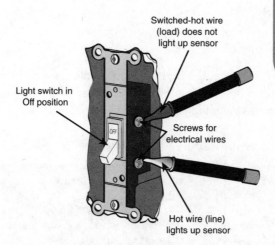

Switched-hot wire (load) does not light up sensor

Light switch in Off position

Screws for electrical wires

Hot wire (line) lights up sensor

If you are installing a two-wire wall switch, proceed to the next section. If you are installing a three-wire switch for use with fluorescent or other nonincandescent lighting, see the "Installing X10-Compatible Wall Switches for Use with Appliances" section in Chapter 5. If you are installing a dimmer switch that uses three or more wires, see the "Installing a Smarthome Two-Way Dimmer Switch" section later in this chapter.

## Installing an X10 Two-Wire Wall Switch

Typical X10 and X10-compatible two-wire light switches have a black wire and a blue wire. When the new switch is installed, connect the black wire to the line (hot) wire and the blue wire to the load (switched-hot) wire. Refer to Figure 4.13.

To complete installation:

1. Make sure that the power is disconnected at the electrical panel.

2. Remove the wires to the light switch (as shown in Figure 4.14).

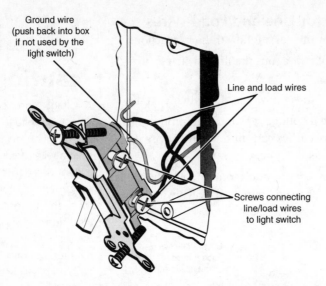

**FIGURE 4.14**

Disconnecting line and load wires from the old light switch.

Ground wire (push back into box if not used by the light switch)

Line and load wires

Screws connecting line/load wires to light switch

3. If the X10 switch uses house and unit control dials, set them for the correct house and unit codes (see Figure 4.15). On some switches, you might need to remove the front switch toggle to access the dials.

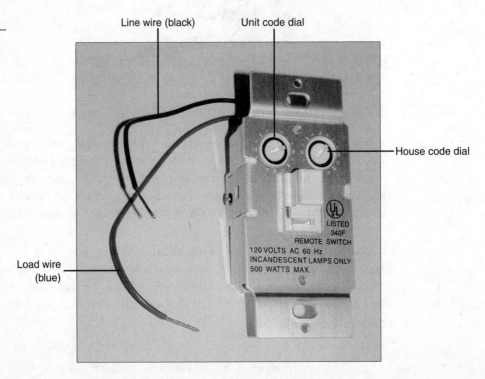

**FIGURE 4.15**

A nondimming X10 light switch that uses house and unit code dials.

Line wire (black)

Unit code dial

House code dial

Load wire (blue)

UL LISTED 340F REMOTE SWITCH 120 VOLTS AC 60 Hz INCANDESCENT LAMPS ONLY 500 WATTS MAX.

4. Connect the black (line) wire from the switch to the line (hot) wire from the wall box. Twist the wires together and use a wire nut to connect the wires to each other.

5. Connect the blue (load) wire from the switch to the load (switched-hot) wire from the wall box. Twist the wires together and use a wire nut to connect the wires to each other.

6. Push the ground wire (if present) back into the box. This type of light switch does not have a connection for the ground wire.

Figure 4.16 shows what the X10 switch looks like after being connected to power wires.

**FIGURE 4.16**

Connecting a nondimming X10 light switch to power wires.

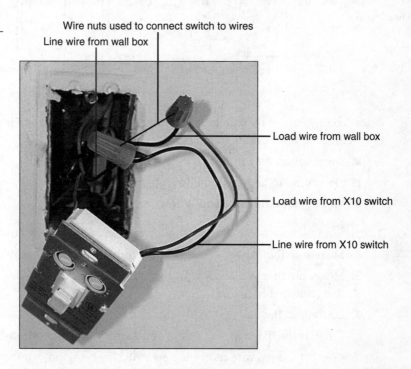

Wire nuts used to connect switch to wires

Line wire from wall box

Load wire from wall box

Load wire from X10 switch

Line wire from X10 switch

Figure 4.17 shows a typical nondimming X10 wall switch after installation.

## Installing a Smarthome Two-Way Dimmer Switch

As a tour through the websites listed in the sidebar "Light Switch Comparisons and Shopping Guides," earlier in this chapter suggests, there are quite a few different types and models of X10-compatible wall switches on the market. When I began to automate my home's lighting, I used the two-wire X10 switch shown in the previous section for porch lighting, but I wanted the den to use a switch with a built-in dimmer, two-way operation, and the capability to store scenes. I chose the Smarthome 2380. It uses a neutral wire and includes a built-in ground wire and a traveler wire for support of three-way or additional switches. Consequently, its installation is more complex than the installation of a two-wire switch. This section shows you how to install this type of switch. To learn how to control this and similar switches' special functions, see Chapter 6.

**FIGURE 4.17**

A nondimmable X10 wall switch after attachment to the wall (left) and after the switch plate has been attached (right).

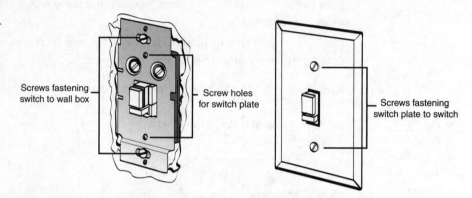

Screws fastening switch to wall box

Screw holes for switch plate

Screws fastening switch plate to switch

Before continuing, make sure that you have read and followed the instructions in these earlier sections of this chapter:

- "Installation Preparations"
- "Preparing to Remove the Old Light Switch"
- "Testing for Line and Load Wires"

To connect the Smarthome 2380 or similar switches, follow these directions:

1. Make sure that power to the switch is turned off at the electrical panel.

2. Make sure that you know which wire is the line (hot) wire and which is the line (switched-hot) wire.

3. Disconnect the line and load wires from the old switch.

4. Connect the black wire from the new switch to the line wire with a wire nut.

5. Connect the red wire from the new switch to the (load) wire with a wire nut.

6. Remove the wire nut from the neutral wires at the back of the wall box and connect the white wire from the new switch to the neutral wire(s) in the switchbox with a wire nut.

7. Connect new switch's ground wire to the bare copper ground wire from the wall box. If the new switch does not have a ground wire, push the ground wire back into the wall box.

8. If the new switch has a traveler wire (used for three-way installations) but there are no additional switches to be connected, cap the wire with a wire nut.

Figure 4.18 shows what a Smarthome 2380 dimmer switch looks like after it has been connected to the wall box wiring.

**FIGURE 4.18**

Connecting a dimmable Smarthome wall switch to wall box wiring.

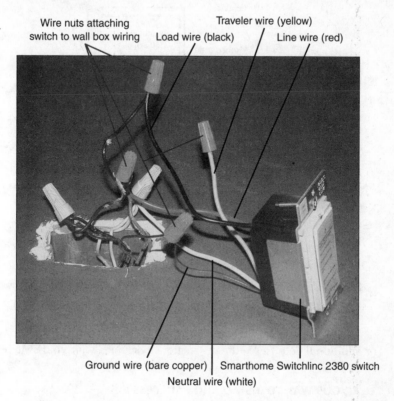

Wire nuts attaching switch to wall box wiring

Traveler wire (yellow)

Load wire (black)

Line wire (red)

Ground wire (bare copper)

Neutral wire (white)

Smarthome Switchlinc 2380 switch

After connecting the switch to the appropriate wires, complete the process:

1. Push the wires back into the switchbox.

2. Reattach the switch to the switchbox with the mounting screws provided.

3. If the switch uses house and unit wheels, set them before continuing.

4. Reconnect power to the switch.

5. If the switch uses a tabletop controller to set house and unit codes, set them now. To set the house and unit codes on the SwitchLinc 2380, press and hold the Set button at the top of the switch toggle for three seconds, and then use a tabletop controller to send the desired house and unit code (refer to Figure 4.19). For other switches, see the instructions packaged with the unit. Be sure to record the house and unit codes you use.

6. Try the switch. If the switch controls dimmable lights, try the dimming feature.

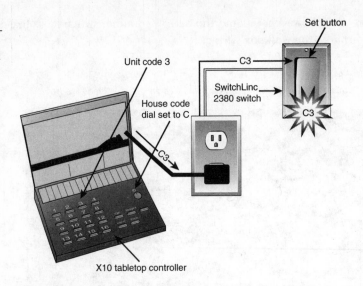

Set button

Unit code 3

C3

SwitchLinc
2380 switch

House code
dial set to C

C3

C3

X10 tabletop controller

7. Use your X10 or X10-compatible remote control or tabletop controller to turn the light off and on and dim the light.

8. Attach the wall plate. You need to order a matching Decora wall plate if you are replacing a toggle switch with a paddle-type switch such as the SwitchLinc 2380.

For additional details, see the instructions packaged with your switch.

---

**CLICK YOUR WAY TO INSTALLATION SUCCESS**

Check out the great Flash-based tutorial at the Smarthome website to learn more about installing X10-compatible light switches, including three-way switches. Your browser needs to have Macromedia Flash installed to view the tutorial at www.smarthome.com/Flash/238xinstall.swf.

If you need Macromedia Flash (required to view the tutorial), download the latest version from www.macromedia.com.

Smarthome provides diagrams for basic two- and three-wire switches at www.smarthome.com/x10_smart_switches4.html and for three-way switches at www.smarthome.com/x10_smart_switches3.html.

---

# Using X10 with Fluorescent Lighting

X10 can be used with fluorescent lights, but appliance modules must be used instead of lamp modules for plug-in fluorescent light fixtures. This is because fluorescent lights place a inductive load on the switch when they are started. Lamp modules are not designed to handle this load, and will be damaged.

If your fluorescent lights are built-in, use X10 or X10-compatible switches that are rated to handle inductive loads. In most cases, a 15-amp switch will be sufficient. Check the amperage rating for the light fixture to verify that a 15-amp switch will be sufficient.

If you prefer not to replace the light switch, you can also install an inline relay module that's rated for fluorescent lighting. These modules can be installed inside the fixture, connecting to the existing fixture wiring.

For more information about these types of switches and modules, see Chapter 5.

# Using X10 with Halogen Lighting

X10 control can be used with halogen lighting as long as the switch is rated for low-voltage lighting. Both dimming and nondimming switches are available for use with halogen and other low-voltage lighting, but note that very low-cost X10 switches are not suitable for use with halogen lighting.

Typically, X10 and X10-compatible switches that use the neutral wire (white wire) are suitable for use with halogen and other low-voltage lighting. However, be sure to check the specification sheet for the switches you are considering before you buy.

# Using X10 with Aquarium Lighting

Aquarium lighting generally uses fluorescent or metal halogen fixtures. By connecting your lighting to an X10 module, you can turn on and turn off the lights remotely or on a time-delayed basis so that your fish and your plant life get enough light to thrive.

Be sure to use appliance-rated X10 modules, such as plug-in modules or inline relay modules, rather than lamp modules to run your aquarium lighting.

# Choosing the Best X10 Controller for Home Lighting

Simple X10 remote controls can control individual lights and dim incandescent lights connected to dimmer-capable X10 lamp modules or switches. By using an X10 or X10-compatible computer interface, you can create macros and scenes that turn on and turn off lights and adjust dimming levels with any dimmable module or switch (see Chapter 11 for details).

However, if you want to store different ramp rates, preset dim rates, or other scene commands in a particular switch's memory without using a computer interface, you need to use a tabletop Maxi Controller such as the one shown in Figure 4.19. This type of controller can send house and unit codes without sending an On, Off, Bright, or Dim command at the same time. Each ramp rate, preset dim level, or other scene command is stored using a unique house/unit code combination. In other words, I can send a command such as C3 ON to turn on the switch shown in Figure 4.19 at its normal level. But, if I store a command such as "Dim to 50% over a two-minute period" as D14 in the switch's scene memory, I can send that command with a tabletop maxi-controller or a computer interface. To learn more about programming switches with scenes, see Chapter 6.

# Troubleshooting X10 Home Lighting

If you're having problems getting your X10 lighting to work, consult the troubleshooting checklist in the following sections for help.

## Can't Turn Lights On and Off

The first and most obvious issue to check is the house and unit codes. If your X10 or X10-compatible module isn't set to the same house code as your remote or tabletop controller, it will not be able to pick up X10 signals. If your X10 or X10-compatible module is set to a unit code different from the unit code you selected, it won't work.

Make sure that you use the same house code for your modules and a unique unit code for each module you want to control individually. Make sure that you are pressing the correct key for your light's unit code. With simple X10 (one-way) modules, you will need to physically inspect the module or light switch to see its settings. If your X10 module can be programmed with a remote, try reprogramming it to the desired house and unit codes.

If someone turns off a lamp using its own switch, the lamp must be turned on again before it can be controlled through an X10 or X10-compatible module. Remind family and visitors to use the X10 or X10-compatible remote or tabletop controller to control these lamps.

If one remote can't control the lamp, try another. The remote's batteries might be run down or, if the remote uses a programmable chip, it might need to be reprogrammed. Consult the remote's instructions for details.

If none of your X10 or X10-compatible modules can be controlled with a wireless remote but its batteries are okay, your transceiver module might be unplugged, set to the wrong house code, or have failed.

If none of your X10 or X10-compatible modules can be controlled with a tabletop controller, the controller might be set to the wrong house code, be unplugged, or have failed.

## Can't Dim Lights

First, make sure that the light you want to dim is connected to a dimmable X10 module or switch. Fluorescent lights can't be dimmed and must be controlled by appliance-rated modules that don't support dimming. If you try to dim such lights, the module controlling the light ignores the dimming command.

Second, make sure that you have selected the correct light. If you can't turn off or turn on the light with your X10 remote, you can't dim it either. Double-check the house and unit codes.

## Can't Bring Light to Full Brightness

If you can't bring the light to full brightness, make sure that a three-way lamp isn't set to use the lower-wattage settings. If the module or switch is programmable to use a preset dim setting, consult the instructions to learn how to override the setting.

## Lights Operate Erratically

If you have problems with consistent operation of X10 or X10-compatible lamp modules, try a different house code (don't forget to change the modules, remotes, and transceivers or tabletop controllers to match); you might be picking up signals from a nearby home or apartment that also uses X10.

If changing house codes doesn't improve reliability, see Appendix B, "Troubleshooting X10," for advanced troubleshooting tips and tools.

# THE ABSOLUTE MINIMUM

- X10 lamp modules are designed to work with incandescent lamps.
- All X10 lamp modules support dimming, enabling you to dim a light without a separate dimmer switch.
- X10 appliance modules don't support dimming, but they can be used with fluorescent lights.
- You can choose from a wide variety of X10-compatible lamp module types, including those that support advanced programming, two-way (transmit-receive) operation, and pass-through connections for normal AC-powered devices.
- Some X10 tabletop controllers enable you to dim selected lamps at the same time.
- You can retrofit screw-in lamps with a screw-in X10 lamp module.
- X10 and X10-compatible light switches enable you to use X10 control with built-in incandescent, fluorescent, and halogen lighting.

*continues*

- Some types of X10 and X10-compatible light switches require a neutral (white) wire. Check the specific wall box you want to rewire before you order your switch.

- Be sure to turn off the circuit powering the light switch you are working on before you start the upgrade process.

- A *voltage sensor*, a simple hand-held device that can detect AC voltage without touching the wire, is a very useful tool for working safely on household wiring.

- When you install a dimming X10 switch, you need to make sure that you connect the black wire from the switch to the hot (line) wire, and the red wire from the switch to the switched-hot (load) wire.

- X10 light switches made for fluorescent lighting do not support dimming.

5

# USING X10 TO CONTROL APPLIANCES

Although most X10 users start by controlling lamps and lighting, there's no reason to stop there. Appliances from TVs and stereos to air conditioners are also "X10-able," enabling you to start, and stop them with a click of your remote control or with signals from other X10 and X10-compatible devices. In this chapter, you'll learn how to put X10 in charge of your appliances.

# X10 Appliance Module Types

You can control almost any appliance with X10, providing you choose the right type of module:

- For appliances up to 15 amps, use plug-in X10 or X10-compatible appliance modules. These are available in two-prong (polarized) or three-prong (polarized and grounded) forms, with or without pass-through connectors. Figure 5.1 shows typical examples. Plug-in appliance modules also support motors up to 1/3 horsepower, 400 watts for TVs, and up to 500 watts for incandescent lights.

**FIGURE 5.1**

Typical appliance modules made by X10 (left) and Smarthome (center and right).The center and right-side modules are programmed with a remote and also feature pass-through outlets.

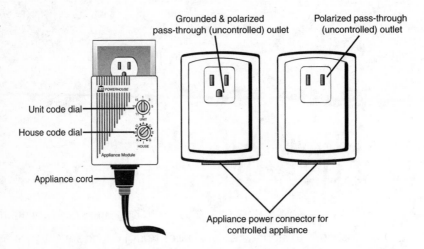

Grounded & polarized pass-through (uncontrolled) outlet

Polarized pass-through (uncontrolled) outlet

Unit code dial

House code dial

Appliance cord

Appliance power connector for controlled appliance

- For plug-in appliances with loads up to 20 amps, and for appliances that are semi-permanently installed (such as air conditioners, electric dryers, and electric stoves), use X10 outlet modules to replace normal electrical outlets. These are available in 15-amp and 20-amp ratings, 110-volt and 220-volt ratings, as well as split and duplex/one-address versions. See Figure 5.2 for typical examples. Note that outlet modules use the traditional X10 house and unit code dials.

- For permanently wired-in appliances, motors, or fluorescent lights that use (or can use) wall-mounted on/off switches, use X10 switches rated for appliances, also referred to as *relay switches*. These switches are available in 110-volt or 220-volt ratings and 15-amp or 20-amp ratings.

Switches made by X10 use code wheels for programming, whereas some X10-compatible switches are programmed with a remote. Consult the instruction manual of the switch you are considering for installation and programming details (see Figure 5.3).

**FIGURE 5.2**

Typical X10 outlet modules. They are installed in place of a normal electrical outlet.

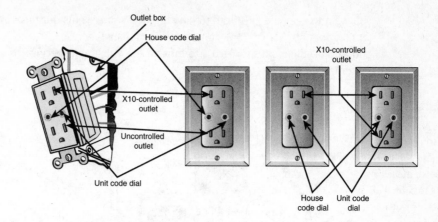

**FIGURE 5.3**

A typical X10 appliance switch after removing the toggle plate to reveal the house and unit code dials.

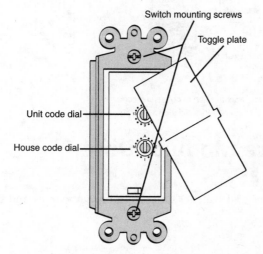

■ For permanently wired-in appliances, motors, or fluorescent lights that use built-in on/off switches, use an X10 or X10-compatible inline appliance switch. Some inline appliance switches support up to 30-amp loads, making them suitable for use with electric water heaters (see Figure 5.4). Appliance relays might use the traditional X10 house and unit code dials, or might be programmed with an X10 remote.

## UNDERSTANDING THE LOCAL CONTROL FEATURE

Most X10 modules support a feature called *local control*, which enables you to turn on and turn off an appliance or lamp with its own switch. If you want the ability to turn on a device, even if the remote is missing or in another room, make sure to specify a module that features local control. However, if you want to use an X10 outlet module to prevent a device from being used, make sure to specify an outlet that does *not* feature local control. For example, if you want to keep the kids from turning on the TV after lights-out time, install an X10 out-let that does not feature local control and use a mini-timer (see Chapter 6, "Using Timers and Advanced Remotes for X10") to turn off the outlet at a specified time. The TV can't be turned on until you turn it on with X10 signals.

**FIGURE 5.4**

Using a 30-amp X10-compatible inline appliance switch made by Elk to control an electric water heater.

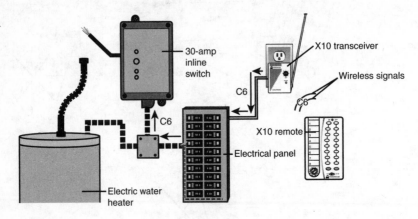

arrows – transmission of house/unit code
C6 – house/unit code

# How X10 Appliance Modules Differ from Lamp Modules

X10 appliance modules and switches differ from lamp modules and switches in sev-eral important ways:

- Lighting support
- Electrical loads
- Programmability

The following sections discuss these differences in more detail.

## Lighting Support

X10 appliance control devices, unlike lamp control devices, don't support dimming, even when used with incandescent or other dimmable lights. Therefore, if you want to dim your lights, make sure that you're *not* using an appliance control device to control your lamps or light fixtures.

Also, X10 appliance modules do not respond to the All Lights On command avail-able with many tabletop controllers and computer interfaces. They do respond to the All Units Off command, however. See Chapter 6 for more information about controllers that support these commands.

Although appliance control devices don't support dimming or All Lights On, they do have three advantages over lamp modules when used in lighting applications:

- Appliance control devices can be used with fluorescent lights, which are often used in kitchens, garages, and workshops.

- Appliance control devices can be used to control combination fan/light fixtures.

- Appliance control devices can be used with higher wattage incandescent lights than lamp control devices.

## Support for Motor and Electrical Loads

X10 appliance control devices are rated to handle resistive (ampere) and motor (horsepower) loads, whereas lamp modules are not. If you use an appliance, motor, or fluorescent light with an X10 lamp control device, you could damage whatever is plugged into the control device. Make sure that you use lamp modules only for incandescent lamps; use appliance modules for other applications.

X10 appliance modules are labeled to indicate the electrical loads they are designed to handle. Figure 5.5 provides a typical example.

**FIGURE 5.5**

Electrical markings on a typical X10 appliance module. Module courtesy of X10 (USA) Inc.

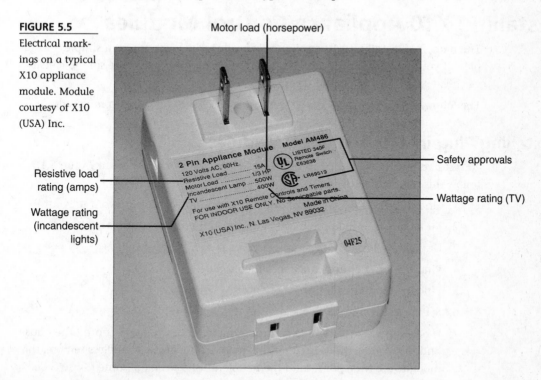

Motor load (horsepower)

Resistive load rating (amps)

Wattage rating (incandescent lights)

Safety approvals

Wattage rating (TV)

## Programmability

Most X10 appliance control modules, regardless of their form, are relatively simple devices. Usually, they are programmed using the traditional house code and unit code wheels, and are designed for one-way (receive-only) operation.

However, if you want to use an X10 appliance module with remote access, particularly via the Internet (see Chapter 12, "Accessing X10 Home Control via Your Home Network and the Internet," for details), consider using a plug-in module that supports two-way operation. Two-way operation enables a module to send status messages back to the controller.

If you want to use an appliance module to control devices that will be part of a scene, such as "dim lights, turn on air conditioner, turn off fan," you can use computer control (see Chapter 11, "Accessing X10 Home Control via Your Home Computer," for details). However, if you want to store scene commands within the module itself so that you can trigger them from a remote control or tabletop controller, use appliance modules with scene storage capability. See Chapter 6 for details about creating scenes.

# Installing X10 Appliance Control Modules

The process of installing X10 appliance control modules ranges from simple to complex. If you can use two or more module types to perform a task, be sure to consider electrical safety factors in your decision.

The following sections cover the process for each type of installation in detail.

## Installing Plug-in X10 Appliance Modules

To install a plug-in X10 appliance module, such as the ones shown in Figure 5.1, follow this basic process:

1. Find a suitable AC electrical outlet near the appliance you want to control.
2. Make sure that the power switch on the lamp or appliance is set to On.
3. Unplug the lamp or appliance from its outlet.
4. Plug the lamp or appliance into the module.
5. Plug the module into the AC outlet.
6. Set the house and unit code dials to the desired settings.
7. If necessary, set the remote control or tabletop controller to control the house and unit code settings used for this module. If you use a wireless remote, the module, the transceiver, and the remote must all use the same house code.
8. Turn the module on and off remotely.

**TRACKING YOUR HOUSE AND UNIT CODES**

Remember, you need to use the same house code for all devices controlled by a particular X10 remote or tabletop controller. Use a unique unit code for each device you want to control independently. The worksheet in Chapter 2, "Getting Started with X10 Home Automation," is helpful for keeping track of the house and unit codes you're using.

## Setting House and Unit Code Dials

If your X10 appliance module uses house and unit code dials, use a small screwdriver to set the dials. With this type of module, you can set it before you plug it into the outlet, as shown in Figure 5.6.

**FIGURE 5.6**

Setting the house code dial on a typical X10 appliance module. Module courtesy of X10 (USA) Inc.

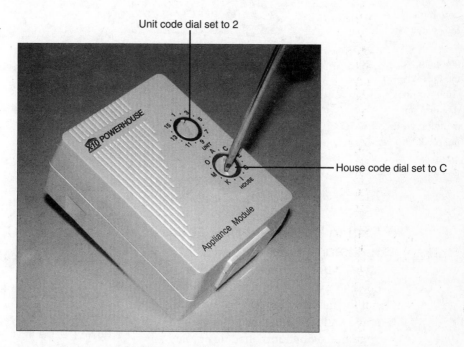

Unit code dial set to 2

House code dial set to C

## Setting House and Unit Codes with a Black & Decker freewire Module

Black & Decker's freewire system (refer to Chapter 4, "Using X10 to Control Home Lighting," for more information) includes an X10-compatible appliance receiver module (see Figure 5.7). This unit has the same ratings as other appliance modules. However, the house and unit code dials on the freewire module are concealed beneath a hinged cover.

The unit code wheel is divided into colors. Each color can be used to represent a zone or room. For easiest operation when using a freewire remote, you should use the zone system when installing modules. For example, you could use the yellow zone for modules in the living room. With the freewire remote control, you can turn off each module in a group with the cover closed, or by opening the cover and using the round on/off buttons to turn off the selected group.

**FIGURE 5.7**

The Black & Decker freewire system's appliance receiver (top) has a color-coded unit code wheel for easy grouping of modules. The remote control (bottom) can control individual modules or a group of modules.

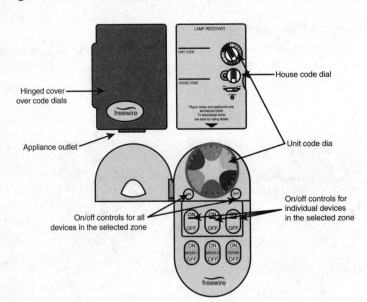

## Setting House and Unit Codes with an X10 Remote

If your X10-compatible appliance module doesn't have house and unit code dials, consult the module's instructions for setting the house and unit codes. To program a Smarthome appliance module or relay switch, for example, press the Set button on the module or switch, and then use a remote, tabletop controller, or computer interface to send the house and unit code you want to use with the module or switch. Figure 5.8 illustrates this process.

**caution**

In the example shown in Figure 5.8, the module uses the *first* X10 code you send. Make sure that code is recorded on your worksheet (as discussed in Chapter 4) because you can't look at the unit to determine its settings.

If you forget the code you sent to the unit, unplug it, press its reset button, and start over.

**FIGURE 5.8**

Using an X10 tabletop controller to program a newly installed Smarthome appliance module with the desired house and unit code.

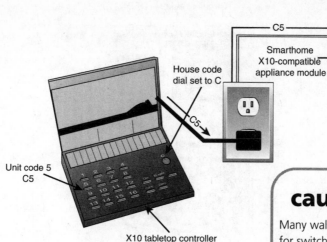

House code dial set to C

C5

Smarthome X10-compatible appliance module

C5

Unit code 5 C5

X10 tabletop controller

## Installing X10-Compatible Wall Switches for Use with Appliances

The process of installing X10-compatible wall switches for use with appliances is similar to the process used for installing an X10 light switch (refer to Chapter 4). However, relay wall switches made for appliances always use the neutral wire, unlike the simple on/off switch installed in Chapter 4.

To install an X10-compatible wall switch that uses a neutral wire, follow this procedure:

1. Turn off the wall switch.

2. Disconnect power to the switch by turning off the appropriate circuit breaker or removing the appropriate fuse (see Figure 5.9).

3. Remove the switch wall plate.

4. Remove the screws holding in the switch.

5. Pull the switch out from the wall box so that the screws holding the wires in place are visible.

6. Make sure that the switch is still turned off.

### caution

Many wall boxes used for switch installations don't have a neutral wire (white) run to the box. If you want to install a switch for lights (refer to Chapter 4) or other uses (this chapter) that require a neutral wire, don't do it if the neutral wire is not available. X10-compatible switches made for appliance control always require the neutral wire; installing such a switch without using the neutral wire can create a fire hazard.

If your existing switch doesn't use the neutral wire but you are installing a switch that does, look toward the back of the wall box for two or more white wires connected to each other with a wire nut. For dimmer applications, you can purchase switches that don't require the neutral wire from Smarthome (SwitchLinc RX series).

Don't confuse the neutral wire with the bare copper ground wire. This is not used in most X10-compatible switch installations, whether for lighting (refer to Chapter 4) or appliance control (this chapter).

**FIGURE 5.9**

Shutting off the circuit before replacing an appliance switch with an X10-compatible appliance switch.

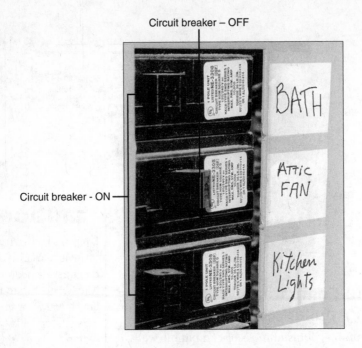

Circuit breaker – OFF

Circuit breaker - ON

BATH

ATTIC FAN

Kitchen Lights

Before continuing, you must test the lines to determine which wire is the *line* wire (carries current at all times—hot) and which line is the *load* wire (carries current when the switch is turned on—switched-hot) using a voltage sensor.

1. Return to the circuit breaker and turn on the power to the switch.

2. Use a voltage sensor to determine which wire is hot (line wire) and which is switched-hot (load wire) (see Figure 5.10).

   The line wire will cause the voltage sensor to light up. Note which wire is the line (hot) wire and which is the load (switched-hot) wire. You need to connect these wires to the correct leads on the new switch.

3. Shut off the power to the switch at the electrical panel.

4. Remove the screws connecting the power wires to the switch (see Figure 5.11).

To connect the new switch, follow these directions:

1. Connect the line wire from the wall box to the switch connector used for the hot (line) wire. Most switches use a screw connection as in Figure 5.12, but a few use a black wire marked *Line*.

2. Remove the wire nut from the neutral (white) wires at the back of the wall box.

3. Connect the neutral wire from the wall box to the switch connector used for the neutral wire. Most switches use a screw connector as in Figure 5.12, but a few use a white wire marked *Neutral*.

4. Connect the load wire from the wall box to the switch connector used for the switched-hot (load) wire. Most switches use a screw connection as in Figure 5.12, but a few use a red wire marked *Load*.

**FIGURE 5.10**

Testing to determine line (hot) and load (switched-hot) wires.

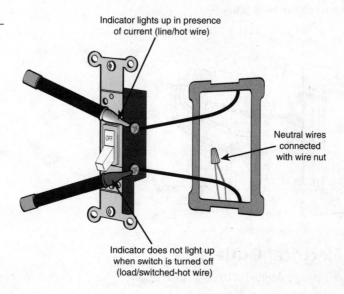

Indicator lights up in presence of current (line/hot wire)

Neutral wires connected with wire nut

Indicator does not light up when switch is turned off (load/switched-hot wire)

**FIGURE 5.11**

Removing the existing appliance power switch.

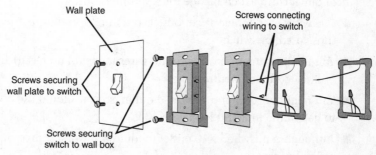

Wall plate

Screws connecting wiring to switch

Screws securing wall plate to switch

Screws securing switch to wall box

Figure 5.12 shows what a typical appliance switch using the neutral line looks like after it has been connected to the wall box wiring.

After connecting the switch to the appropriate wires, complete the process:

1. Push the line, load, neutral, and ground wires back into the switchbox (the ground wire is not used).

2. Reattach the switch to the switchbox.

3. Reconnect power to the switch.

4. Follow the instructions provided with the switch for setting house and unit codes. In most cases, these codes are set by adjusting code wheels, which might require removing the switch toggle plate.

5. Turn on and turn off the device using the switch.

6. Use your X10 remote control or tabletop controller to turn the device off and on.

7. Reattach the wall plate.

**FIGURE 5.12**

Connecting an
X10 wall switch
for appliances to
wall box wiring.

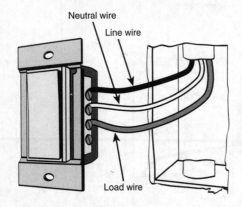

Neutral wire

Line wire

Load wire

## Installing X10 Electrical Outlets

Even if you have installed X10 or X10-compatible light switches, installing an X10 electrical outlet can be a challenge for several reasons:

- The wires used for electrical outlets are thicker and harder to bend than those used for switches.

- You use line, neutral, and ground wires to install an electrical outlet instead of line, load, and neutral wires.

- You might encounter a miswired outlet, so you should use a voltage sensor to determine line and load wires.

- Although a miswired X10 outlet module will work, it presents a fire and safety hazard.

- The outlet module uses most of the space in the electrical box, leaving relatively little room for the wires after the existing outlet has been replaced with the X10 electrical outlet.

- When you push the outlet module back into place, you must make sure that you don't nick the insulation around the wires or trap bare wires between the back of the module and the back of the wall box.

I suggest that you use a plug-in appliance module instead of an outlet module. However, if you decide that you must install an outlet module, be especially careful.

Figure 5.13 shows a typical split (one outlet X10 controlled, the other uncontrolled) outlet module. Note the clear identification of each wire on the rear of the module.

**FIGURE 5.13**

Front (top) and rear (bottom) views of a typical X10 split electrical outlet.

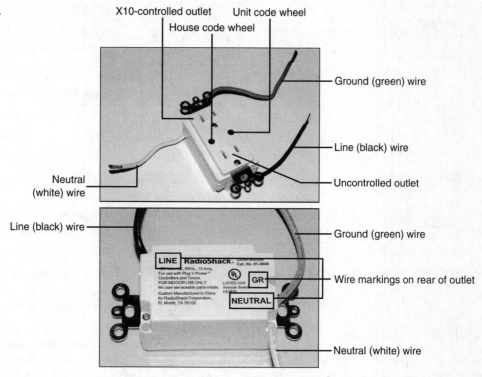

To install an X10 electrical outlet, follow this procedure:

1. Set the house and unit code dials to appropriate values (use the worksheet in Chapter 2 for a reference). Refer to Figure 5.6 earlier in this chapter.

2. Shut off the power to the outlet at the electrical (circuit breaker or fuse) box.

3. Use a voltage sensor to verify the power is out (see Figure 5.14).

4. Remove the faceplate over the existing outlet.

5. Remove the screws holding the outlet to the wall box.

6. Pull the outlet out of the wall box.

7. Depending on the outlet and the original installer's preferences, the wires might be held in place by screws on the sides of the unit or by locks inside the outlet. The outlet shown in Figure 5.15 uses a screw to secure the bare copper ground wire, but internal locks to hold the line and neutral wires. To release the locks, insert a small straight-bladed screwdriver into the slot next to the wire hole and wriggle the screwdriver until the wire releases.

**FIGURE 5.14**

Using a voltage tester to verify that the electrical supply to the outlet has been shut off.

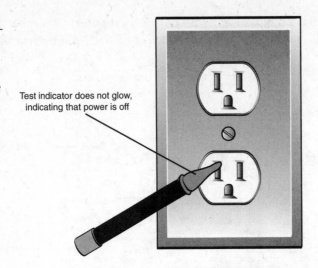

Test indicator does not glow, indicating that power is off

**FIGURE 5.15**

Releasing wires locked into the rear of an outlet.

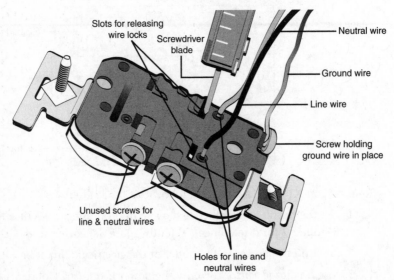

Slots for releasing wire locks

Screwdriver blade

Neutral wire

Ground wire

Line wire

Screw holding ground wire in place

Unused screws for line & neutral wires

Holes for line and neutral wires

8. Connect the line (black), neutral (white), and ground (green) wires from the new X10 outlet to the corresponding wires in the wall box using wire nuts (usually provided with the new outlet). Note that the ground wire is often a bare copper wire. Figure 5.16 shows the outlet after being secured to the wires from the wall box.

9. Push the wires back into the box. You might need to bend the wires to provide sufficient clearance for the outlet because X10 outlets tend to be deeper front-to-back than conventional outlets.

**FIGURE 5.16**

The X10 outlet
after being wired
into the wall
box.

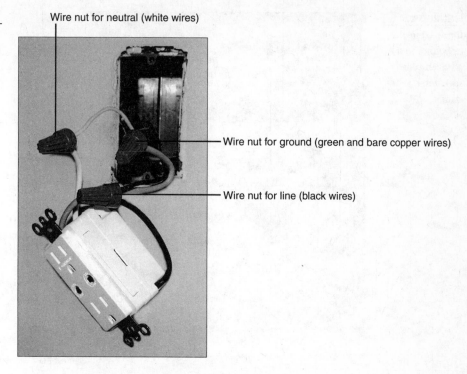

**FIGURE 5.16**

The X10 outlet
after being wired
into the wall
box.

Wire nut for neutral (white wires)

Wire nut for ground (green and bare copper wires)

Wire nut for line (black wires)

10. Attach the X10 outlet to the box using the screws provided with the outlet.

11. Attach the new outlet cover to the outlet.

12. Turn on the power at the electrical box.

13. If the outlet is a split type (one outlet uncontrolled), plug a device into the uncontrolled outlet and turn it on. It should run normally.

14. Plug a device into the controlled outlet (or either outlet, if both are X10 compatible) and use the X10 remote to turn on and turn off the device. Figure 5.17 shows you what your outlet should resemble after you complete installation and plug in an appliance.

15. Repeat step 13 with the other outlet if both outlets are X10 controlled.

16. If both outlets work, you're all set!

## Installing X10-Compatible Appliance Relay Modules

To install an X10-compatible appliance inline relay module, such as the one shown in Figure 5.18, see the instructions packaged with the module. You will need to connect this module to the wiring running to the device you want to control.

**FIGURE 5.17**

Connecting an appliance to the X10-controlled socket in a split outlet.

**FIGURE 5.18**

An X10-compatible inline relay module made by Advanced Control Technologies, Inc.

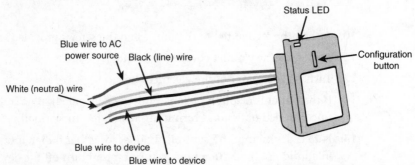

# Using Appliances with X10 Appliance Modules

Connecting your appliance to an X10 appliance module is simple:

1. Turn off the appliance.

2. Plug the appliance into an X10-controlled outlet.

3. Turn on the appliance.

4. Select the appropriate button on the X10 remote control or tabletop controller to activate that appliance.

## Programming Your Appliance to Work with Other Devices

If you want your appliance to turn on at the same time as another X10 device, set both for the same house and unit codes. However, keep in mind that this simplistic approach will prevent you from using the devices independent of one another unless you get out of your easy chair and turn them on or off yourself.

An X10 timer enables you to run an appliance, such as a coffeemaker or fan, when you want it to run. To automate remote operation of your appliance, use a programmable X10 control module. An X10-to-computer interface enables you to control an appliance remotely via your home network or the Internet.

See Chapter 6 for more information about X10 timers, and Chapters 10–12 for more information about controlling your X10 system remotely via telephone, computer, and the Internet.

# Troubleshooting X10 Appliance Control

X10 appliance control is fairly straightforward. But, if you're having problems, use the suggestions in this section to get your installation squared away.

## Incorrect House and Unit Codes

If your X10 module or switch isn't set to the same house code as your remote, it will not be able to pick up X10 signals. If your X10 module is set to a unit code different from the unit code you selected, it won't work.

---

**PLAN, PLAN, AND PLAN AGAIN**
Use the X10 planning tables in Chapter 2 to make sure that you use the same house code for your modules and a unique unit code for each module you want to control individually.

---

Make sure that you're pressing the correct key for your light's unit code. With modules that use house and unit code dials, you'll need to physically inspect the module or light switch to see its settings. If your X10 module can be programmed with a remote, try reprogramming it to the desired house and unit codes.

## Device Is Turned Off

If a device plugged into or controlled by an X10 or X10-compatible module is turned off using its own on/off switch, X10 cannot control that device until it is turned on again.

Turn the device's own power switch to the On position and retry turning it off and on with your X10 remote.

## Remote Control and Transceiver Problems

If one remote can't control the device, try another. The remote's batteries might be run down. Or, if the remote uses a programmable chip, it might need to be reprogrammed. See the remote's instructions for details.

If none of your X10 devices can be controlled with a remote, your transceiver module might be unplugged, be set to the wrong house code, or have failed.

## Tabletop Controller Problems

If none of your X10 devices can be controlled with a tabletop controller, it might be set for the wrong house code, might not be plugged in, or might be plugged into a surge suppressor.

## No Power to Outlet

It's just as important to turn the power back on after you install a new wired-in-place X10 module, outlet, or switch as it is to turn off the power before you start.

Use a voltage tester to see whether other outlets on the same circuit are working. If none of the outlets are working, you need to turn the power back on at the electrical box.

## Incorrectly Wired Outlet

If other outlets on the same circuit as your newly installed outlet are working, but your outlet has no power, you have a wiring problem. *Shut off the power immediately and recheck your installation!* The wire nuts connecting the outlet to the wall box might have come loose when you pushed the wires back into the box, or you might have miswired the outlet or switch. If your outlet still won't work after you redo the wiring and restart it, it might be damaged.

## X10 Devices Work Erratically

If some of your X10 or X10-compatible devices work some of the time, but not consistently, and you have ruled out the problems discussed in this chapter, you might have signal quality problems. For advanced troubleshooting techniques and tools, see Appendix B, "Troubleshooting X10."

# The Absolute Minimum

- Appliance modules are available in plug-in, outlet, switch, and inline relay versions.

- Plug-in appliance modules support motors and loads of 15 amps, but cannot dim lights.

- Most appliance modules support one-way operation, but a few support two-way operation for scenes and reporting status information.

- Most appliance modules, switches, and outlets are set with house and unit code wheels, but a few use a remote to set these codes.

- Appliance switches typically use line (hot), load (switched-hot), and neutral wires.

- Electrical outlets use only three wires: line, neutral, and ground.

- Electrical outlets are available to handle loads up to 20 amps.

- Problems with X10 appliance modules are often caused by incorrect house and unit codes, devices that are already turned off, remote control and transceiver problems, no power to the outlet, or an incorrectly wired outlet.

# 6

# USING TIMERS AND ADVANCED REMOTES FOR X10

This chapter shows you how to turn on and turn off lights and appliances at preset intervals or randomly to give a lived-in look to your home while you're away, program dimmer switches, and control your home entertainment and X10 devices with a single remote. By adding timers, Maxi Controllers, and universal remotes to your existing X10 home automation system, you can turn it into a more powerful and more useful system.

# X10 Timers

An X10 timer (see Figure 6.1) resembles an alarm clock. However, instead of waking you up, it wakes up specified X10 devices. The Mini Timer shown in Figure 6.1 can control up to eight devices interactively or up to four devices with its built-in timer.

**FIGURE 6.1**

A typical X10 Mini Timer.

Radio Shack's Home Automation Starter Kit #61-3000 features a Mini Timer with an LCD display (see Figure 6.2) that can control eight devices interactively or with its built-in timer. It can store up to 64 on or off commands in its built-in memory.

**FIGURE 6.2**

Radio Shack's #61-3000 Home Automation starter kit includes a Plug 'n Power module (left) and Mini Timer (right).

## What X10 Timers Can Do

An X10 timer can be used in many ways:

- It can turn on or turn off a particular device.
- It can dim or brighten a specified incandescent or other dimmable lamp connected to a lamp module or light switch.
- It can turn on all lights that use the same house code as the timer and are connected to lamp modules or switches.
- It can turn off all devices (lamps and appliances) that use the same house code as the timer.
- It can turn on and turn off specified devices on a timed basis.
- It can adjust on/off times for all devices controlled by the timer.

You will learn how to use each of these features in the following sections.

## Preparing to Use an X10 Timer

Before you install an X10 timer, you need to make sure that you know:

- Which devices you want to control
- What house code is used by your devices
- What unit code is used by each device
- What types of modules are used by your devices

You need to identify the devices you want to control so that you can rank them in order of importance. Although you can control up to eight different unit codes interactively with an X10 Mini Timer, you can control only four different unit codes with the timer feature. Therefore, you must decide which devices are most important to control on a timed basis. For example, you might decide that porch lights, the bedroom lamps, and the coffeepot are the most critical devices to you.

---

**DUPLICATE UNIT CODES EXTEND YOUR TIMER'S REACH**

Although Mini Timers are limited to four different unit codes, that doesn't mean you can control only four different devices. Configure modules for devices you would normally operate at the same time, such as bedside lamps or porch lights, on the same unit code. A single command controls all devices with the same unit code.

---

A Mini Timer, like any other X10 controller, controls only one house code at a time. If you use multiple house codes in your X10 home automation system, use a different timer for each house code you want to control.

**MINI OR MAXI? UNIT CODES MAKE THE DIFFERENCE**

A Mini Timer or Mini Controller can control house codes 1–8. A Maxi Controller can control house codes 1–16. Most Mini Timers and Mini Controllers also use a switch to select house codes 1–4 or 5–8 for interactive control to enable the unit to occupy as little shelf or table space as possible.

Maxi Controllers also use separate unit code and command (On, Off, Bright, Dim) buttons. This enables a Maxi Controller to send addresses for programming some types of modules and switches. Mini Timers and Mini Controllers cannot send addresses separately from commands.

You need to identify the unit codes used by your devices. Mini Timers can control only unit codes 1–4 and 5–8. Timers that can control unit codes 9–16 are not widely available at the present time. Therefore, you must adjust the unit codes on the modules, outlets, or switches you want to control with a Mini Timer to fall into one number range or the other, or purchase and configure an additional Mini Timer. If you need to control devices with unit codes higher than 8, consider using a tabletop Maxi Controller (see the "X10 Tabletop Maxi Controller" section later in this chapter) or a computer-based controller (see Chapter 11, "Accessing X10 Home Control via Your Home Computer," for details).

The module type(s) you use in your automation system are also important if you want to make full use of the All Lights On button. This button triggers lamp modules and light switches, but does not control appliance modules or outlets. However, the All Units Off button turns off all types of X10 modules, including appliance modules and outlets as well as lamp modules and light switches. Use Table 6.1 to plan your Mini Timer home automation project. Table 6.2 provides a completed sample for your review.

**TABLE 6.1**   Timer Planning Sheet

| House Code | Unit Code | Device Type | Location | Module Type | Control with Timer? |
|---|---|---|---|---|---|
| — | — | — | — | — | — |
| — | — | — | — | — | — |

**TABLE 6.2**   Sample Timer Planning Sheet

| House Code | Unit Code | Device Type | Location | Module Type | Control with Timer? |
|---|---|---|---|---|---|
| B | 2 | Porch light | Front Porch | Lamp | Yes |
| B | 3 | TV | Bedroom | Appliance | Yes |

**TABLE 6.2** (continued)

| House Code | Unit Code | Device Type | Location | Module Type | Control with Timer? |
|---|---|---|---|---|---|
| B | 5 | Porch light | Back Porch | Lamp | Yes*<br>*Change to unit code 2 |
| B | 4 | Coffee maker | Kitchen | Appliance | Yes |
| C | 1 | Ceiling light | Bedroom | Lamp | Yes*<br>*Change to house code B |
| C | 2 | Motion detector | Garage | Specialized | No |
| C | 3 | Wireless camera | Garage | Specialized | No |

As you can see in Table 6.2, inventorying your existing X10 modules can be very useful before installing an X10 timer. Note that the back porch light must be moved to unit code 2 to enable it to be controlled by the same timer as other appliances. Also, the house code used for the ceiling light in the bedroom must be changed to B from C to enable it to be controlled by the timer. The security devices in the garage could be controlled by a separate timer, or not timer-controlled at all as in this example.

To adjust the unit or house code for a plug-in module with control dials, use a small screwdriver as shown in Figure 6.3.

**FIGURE 6.3**

Adjusting code dials on an X10 plug-in module.

To adjust the unit or house code for an electrical outlet with control dials, use a small screwdriver as shown in Figure 6.4.

**FIGURE 6.4**
Adjusting code
dials on an X10
wall outlet.

To adjust the unit or house code for a light switch with control dials, you have to remove the switchplate, and then use a small screwdriver as shown in Figure 6.5.

**FIGURE 6.5**
Adjusting code
dials on an X10
light switch.

If you use modules or light switches that are programmed with code sequences, you will need to use a Maxi Controller or a computer interface to configure them. To learn how to use a Maxi Controller, see the "X10 Tabletop Maxi Controller" section, later in this chapter. Computer interfaces are discussed in Chapter 11.

## Setting Up an X10 Mini Timer

Before you plug in your Mini Timer, flip it over and install the appropriate battery in the base. The X10 Mini Timer uses a nine-volt alkaline battery in the base (see Figure 6.6). The Radio Shack Mini Timer shown in Figure 6.2 uses a pair of AA batteries. Batteries provide backup power to maintain settings if the unit is unplugged or an AC power failure takes place.

**FIGURE 6.6**

Installing a nine-volt battery in the Mini Timer.

To install a Mini Timer, simply plug it into an AC electrical outlet. Remember, as with any X10 device, don't plug it into a surge suppressor; surge suppressors prevent X10 signals from being transmitted reliably.

To set the current time with either the X10 or Radio Shack Mini Timer, select Set Clock with the Mode Switch slider (see Figure 6.7) and use the Time buttons to advance to the correct time. After you've selected the correct time, move the mode switch to Run.

Figure 6.8 shows the control panel of the Radio Shack Mini Timer illustrated in Figure 6.2. Compared to the X10 Mini Timer, the Radio Shack Mini Timer does not provide bright/dim control for lamp modules, but other interactive control options are similar.

**FIGURE 6.7**

The control panel of a typical X10 Mini Timer.

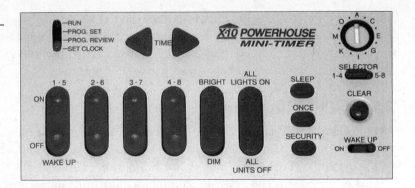

**FIGURE 6.8**

The control panel of the Radio Shack Mini Timer included in the Home Automation Kit #61-3000.

## Using the Timer Interactively

When the mode switch on the Mini Timer is set to Run, the Mini Timer can be used like any tabletop or wireless X10 remote. Press the On button for the unit code of the device you want to start, and the device turns on; press the Off button to turn it off (refer to Figures 6.7 and 6.8).

To turn on all lights using the same house code as the timer, press the All Lights On button with either Mini Timer. To turn off all modules using the same house code as the timer, press the All Units Off button (refer to Figures 6.7 and 6.8).

To adjust the brightness of a particular lamp with the X10 timer, press the On button that corresponds to that lamp's unit code, and then press the Dim or Bright button (refer to Figure 6.7) until the lamp reaches the desired brightness level.

## Using Timed Control

After you've used interactive control to make sure that your timer can communicate with your modules, it's time to learn how to use timed control. Timers can trigger devices to turn on or turn off at the same time every day, just once, or at random times within the hour selected (Security mode).

In this example, let's program porch lights on unit code 2 to come on at 6:00 p.m. and turn off at 11:30 p.m. every day. To adapt this procedure to your use, replace the unit codes and times with those suitable for your situation. The steps are the same for the X10 and Radio Shack Mini Timers.

1. Make sure that the porch lights are set to the same house code as the timer and to unit code 2 (refer to the "Preparing to Use an X10 Timer" section earlier in this chapter for details).

2. Move the Mode Switch slider to Prog Set (see Figure 6.9).

3. Press the Time button to advance the time to 6:00 p.m.

4. Press the On button for unit code 2. The display blinks momentarily. This sets the On time for 6:00 p.m.

5. Press the Time button to advance the time to 11:30 p.m.

6. Press the Off button for unit code 2 to shut off the unit at 11:30 p.m.

7. Set the Mode Switch slider to Run.

The porch light will come on at 6:00 p.m. and turn off at 11:30 p.m.

**FIGURE 6.9**

Setting a timed event.

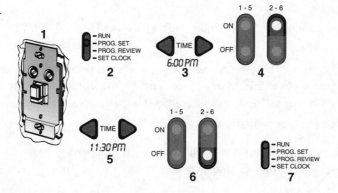

With the X10 Mini Timer, you can store two on and two off commands for each unit code. Therefore, you can also turn on the porch lights in the morning. To turn on the porch lights at 5:30 a.m. and off at 8:00 a.m., follow the same procedure, but substitute 5:30 a.m. for 6:00 p.m. in step 3 and 8:00 a.m. for 11:30 p.m. in step 5.

After you've stored both sets of commands, the porch lights will come on at 5:30 a.m. every day, shut off at 8:00 a.m., come on again at 6:00 p.m. every evening, and shut off at 11:30 p.m. each night.

You can store up to 64 on or off commands in the memory of the Radio Shack Mini Timer. There is no restriction on the number of commands that can be stored for each unit code.

The X10 Mini Timer used in this chapter displays 18:18 in the time display window if you attempt to create a third on or off event for a particular unit number. To clear

18:18 from the display, move the mode switch to Prog Review and press the On or Off button for the unit code you tried to program with a third event. This puts the unit into Review mode.

The Radio Shack Mini Timer displays Full in its LCD display if you attempt to store more than 64 commands. To clear a command, press the number of the unit code you want to remove, press the On or Off button, and then press the Clear button (refer to Figure 6.9).

## Selecting a Timed Event to Occur Just Once

If you want to set a timed event to occur just once, you can do so by pressing the Once button during the programming process with the X10 Mini Timer. For example, let's assume that you want to turn on your Christmas tree at 5:00 a.m. on Christmas Day to greet the children as they hurry down the stairs. Follow this procedure any time after 5:00 a.m. on Christmas Eve:

1. Make sure that the module used for the Christmas tree is set to the same house code as the timer and that you know the unit code. In this case, we'll use unit code 1.
2. Move the Mode Switch slider to Prog Set (see Figure 6.10).
3. Press the Time button to advance the time to 5:00 a.m.
4. Press the On button for unit code 1, and then press the Once button (see Figure 6.10) within four seconds. The display blinks momentarily. This sets the Christmas tree to turn on at 5:00 a.m. the next morning.
5. Set the Mode Switch slider to Run.

At 5:00 a.m., the Christmas tree will turn on automatically. If you really want to surprise the kids, choose a time *after* they're likely to be up.

**FIGURE 6.10**

Setting a one-time event.

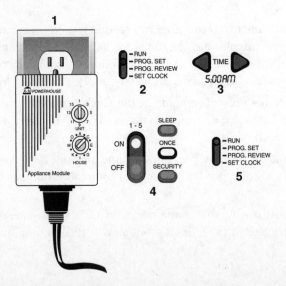

With the Radio Shack Mini Timer, follow steps 1–3 as listed. In step 4, press the Mode button instead of the Once button and hold it down until "Once" shows on the LCD display. Follow step 5 as written.

### Checking and Removing Timed Settings

To check your settings, move the Mode Switch slider to Prog Review (Prog. Set/Review on the Radio Shack Mini Timer). Press any On or Off button to see events programmed for that unit code: The time display shows the on or off time if an event has been programmed. To see whether a second on or off time has been programmed, press the On or Off button again. To remove a timed setting, press the Clear button while viewing an on or off time. After you've finished reviewing or deleting settings, set the Mode Switch slider to Run.

## Using the Security Feature

To vary the exact on and off times for a particular module, press the Security button on the X10 timer within four seconds after you select On or Off during programming. For example, to vary the exact times the porch lights come on, follow this procedure:

1. Make sure that the porch lights are set to the same house code as the timer and to unit code 2 (refer to the "Preparing to Use an X10 Timer" section earlier in this chapter for details).

2. Move the Mode Switch slider to Prog Set (see Figure 6.11).

3. Press the Time button to advance the time to 6:00 p.m.

4. Press the On button for unit code 2 and press the Security button within four seconds (see Figure 6.11). This sets the actual on time to vary within the hour of 6 p.m.

5. Press the Time button to advance the time to 11:30 p.m.

6. Press the Off button for unit code 2 to shut off the unit at 7:00 a.m. and press Security within four seconds. This sets the actual off time to vary within the hour of 11 p.m.

7. Set the Mode Switch slider to Run.

With the Radio Shack Mini Timer, follow steps 1–5 as written. In step 6, repeatedly press the Mode button within four seconds (instead of the Security button) until "Security" is displayed. Follow step 7 as written.

## Sleep, Alarm, and Snooze Features

Use the Sleep button (see Figure 6.12) to turn on or turn off a particular unit code for 15 minutes or multiples of 15 minutes. To turn on a device for 15 minutes, press the On button for the device's unit code, and then press the Sleep button within four seconds. Press the Sleep button twice to turn it on for 30 minutes, and so forth. To turn off a device for 15 minutes, press the Off button for the device's unit code, and then press the Sleep button within four seconds. Press the Sleep button twice to turn it off for 30 minutes, and so forth. Up to two unit codes can be operated in Sleep mode at the same time. The Radio Shack Mini Timer does not support Sleep mode.

**FIGURE 6.11**

Setting up events with the security feature.

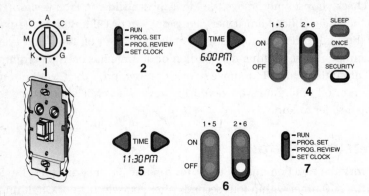

The Wake Up slider switch (see Figure 6.12) triggers a buzzer when an On command is sent to unit code 1 or unit code 5. You can use this feature to make your Mini Timer function as an alarm clock. For example, connect your bedroom lights to a module set for unit code 1 or unit code 5, set unit code 1 (or 5) to receive an On command at 6:30 a.m., and if Wake Up is turned on, the bedroom lights will come on at 6:30 a.m. and the Mini Timer will sound a buzzer. On the Radio Shack Mini Timer, the Wake slider switch performs the same function.

On weekends, leave Wake Up turned off and the buzzer will not come on. To shut off both the buzzer and the module on unit code 1 or unit code 5, move the buzzer switch to Off and move the Mode switch to Set Clock. At the end of the weekend, move the Wake Up switch to On (doing so re-enables the buzzer) and the Mode switch back to Run (the module on unit code 1 or 5 will turn on as scheduled next morning). On the Radio Shack Mini Timer, use the Clock Set position instead of Set Clock to turn off wakeup functions.

When the buzzer sounds and the device on unit code 1 (or 5) is triggered, press any key on either Mini Timer to snooze (turn off) the buzzer for 10 minutes. The device triggered remains on.

**FIGURE 6.12**

The sleep and wakeup controls on a typical Mini Timer.

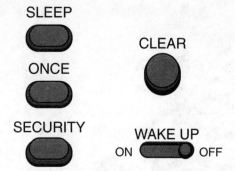

SLEEP

CLEAR

ONCE

SECURITY

WAKE UP

ON    OFF

# X10 Tabletop Maxi Controller

As you've learned in the preceding sections, adding a Mini Timer to your X10 home automation system provides true automation. You no longer need to turn on or turn off lights or other devices manually or with a remote control. However, a Mini Timer is not designed to control multiple devices interactively or to send strings of program codes to intelligent dimmer switches. If you have one or more programmable dimmer switches, or if you want to control groups of devices, you need to add a full-featured X10 tabletop controller (see Figure 6.13), often referred to as a Maxi Controller, to your home automation system.

Like a Mini Timer, the X10 tabletop controller shown in Figure 6.13 can turn on all lights and shut off all units. However, it differs in two significant ways from a Mini Timer or wireless remote control:

■ It can control all 16 available X10 unit codes.

■ It has separate buttons for unit codes and for commands (on, off, bright, dim).

These features enable you to control multiple devices with a single set of commands and send combinations of house codes and unit codes to control programmable X10 dimmer switches, such as the one shown in Figure 6.14. To learn how to install this type of light switch, refer to Chapter 4, "Using X10 to Control Home Lighting."

**caution**

Just because a controller fits on a table and plugs into the wall doesn't mean it supports programmable devices. If the controller uses On/Off buttons for each unit code, it can't be used to control multiple devices or send commands. Mini controllers have Unit Code On and Unit Code Off buttons, whereas Maxi Controllers have Unit Code buttons and separate On and Off buttons. This enables the Maxi Controller to send an X10 address without a command (A10) instead of sending an address with a command (A10 On or A10 Off) as a Mini Controller or Mini Timer does.

**FIGURE 6.13**
X10 Powerhouse Maxi Controller—a typical tabletop controller.

**FIGURE 6.14**
A programmable X10 dimmer switch that must be configured with a Maxi Controller or with a computer interface.

## Setting Up the Maxi Controller

To set up a Maxi Controller, follow this procedure:

1. Determine the house code used by the devices you want to control.

2. Turn the House Code dial (see Figure 6.15) to the house code used by those devices.

3. Plug the controller into an AC outlet, not a surge protector.

Some vendors supply stickers that you can use to indicate the type of module and location for each unit code. Don't apply these stickers right away; instead, keep notes on a separate piece of paper until you've completed your project.

**FIGURE 6.15**

Control buttons and the House Code dial on a typical X10 tabletop Maxi Controller.

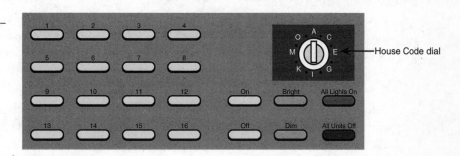

House Code dial

## Controlling Devices

To control a single device, press the unit code number for that device, and then the command key (refer to Figure 6.15). For example, to turn on a lamp connected to a module at unit code 1, press the 1 button, and then press the On button. To turn off the lamp, press 1, and then press the Off button.

To control multiple devices at the same time, press the unit code number for each device, followed by the command key. For example, to turn on lamps connected to modules at unit code 1 and unit code 2, press 1, 2, and then press the On button. To turn off the lamps, press 1, 2, and then press the Off button.

You can also dim or brighten two or more lights at the same time. For example, to dim lamps on unit codes 1 and 2, press 1, 2 and then press Dim until the desired brightness level is reached.

## Using All On/All Off Commands

The All Lights On and All Units Off command buttons (refer to Figure 6.15) work the same way on a tabletop Maxi Controller as on the X10 Mini Timer discussed earlier in this chapter:

- Press the All Lights On button to turn on all lights connected to X10 lamp modules or light switches using the same house code as the controller.

- Press the All Units Off button to turn off all X10 devices (including lights and appliances) using the same house code as the controller.

## Configuring Programmable Modules

If you plan to install programmable dimmer switches or modules to your X10 home automation system, adding an X10 tabletop Maxi Controller should be on your "must buy" list. Its capability to send combinations of house and unit codes to a programmable dimmer switch or module is essential, especially if you are not ready to add computer control to your X10 home automation system.

Before you can send commands to the dimmer switch or module, make sure that you have the instruction manual for the switch or module (you can usually obtain electronic versions in Adobe Acrobat format from the vendor). The instruction sheet lists the codes you need to send to program preset dimming levels, dimming rates, and other advanced features, as well as the method used to program house and unit codes for the device.

You'll need to keep a small screwdriver handy because many modules use different house and unit code combinations for some types of programs. You must change the house code frequently when sending strings of commands. Here are some examples based on commands used by ToggleLinc and SwitchLinc programmable dimmer switches made by Smarthome (www.smarthome.com).

To prepare the switch or module to accept programming commands, send the following codes with the tabletop Maxi Controller: O16, N16, M16, P16, M16.

To send these commands, follow this procedure (see Figure 6.16):

1. Turn the House Code dial to O.
2. Press the 16 key.
3. Turn the House Code dial to N.
4. Press the 16 key.
5. Turn the House Code dial to M.
6. Press the 16 key.
7. Turn the House Code dial to P.
8. Press the 16 key.

9. Turn the House Code dial to M.

10. Press the 16 key.

11. Turn the House Code dial back to the normal house code used (for example, B).

## Configuring a Preset Dimming Level

To set the switch or module to turn on at a preset dimming level, press the Unit Code button for that switch, followed by the Dim button. Release the Dim button when the lamp is at the appropriate brightness. Then send these commands to store this level: O16, P16, N16, M16.

To send these commands, follow this procedure:

1. Turn the House Code dial to O.

2. Press the 16 key.

3. Turn the House Code dial to P.

4. Press the 16 key.

5. Turn the House Code dial to N.

6. Press the 16 key.

7. Turn the House Code dial to M.

8. Press the 16 key.

9. Turn the House Code dial back to the normal house code used (for example, B).

When you turn on the switch or module, the lamp connected to it will turn on at the brightness level stored in memory. Scene-capable dimmer switches store scenes and bright/dim ramp rates the same way.

## Creating a Scene

Many, but not all, programmable light switches and modules are also capable of storing a scene. Switches and modules with this feature are sometimes referred to as *scene-capable*. An X10 *scene* is a particular action (such as dimming the light to a particular level at a particular rate or turning on a fan) that is assigned its own house and unit code; think of it as a sort of macro. You can create scenes with a tabletop Maxi Controller as described in this section, or with an X10 computer interface (see Chapter 11).

---

**SCENE MEMBERSHIP VERSUS SCENE STORAGE**

Don't confuse a module or switch's capability to store a scene with the capability to be in a scene. Any X10 module or switch can be part of a scene controlled by an X10 or X10-compatible computer interface and program. However, only modules or switches with scene memory can store a scene that can be triggered with a house/unit code from a tabletop controller or wireless remote. For example, I have a scene-capable light switch in my den that is normally addressed as C2. However, I have stored a preset dim level and ramp rate as a scene using C13. When I want to use the den light normally, I send C2 ON. But when I want to trigger the scene, I send C13 ON.

---

The specifics of how to create a scene vary with the programming codes understood by the module or light switch. The examples in this section, like those in the previous section, are based on the codes supported by ToggleLinc, SwitchLinc, and other Smarthome products. If you use other brands of scene-enabled modules or switches, consult the documentation for your product for details.

To prepare the module to receive a new scene, enter these commands: O16, N16, M16, P16, M16.

To send these commands, follow this procedure:

1. Turn the House Code dial to O.
2. Press the 16 key.
3. Turn the House Code dial to N.
4. Press the 16 key.
5. Turn the House Code dial to M.
6. Press the 16 key.
7. Turn the House Code dial to P.
8. Press the 16 key.

9. Turn the House Code dial to M.

10. Press the 16 key.

11. Turn the House Code dial back to the normal house code used (for example, B).

Let's assume that the unit code for the switch is 2. To create a scene with a low light level, press 2 on the controller, and then press the Dim key and release it when the light level reaches the desired level. To store that level as a scene, send the following commands, followed by the unit code you want to use to identify that scene.

The scene commands are M16, N16, O16, P16.

To send these commands, follow this procedure:

1. Turn the House Code dial to M.

2. Press the 16 key.

3. Turn the House Code dial to N.

4. Press the 16 key.

5. Turn the House Code dial to O.

6. Press the 16 key.

7. Turn the House Code dial to P.

8. Press the 16 key.

9. Turn the House Code dial back to the normal house code used (for example, B).

Finally, send the unit code you want to use to identify the scene. Make sure that you don't use an existing unit code. For example, if house code B is already controlling unit codes 1–6, you could use any unit code from 7–16. If you want to use a Mini Timer or Mini Controller to control the scene, make sure that you assign it a unit code from 1–8. However, if you plan to use a Maxi Controller or wireless remote that supports all unit codes 1–16, you can assign any unit code to the scene.

For example, to use B16 as the code for this scene, do the following:

1. Make sure that the house code is set to B.

2. Press the 16 button.

To activate the switch or module in its normal mode, follow these steps:

1. Make sure that the house code is set to the correct value (B, in this example).

2. Press the button for the module's normal unit code (2, in this example).

3. Press On, Off, Bright, or Dim.

To activate the scene, do the following:

1. Make sure that the house code is set to the correct value (B, in this example).

2. Press the button for the scene code (16, in this example).

3. Press On to activate the scene.

Most scene-enabled modules can store multiple scenes. For example, the SwitchLinc two-way switch I installed can support up to 64 scenes. Check with the vendor of the switch or module you're considering to determine how many scenes a particular model can store. *Each scene must use a unique house/unit code combination.*

Use Table 6.3 to record scene settings you create. Table 6.4 shows a completed sample.

## caution

As you can see from the examples in this chapter, certain house and unit codes are reserved by programmable modules and switches for sending and storing commands. Do *not* use these house and unit codes for other devices. The easiest way to avoid conflicts is to avoid using the house codes used for programming with any of your devices. For example, with Smarthome devices, you might want to avoid using house codes M, N, O, and P. Consult the documentation for other brands to determine which house and unit codes are reserved for configuring programmable modules.

**TABLE 6.3**  Scene Settings Worksheet

| Module Type | Brand/Model | Location | Default House/Unit Code |
|---|---|---|---|
| — | — | — | — |
| Scene 1 Description | Scene 1 House/Unit Code | | |
| — | — | | |
| Scene 2 Description | Scene 2 House/Unit Code | | |
| — | — | | |
| Scene 3 Description | Scene 3 House/Unit Code | | |
| — | — | | |

**TABLE 6.4** Sample Scene Settings Worksheet

| Module Type | Brand/Model | Location | Default House/Unit Code |
|---|---|---|---|
| Light switch | Smarthome 2380W | Bedroom | B6 |
| Scene 1 Description | Scene 1 House/Unit Code | | |
| Dims to 25% | B16 | | |
| Scene 2 Description | Scene 2 House/Unit Code | | |
| Dims to 50% | B15 | | |
| Scene 3 Description | Scene 3 House/Unit Code | | |
| Gradually brightens from 0–100% (wake up) | B14 | | |

# X10 Universal Remote

If don't want to add yet another remote to your growing collection of them and you use X10 interactively, consider using a universal remote that can control both X10 devices and some, or all, of your home entertainment devices.

At first glance, this might seem to be an impossible requirement. After all, X10 uses commands sent via AC power line signals, whereas home entertainment devices use infrared *(IR)* line-of-sight signals. However, by using a remote control capable of sending X10 and home entertainment signals (see Figure 6.17), you can control both types of devices with a single remote control.

**FIGURE 6.17**

X10's UR74A Universal Learning Remote control works with typical X10 RF transceivers (inset) and with most major brands of TV, VCR, and other home entertainment products.

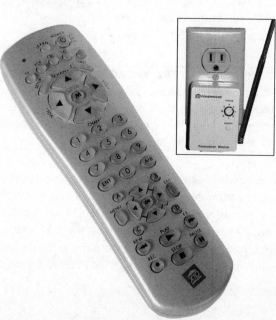

# Setting Up a Universal Remote

To set up a typical universal remote for use with your home entertainment hardware, such as the UR74A 5-in-1 Universal Learning Remote shown in Figure 6.17, install the appropriate batteries, and then use the code listing supplied with the remote or use the learning feature.

Here's how to teach the remote to control your electronics:

1. Turn on the TV or other electronic device you want to control with the universal remote.

2. Press and hold the SETUP button (see Figure 6.18) until the red LED indicator light glows steadily.

3. Release the SETUP button.

4. Press and release the mode button for the device you want to control. For example, to control a TV, press the TV button.

5. Enter the three-digit code from the library code table for the device. After you've entered the last digit, the red LED will turn off.

6. Point the remote at the device and press POWER. If the device turns off, continue to the next step.

7. Point the remote at the device and press POWER to turn the device on again.

8. Press CHANNEL +. If the device responds, you have successfully programmed your remote to use that device.

If the device does not work at step 7 or step 8, start the process over again with the next code number for the brand of device. For other types of X10 universal remotes, see the instructions packaged with the remote.

---

**IF AT FIRST YOU DON'T SUCCEED, TRY, TRY AGAIN**

Many brands of electronic equipment have multiple codes you might need to try before you find the right code. For example, some brands list as many as 28 codes. If you lose your code sheet, contact the vendor for a replacement. Most remote vendors post code listings on their websites.

---

Use the learning feature to teach the universal remote any codes it did not receive from the code used to configure basic features. For example, if you find a code that supports all of your television's features except the FM radio button, you can use the learning feature on the new remote to understand the FM command: Transmit the FM radio command from your original remote to the learning remote while you select an unused button for configuration as the FM radio button.

**FIGURE 6.18**

The control panel of the UR74A remote.

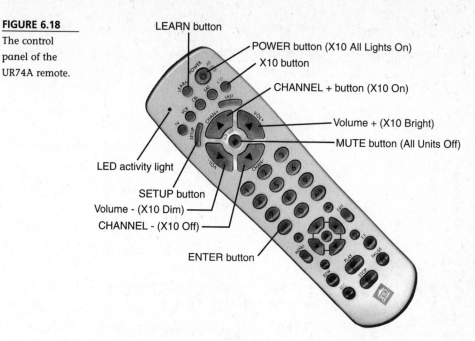

LEARN button

POWER button (X10 All Lights On)

X10 button

CHANNEL + button (X10 On)

Volume + (X10 Bright)

MUTE button (All Units Off)

LED activity light

SETUP button

Volume - (X10 Dim)

CHANNEL - (X10 Off)

ENTER button

Right out of the box, the remote is ready to work with X10 devices using house code A. To change house codes, follow this procedure:

1. Press the X10 button (refer to Figure 6.18).

2. Press and hold the SETUP button until the LED *(light emitting diode)* activity light above the TV and VCR button blinks.

3. Enter the number corresponding to the house code from Table 6.5. For numbers 1–9, press the number key. To enter numbers 10–16, press each digit. To enter 10, press 1, and then press 0, and so on.

4. Press the ENTER button to store the new house code.

**TABLE 6.5**   Remote Control Numbers/X10 House Code Cross-Reference

| Number to Enter on Remote | Equivalent House Code |
|---|---|
| 1 | A |
| 2 | B |
| 3 | C |
| 4 | D |
| 5 | E |
| 6 | F |
| 7 | G |

**TABLE 6.5** (continued)

| Number to Enter on Remote | Equivalent House Code |
|---|---|
| 8 | H |
| 9 | I |
| 10 | J |
| 11 | K |
| 12 | L |
| 13 | M |
| 14 | N |
| 15 | O |
| 16 | P |

## Using the Remote to Control Home Entertainment

After you've configured your remote to work with your television and other home entertainment devices, it works like any other universal remote. Press the button for the device you want to control, such as the TV, and then press the button for the command you want to send. For example, to turn on the TV and switch it to channel 7, use this procedure:

1. Press the TV button.

2. Press the POWER button.

3. Press the 7 key on the keypad.

4. Press ENTER (if necessary; required by some types of TVs).

If you are unable to control all the features of your home entertainment device with the universal remote, try these solutions:

■ Try a different device code from the list for your brand of home entertainment hardware.

■ Contact the vendor to determine the correct remote code for the device. The Universal Remote Codes website at www.xdiv.com/remotes/ is a helpful place to start your search; you can also try searches on Google (www.google.com) and other Internet search engines.

■ Use the universal remote's learning feature to learn specific commands from the device's original remote control (if you have it).

■ Keep the original remote control handy (if you still have it) in case you need to use it for specific situations.

## Using a Universal Remote with X10 Devices

The 5-in-1 X10 Universal Learning Remote is preprogrammed to work with an X10 RF transceiver such as the one shown in Figure 6.17. To control an X10 device, do the following:

1. Press the X10 button on the remote control.

2. Press the unit number of the device you want to control. For example, if you want to control a device using unit code 11, press the 1 key twice.

3. To turn on the unit, press the CHANNEL + button. To turn off the unit, press the CHANNEL - button.

4. To dim a lamp connected to a lamp module or switch, press the VOLUME - button. To brighten it, press the VOLUME + button.

5. To turn on all lamps connected to lamp modules or switches on the same house code, press the POWER button.

6. To turn off all X10 modules (including appliance modules) on the same house code, press the Mute (M) button.

## X10 IR Controllers and Universal Remote Controls

If you don't have an RF transceiver in your X10 home automation system, you can also use an X10 universal remote with an IR-based tabletop controller such as the X10 IR543 Command Center (see Figure 6.19). It plugs into an AC electrical outlet, just as with the other devices discussed earlier in this chapter. It can control unit codes 1–4 or 5–8 interactively (you select the device numbers with a top-mounted selector switch), and you can control groups of devices, just as with an X10 Maxi Controller. You can control unit codes 9 and 10 through IR signals. However, because it lacks buttons for unit codes 9–16 and cannot send IR signals to unit codes above 10, it cannot be used to configure programmable modules or switches.

Although the Command Center can be used as a tabletop controller, its primary function is to receive IR signals from an X10 universal remote control. Although some vendor websites suggest that you need one of these to enable your X10 universal remote to work properly, you can do without this device if you already have an RF transceiver and your X10 universal remote can send RF signals, as the 5-in-1 model shown earlier in this chapter can do.

Consult the instructions for your X10 universal remote to determine whether you need to reconfigure it to work with an X10 IR controller. For example, the UR74A must be reprogrammed from device code 999 (X10 RF transceiver) to code 998 to use the IR543.

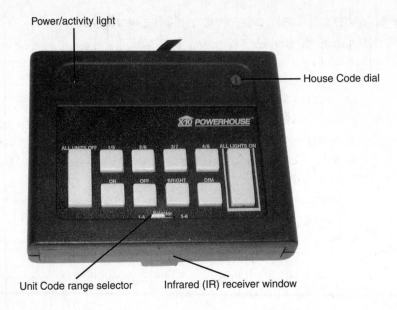

Power/activity light

House Code dial

Unit Code range selector

Infrared (IR) receiver window

To reprogram your X10 universal remote to work with the IR543, follow this proce-dure:

1. Press and hold the SETUP button until the LED indicator lights steadily (refer to Figure 6.18).

2. Release the SETUP button.

3. Press and release the X10 button.

4. Press 9, 9, 8 and then press the ENTER button. This programs the remote to control the IR Mini Controller.

To reprogram the controller to work in standard mode, follow the same instructions but, in step 4, press 9, 9, 9, and then press the ENTER button.

If you want to use the X10 Universal Remote with both a wireless transceiver and the IR543, program an unused device type button (except the TV button) on the remote to use code 998 (the code for the IR543).

Table 6.6 compares the control options available with the X10 Universal Remote when used with a wireless transceiver and with the IR543 IR Mini Controller.

**TABLE 6.6** Wireless Transceiver and IR543 with X10 Universal Remote

| Feature | Wireless Transceiver | IR543 |
|---|---|---|
| Number of unit codes controlled | 16 | 10 |
| Can control groups of devices (for example: 1, 2, ON) | No | Yes |

# THE ABSOLUTE MINIMUM

■ More powerful wireless and tabletop controllers improve the capability of any X10 home automation system.

■ An X10 timer can be used to turn on and turn off devices with timed settings, randomly, or interactively.

■ The commonly sold Mini Timer cannot be used with device codes above 8.

■ All Lights On commands provided by many types of remotes and controllers work with X10 light switch and lamp modules only.

■ All Units Off commands provided by many types of remotes and controllers turn off all types of X10 modules, including appliance modules.

■ A Mini Timer works with only one house code at a time.

■ A Mini Timer can be used as an alarm clock.

■ A tabletop Maxi Controller works with all unit codes 1–16.

■ A tabletop Maxi Controller can send programming codes as well as on, off, bright, and dim commands.

■ To configure programmable modules with a tabletop Maxi Controller, you must change the House Code dial several times during the programming process.

■ You can use a tabletop Maxi Controller to create and store one or more scenes in a scene-capable module or light switch's nonvolatile memory.

■ Each scene stores a particular set of actions, and is started by sending the unique house/unit code assigned during scene creation.

■ After a scene has been stored in a module or light switch, it can be triggered by any remote that can send the appropriate house/unit code.

■ An X10 universal remote can control X10 devices via radio frequency (RF) or via infrared (IR), depending on the type of receiver you have.

■ An X10 universal remote can also be configured or trained to replace remote controls for televisions and other types of home entertainment equipment.

# PART

# Using X10 for Advanced Home Control

7

# USING X10 TO CONTROL HVAC SYSTEMS

If X10 home automation is smart enough to control your lighting, is it smart enough to help you heat and cool your home? The answer is "Yes!" Whether you're interested in adding interactive control to a whole-house fan, an automatic feature to central heating and air, or a thermostatic control to portable heating and cooling devices, this chapter shows you how X10 home automation can help you save money and help make your life easier.

# Integrating X10 with HVAC Systems

You can use X10 to view and control your home's heating, ventilating, and air conditioning *(HVAC)* in a variety of ways:

- Temperature monitors can be used to detect the temperature in different rooms.
- Thermostats can be used to control HVAC interactively or from your computer desktop. By adding telephone (see Chapter 10, "Accessing X10 Home Control via Telephone") or web-based (see Chapter 12, "Accessing X10 Home Control via Your Home Network and the Internet") remote access, you can literally turn up the heat or the AC from anywhere.
- You can replace your existing HVAC controller with an X10 PLC–based unit.

The following sections discuss the various approaches in greater detail.

# Using X10 for Temperature Monitoring

One big problem with typical household thermostats is that they measure heat at just one location: the thermostat itself. If the thermostat is in an unusually hot part of the house (such as a location that receives direct sun for part of the day), the remainder of the house will be chilly in all seasons. The heat won't run much in the winter, and the air conditioning will be blasting away in the summer.

You can use X10 temperature monitors to determine the temperature variations in different parts of your home and apply this information in a variety of ways. If your home has zone heating or AC, you can adjust the heating or cooling in different rooms based on this information. If parts of your home are subject to potentially dangerous temperature extremes, you can monitor these locations and receive a warning of low temperatures before damage (such as frozen water pipes) can take place. Temperature monitors can also be used to provide thermostatic control of portable heating and cooling devices; see the "Using X10 Control for Heating and Cooling Appliances" section later in this chapter.

## TempLinc

The Smarthome TempLinc model 1625 (shown in Figure 7.1) is a leading X10 temperature monitor. It has three components:

- A temperature sensor; this is a small box that can be attached to a wall or other location with double-stick tape or screws (both included).
- An X10 transceiver, which is a modified version of the Smarthome PowerLinc II; this plugs into an AC outlet.
- An interface cable to connect the sensor and the X10 transceiver.

**FIGURE 7.1**
Smarthome's
TempLinc model
1625 tempera-
ture sensor.

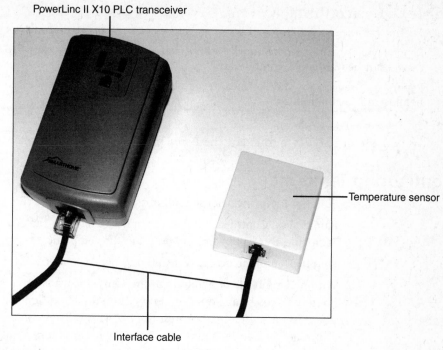

PowerLinc II X10 PLC transceiver

Temperature sensor

Interface cable

## Programming TempLinc

TempLinc can be programmed to monitor temperatures and transmit changes as frequently as they occur or only on request. When an X10 HVAC control is added to the HVAC system, TempLinc also can be used as a thermostat to provide heating and cooling control. TempLinc can be configured to work in Fahrenheit (F) and Celsius (C) temperature scales.

Table 7.1 lists the codes supported by TempLinc; these are the same codes used by the popular RCS family of programmable X10 thermostats.

## Table 7.1    Programming Codes Used by TempLinc and RCS Programmable Thermostats

| Operation Mode | Code (Fahrenheit) | Code (Celsius) | Examples |
|---|---|---|---|
| Reports when temperature changes | House code +1 | House code +9 | B1, B9 |
| Reports on user request | House code +2 | House code +10 | B2, B10 |
| Thermostat mode (cooling) | House code +3 | House code +11 | B3, B11 |
| Reports when temperature changes and thermostat cooling mode combination | House code +4 | House code +12 | B4, B12 |
| Reports on user request and thermostat cooling mode combination | House code +5 | House code +13 | B5, B13 |

## Table 7.1 (continued)

| | | | |
|---|---|---|---|
| Thermostat mode (heating) | House code +6 | House code +14 | B6, B14 |
| Reports when temperature changes and thermostat heating mode combination | House code +7 | House code +15 | B7, B15 |
| Reports on user request and thermostat heating mode combination | House code +8 | House code +16 | B8, B16 |

Use these codes to configure the TempLinc as described in the following section.

## Configuring TempLinc

To program the TempLinc's house and unit code:

1. Plug a Maxi Controller into an AC outlet other than the one used for the TempLinc; this will be used to program the TempLinc.

2. Plug the TempLinc transceiver into another AC outlet.

3. Within one minute of plugging in the TempLinc transceiver, send the same house/unit code three times in a row using the Maxi Controller. For example, to use F2 for the TempLinc, press the F, 2, F, 2, F, 2 keys on the Maxi Controller (shown in Figure 7.2). For more information about the Maxi Controller, refer to Chapter 6, "Using Timers and Advanced Remotes for X10."

**FIGURE 7.2**

A Maxi Controller is used to program the TempLinc.

Select the house code you want to use for TempLinc

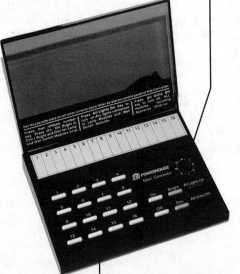

Use the number keys only to program the unit code, TempLinc operating mode, and temperature set point

---

**HOUSE/UNIT CODES TO AVOID**

TempLinc uses unit codes 11–16 along with preset dim levels to report the current temperature; for details, see the "How TempLinc Reports Temperatures" section later in this chapter. For this reason, you should not use house codes M–P with TempLinc because M16, N16, O16, and P16 are used to program intelligent light switches and modules (refer to Chapter 6). Choose a house code between A and L that does not already have unit codes 11–16 assigned to other devices.

Be sure to write down the house and unit code you used. This information will be used to configure other X10 devices and software to work with TempLinc.

---

4. Using the Maxi Controller, send the same house code you used in step 3 and a unit code that corresponds to one of the modes in Table 7.1. For example, to set TempLinc to operate in the Report on Change mode, press the F, 1 keys (assuming that the TempLinc is using house code F as in step 3).

If the TempLinc will be used as a thermostat to control an HVAC system or other heating/cooling device, you must also program the temperature setpoint. The *setpoint* is the temperature you'd like to maintain. The setpoint is sent in two pieces: as the first digit (tens) and the second digit (ones). For example, to set the setpoint to 72° Fahrenheit using a house code of F, you'd send F7 F2 (F7 = 70, F2 = 2).

Although each programming step has been written down separately in this section for clarity, you should actually send the codes in quick sequence to avoid the TempLinc timing out or receiving erroneous X10 commands from another source. For example, to program TempLinc to be identified as F2 in your system and to work in Report on Change mode, send these codes in sequence:

<u>F2</u> <u>F2</u> <u>F2</u> (Sets house/unit code)

**F1** (Sets operating mode)

To program TempLinc to be identified as B6 in your system and to work as a thermostat (Cooling mode) with a setpoint of 68° Fahrenheit, send these codes in sequence:

<u>B6</u> <u>B6</u> <u>B6</u> (Sets house/unit code)

**B3** (Sets operating mode)

*B6 B8* (Sets temperature setpoint)

# How TempLinc Reports Temperatures

As you have learned in previous sections, the X10 protocol can transmit house codes, unit codes, and preset dim levels. These three elements of the protocol are used by TempLinc and other types of X10 or X10–compatible temperature sensing and thermostat devices to report the current temperature.

TempLinc uses unit codes 11–16 in the selected house code, along with preset dim levels, to report the current temperature when the temperature changes or the unit is queried. TempLinc's documentation includes a translation table in which you can look up the house code and preset dim level transmitted by TempLinc to determine the correct temperature in Fahrenheit or Celsius. Refer to TempLinc's instructions for more detail.

If your home computer is configured to connect to your X10 system with an interface, you might be able to see the temperature on your computer screen. X10 PLC-compatible software programs such as Smarthome Live! (see Chapter 12), HomeSeer (see Chapters 11, "Accessing X10 Home Control via Your Home Computer," and 12), and many others can read this information and translate it into a user-friendly display. However, even if your software cannot translate the codes for you, you still can set the interface to report on request, query the house and unit code, and receive the unit code and preset dim value. Look up this information in the translation table provided with TempLinc to determine the current temperature.

---

**MAKE YOUR PC TEMPERATURE-SAVVY**

If you have a Smarthome PowerLinc or PowerLinc II (serial) interface, you can download a Microsoft Windows–based program that will display TempLinc information onscreen even if you don't use a full-featured X10 PLC home management program. This program also supports TempLinc's Thermostat mode. Get the program from the TempLinc page at Smarthome.com:

www.smarthome.com/1625.html

---

## Using TempLinc's Thermostat Mode

You can use TempLinc in Thermostat mode to

- Control X10 PLC HVAC systems
- Control small heaters, fans, and window AC units

To learn more about controlling portable heaters, fans, and window AC units, see "Using X10 Control for Heating and Cooling Appliances" section later in this chapter.

# Thermostat Setback Devices

If you want to use X10 to help control your HVAC system but don't want to go to the trouble and expense of replacing the thermostat and HVAC control system, you still can use X10 to save on your heating bills by installing an X10 PLC thermostat setback module, such as the X10.com TH2807 (shown in Figure 7.3). The TH2807 is sold by many X10 hardware vendors, and sells for about $20 (or about one-tenth the cost of a full-blown X10 HVAC control system).

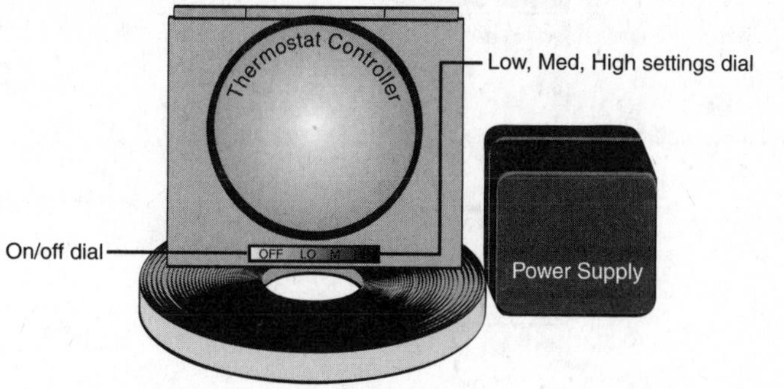

**FIGURE 7.3**

The TH2807 thermostat setback module works with any conventional or programmable thermostat.

Thermostat Controller

Low, Med, High settings dial

On/off dial

OFF LO M

Power Supply

## Installing and Using the TH2807 Thermostat Setback Module

The TH2807 installs on the wall below your normal thermostat and is plugged into a standard X10 appliance module (refer to Chapter 5, "Using X10 to Control Appliances," for examples). The TH2807 has a simple sliding control that enables you to select a temperature reduction of about 5° (low), 10° (medium), or 15° (high) when the unit is triggered. When the TH2807 activates, a small heater inside the unit is turned on. Heat from the heater is picked up by your thermostat, making the thermostat "think" that the room is warmer than it actually is. Because the thermostat thinks the room is warmer, it doesn't turn on the heat as often as usual. For example, you can leave your thermostat set to a comfortable 72° at all times, but when the TH2807 is activated, the room will be up to 15 degrees cooler, depending upon how the unit is set. Figure 7.4 demonstrates how the TH2807 works.

You can also use the TH2807 in the summer if your home has central air conditioning: When the unit is triggered, the small heater comes on and warms the thermostat, which obediently turns on the air-conditioning unit.

Because the TH2807 is controlled by an standard X10 or X10–compatible appliance module, it can be triggered by a wireless X10 remote control and transceiver as you saw in Chapter 5, a tabletop Mini Timer or Maxi Controller as shown in Chapter 6, a security system as you'll see in Chapter 9, "Using X10 to Provide Security," or by a home computer interface (see Chapter 11) or web-based interface (see Chapter 12).

The TH2807 is best suited for use with a traditional nonprogrammable thermostat. If you prefer to combine the power of a programmable thermostat with full remote capabilities, you need to consider an X10 HVAC controller and thermostat combination.

**FIGURE 7.4**

How the TH2807 thermostat fools your thermostat into thinking the room is warmer than it actually is.

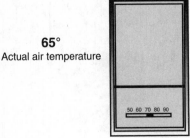

**Furnace
stays OFF
77°**
Thermometer in thermostat reading

**65°**
Actual air temperature

**72°**
Thermostat setting

50 60 70 80 90

**Setback unit
turned ON**

# X10-Compatible HVAC Controllers and Thermostats

The ultimate in X10 home climate control involves replacing your existing thermostat with an X10 thermostat and connecting an X10 controller to your existing furnace and air conditioning system. This solution enables you to control and monitor your HVAC very precisely via telephone, home computer, and Internet, and support a full range of day and time programmability as well as the latest multistage HVAC systems and heat pumps.

Some of the most widely supported X10-compatible HVAC controllers and thermostats are those made by Residential Control Systems, Inc. (RCS). The latest RCS product for X10 HVAC control is the TXB16 thermostat and controller, which replaces the popular TX15-B model. The TXB16 thermostat and controller are used in this chapter to show how X10 can be used to control an HVAC system.

---

**DROPPING IN ON RCS**

Visit the RCS website at www.resconsys.com.

The TXB16, like its predecessor, has two major components:

- A Wall Display Unit, which replaces the standard or programmable thermostat
- An HVAC Control Unit, which is connected directly to your HVAC system and to the Wall Display Unit

Other parts of the TXB16 kit include

- A TW523 X10 interface used by the HVAC Control Unit
- An RJ-11 cable to connect the TW523 to the HVAC Control Unit
- A 12V DC power "brick" that connects the HVAC Control Unit to a 115-volt outlet

Figure 7.5 shows how the TXB16's components are retrofitted to a typical HVAC system.

**FIGURE 7.5**

A conventional thermostat/ HVAC system (top) compared to a TXB16 system (bottom). The images are not drawn to scale.

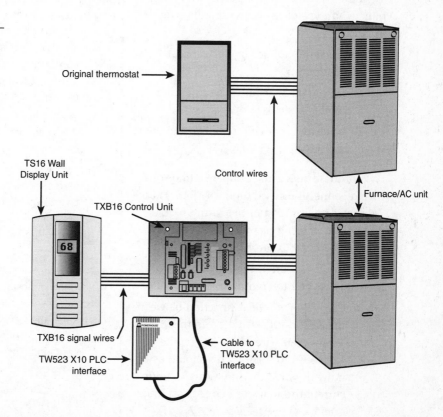

Original thermostat

TS16 Wall Display Unit

TXB16 Control Unit

Control wires

Furnace/AC unit

68

TXB16 signal wires

TW523 X10 PLC interface

Cable to TW523 X10 PLC interface

**TEST BEFORE YOU INSTALL THE TXB16**

Although test procedures for the TXB16 Control Unit and the TS16 Wall Display Unit are listed near the end of the installation and instruction manual for the TXB16, you should perform these tests *before* installation. This ensures that the units are working properly, and that you understand how to read the status LEDs on the TXB16 Control Unit and the display of X10 commands and HVAC modes on the TS16 Wall Display Unit. You will need an X10 Maxi Controller for some tests.

## Installing the TXB16 Control Unit

The TXB16 Control Unit is connected to the HVAC system using the wiring that originally ran to the thermostat. In effect, the TXB16 Control Unit replaces the temperature control functions of the original thermostat, and the TS16 Wall Display Unit replaces the display and user interface functions of the original thermostat.

Before you install the TXB16 Control Unit or any other HVAC controller, you should determine what type of heating system is already in place:

- Conventional gas or electric heating or heat pump
- Integrated or separate heating and cooling systems
- Single-stage or two-stage heating or cooling

Each of these affects the jumper settings and wiring connections used on the TXB16. Figure 7.6 shows the location of the wiring blocks and DIP *(dual inline package)* switch bank inside the TXB16 Control Unit.

Proper configuration of the TXB16 Control Unit requires you to do the following:

- Correctly wire the connection between the existing HVAC unit and the J5 seven-screw wire connector on the TXB16 Control Unit. This should essentially be wired the same way as your current thermostat's heating, cooling, and fan wires (see Figure 7.7) .

**caution**

You can make a real mess of your HVAC system if you don't properly install HVAC thermostats and controllers. Although most projects in this book are suitable for nonexpert installation, so many variations are possible in HVAC systems that it's easy to make a mistake. For this type of installation, you might want to hire an HVAC specialist—particularly one experienced in X10 installations. However, if you prefer to do it yourself, check the following:

- Find out from your builder or HVAC contractor the details of your HVAC system.
- If you've previously replaced a thermostat, take a look at how it's wired. You'll make the same types of connections to the TXB16 Control Unit.
- Note the wire colors used by your thermostat and their connections. They might not match the standards listed in the TXB16 Control Unit documentation. For example, my home uses a blue wire for the fan rather than the normal green wire.
- Use a digital camera set for close-up mode to photograph the wire connections in your current thermostat before you disconnect it.

**FIGURE 7.6**

Major internal components of the TXB16 Control Unit.

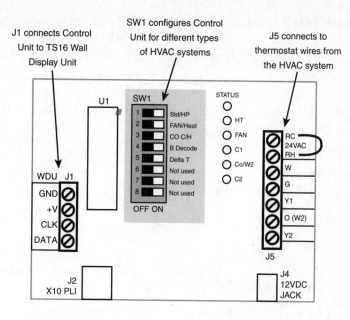

**FIGURE 7.7**

A comparison of the wiring in a typical programmable thermostat with the J5 connection in the TXB16 Control Unit.

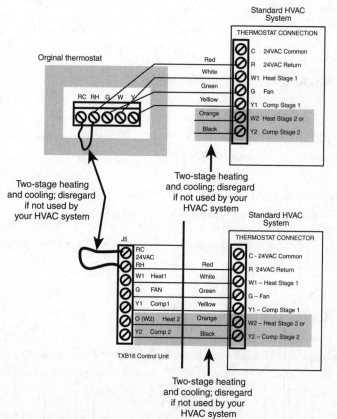

■ Properly configure the SW1 bank of DIP switches to match the type of system (gas, electric, or heat pump), the matching X10 decode table, and heat pump changeover settings. See Table 7.2 for a quick reference (right = on; left = off).

**TABLE 7.2** SW1 DIP Switch Quick Reference (TXB16 Control Unit)

| Switch | Electric | Gas | Heat Pump |
|--------|----------|-----|-----------|
| SW1-1 | Off | Off | On |
| SW1-2 | On | Off | Off |
| SW1-3 | Off | Off | # |
| SW1-4 | * | * | * |
| SW1-5 | @ | @ | @ |

*# Select Off for systems that perform changeover with cooling (used by most heat pumps); select On for systems that perform changeover with heating.*

*\* Leave set to Off unless TS15 Wall Display Unit is used; an On setting forces the Control Unit to use TX15-compatible X10 decode table (table B).*

*@ Select Off for 1° setpoint operation. Select On to use +/– 1° setpoint, which provides a greater temperature variation but less HVAC system cycling.*

Additional DIP switches should be ignored.

The four-screw J1 connection is used for the connection to the TS16 Wall Display Unit (discussed in the next section). J2 is used for the connection to the TW523 or equivalent X10 interface included with the kit, and J4 is a connection to the 12V DC transformer (also included with the kit).

---

**YOU NEED AC OUTLETS TO MAKE YOUR HVAC SYSTEM X10 PLC-READY**

If your HVAC system is not located in a space that has a standard paired 115V AC wall outlet, you need to install one or determine whether there's a paired outlet nearby. Both the TW523 X10 interface module and the 12V DC transformer must be connected to an AC outlet.

---

## Installing the TS16 Wall Display Unit

The TS16 Wall Display Unit is used in place of a standard or programmable thermostat. Remove the LCD display and pushbutton front panel to reveal the wiring connectors. The J1 connector on the right side is used for the four-wire connection from the TXB16's J1 connection, whereas the J2 connector on the left side is used for an optional RS15 remote sensor (see Figure 7.8). The TXB16 supports up to three remote sensors (one can be located outside). It can use a remote sensor in place of its onboard sensor, or average the results from the remote sensors to determine when to trigger heating or cooling.

**FIGURE 7.8**

Wiring connections from the TS16 wall display unit (center) to the RS15 temperature sensor (left) and the TXB16 Control Unit (right).

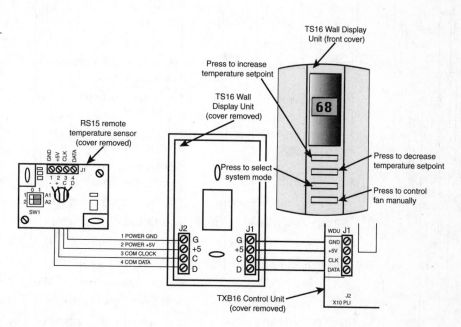

## Operating the TXB16

After you've installed the TXB16, you control the system through the TS16 Wall Display Unit or through X10 commands. The X10 house code address, temperature setpoints, and HVAC mode settings are controlled through the Wall Display Unit's front-panel pushbuttons (refer to Figure 7.8).

If you use additional remote sensors, the WDU is also used to select which sensor temperature readings (internal, external, or an average) are used to trigger the HVAC system.

After you've set the X10 house code, it is expressed numerically on the TS16 display (1 = A, 2 = B, and so on through 16 = P). For maximum flexibility, choose a house code you are not using for any other X10 modules or scene commands. This will enable you to use a full-featured X10 decode table to control your HVAC system.

The TXB16 can use one of four X10 decode standards, unless you use SW1-4 DIP switch on the Control Unit to force the system to use the TX15-compatible X10 decode table B. By default, the TXB16 uses the receive-only P decode table; but you can switch between the receive-only P and B decode tables and the limited receive-only decode table L via X10 commands. Table L uses only two unit codes: 7 (system on/off) and 8 (setback on/off). Table L is designed for use in X10 systems that support only one house code, which is also used by other types of modules. Table 7.3 compares the features of the decode tables.

**TABLE 7.3** TXB16 Decode Tables Compared

| Unit Code | Decode Table P | Decode Table B | Decode Table L |
|---|---|---|---|
| 1 | Sets temperature setpoint | Sets temperature setpoint or Thermostat mode | — |
| 2 | Sets temperature setpoint | Sets emperature setpoint or Thermostat mode | |
| 3 | Sets temperature setpoint | Sets temperature setpoint or Thermostat mode | — |
| 4 | Sets temperature setpoint | Sets temperature setpoint or Thermostat mode | — |
| 5 | Sets temperature setpoint | Sets temperature setpoint | — |
| 6 | Sets temperature setpoint | Sets temperature setpoint | — |
| 7 | Sets temperature setpoint | Sets temperature setpoint | System on/off |
| 8 | Sets temperature setpoint | Sets temperature setpoint | Setpoint on/off |
| 9 | Sets Thermostat mode | Sets temperature setpoint | — |
| 10 | Sets Thermostat mode | Sets temperature setpoint | — |
| 11 | Sets Thermostat mode | Sets temperature setpoint | — |
| 12 | SetsThermostat mode | Sets temperature setpoint | — |
| 13 | Setback on/off | Sets temperature setpoint | — |
| 14 | Sets optional setback values | Sets temperature setpoint | — |
| 15 | Sets optional setback values | Sets temperature setpoint | — |
| 16 | Sets optional setback values | Sets temperature setpoint | — |
| Preset dim command to switch to this decode table | Unit code 4,preset dim 90% | Unit code 4,preset dim 94% | Unit code 4, preset dim 97% |

For details of how each unit code is used by each table, download the TXB16 X10 protocol manual from the RCS website (www.resconsys.com).

Unless the system is locked into the Decode Table B mode with SW1-1, you can switch between decode tables with the following X10 commands:

■ All Lights On—Send this command to the house code used by the TXB16 to switch the decode table to B.

■ All Units On—Send this command to the house code used by the TXB16 to switch the decode table to P.

■ You can use unit code 4 with certain preset dim values to switch among the P, B, and L decode tables; see Table 7.3 for details.

The commands supported by decode tables P (the default), B, and L are simple enough that you can control your furnace with a simple wireless X10 remote or tabletop Maxi Controller. By using a Mini Timer, you can create programs to adjust the temperature according to the time of day (refer to Chapter 6 for Mini Timer programming details).

Regardless of the decode table selected, you can also control the TXB16 with bidirectional commands based on the preset dim commands originally developed for X10 lighting control. Table 7.4 provides a simple overview of how the unit codes are used in this mode. For details, download the TXB16 X10 protocol manual from the RCS website.

**Table 7.4**   TXB16 Bidirectional Preset Dim Decode Table Overview

| Unit Code | Usage |
|-----------|-------|
| 1 | Send new temperature setpoint |
| 2 | Send new temperature setpoint |
| 3 | Send new temperature setpoint |
| 4 | Send commands |
| 5 | Request status |
| 6 | Report status |
| 7 | Reserved |
| 8 | Reserved |
| 9 | Send new temperature setpoint |
| 10 | Echo command back |
| 11 | Report current temperature |
| 12 | Report current temperature |
| 13 | Report current temperature |
| 14 | Report current temperature |
| 15 | Report current temperature |
| 16 | Report current temperature |

The bidirectional preset dim commands supported by the TXB16 are best controlled through an X10 PLC–compatible home management software program such as HomeSeer (discussed in Chapter 11), Home Control Assistant, HAL Deluxe, Stargate, or Stargate Lite, among others.

**"ROLL YOUR OWN" HOME TEMPERATURE CONTROL**

Even if your home control software doesn't include specific support for a TXB16, you can create a separate command for each of the commands you want it to execute. For example, if you want to switch the decode table to P, set the mode to cool, and set the setpoint to 75° F, you could create a macro or series of commands like this:

1. House code/All Units On (switches TXB16 to decode table P)

2. House code/Unit Code 10 On (sets mode to cool)

3. House code/Unit Code 3 Off (sets temperature setpoint to 75° F)

To check the current temperature, send the following command from the bidirectional preset dim commands list using your home automation software's advanced command menu:

House code/Unit Code 5 Preset Level 1 (same as preset dim 0%)

A preset level dim reply will be sent back on House code/Unit Code 11–16, preset dim level 1–32 (0–100%). To view the reply, switch your home automation software to an X10 monitoring mode (see Chapter 11 for examples). Look up the actual temperature in the TXB 16 X10 protocol manual, which is available on the RCS website.

# Using X10 Control for Heating and Cooling Appliances

You don't need to replace your existing thermostat with an X10 HVAC controller to use X10 to help make your home more comfortable. You can use X10 to control

- Attic fans
- Space heaters
- Room and window fans
- Room air conditioners

Depending on your situation, you can control these devices interactively or add intelligence by using a TempLinc module to automate the process.

## Installing X10 Control for Attic and Whole-House Fans

Attic and whole-house fans can reduce or eliminate the need for air conditioning, and help reduce air-conditioning bills by up to 30%. It's easy to use X10 to control a whole-house fan if it is connected to a wall-mounted On/Off switch that uses a neutral wire: just replace the switch with an X10–compatible appliance-rated 15-amp wall switch such as the Leviton Decora DHC model 6291 (about $40). It uses a three-wire connection (see Figure 7.9). For wiring details, refer to Chapter 5.

**FIGURE 7.9**

Installing a
Leviton wall
switch for use
with fans and
other appliances.

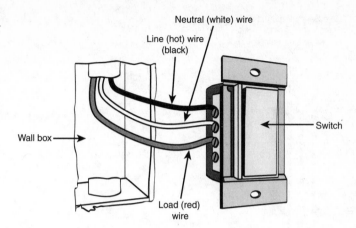

Neutral (white) wire

Line (hot) wire
(black)

Switch

Wall box

Load (red)
wire

To set the wall switch's house and unit codes, remove the paddle-type switch plate
from the front panel and set the X10 House Code and Unit Code dials as desired (see
Figure 7.10).

**FIGURE 7.10**

Adjusting house
and unit codes
on the Decora
DHC model
6291.

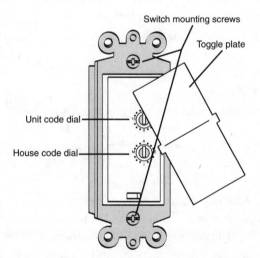

Switch mounting screws

Toggle plate

Unit code dial

House code dial

You can also use a quieter switch that also supports two-way communications and
scene commands: the Smarthome SwitchLinc Relay two-way switch #23883 (about
$70). As with the SwitchLinc switches discussed in Chapter 4, "Using X10 to Control
Home Lighting," and Chapter 5, the SwitchLinc Relay is configured through a Maxi
Controller:

1. Press the Set button on the top of the switch toggle (see Figure 7.11).

2. Send the desired house/unit code from a Maxi Controller within 30 seconds.
   For example, to set the switch to use house code E and unit code 4, set the
   Maxi Controller to use house code E, and then press the 4 button.

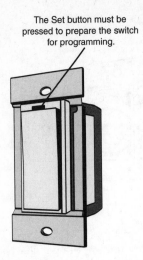

**FIGURE 7.11**

Preparing a SwitchLinc Relay two-way switch for programming.

The Set button must be pressed to prepare the switch for programming.

## Controlling the Whole-House Fan with X10

After you've installed an X10 switch to control a whole-house (or attic) fan, you can use these methods to control the fan's operation:

- To run the fan interactively, use any X10 or X10—compatible remote or tabletop controller to send an On command to the switch's house and unit code—this turns on the fan. To turn off the fan, send an Off command to the fan's house and unit code.

- To run the fan at particular times, you can use a Mini Timer (refer to Chapter 6 for details); remember to use a unit code of 1–8 for the fan (Mini Timers don't support unit codes 9–16). You can also use an X10 PLC-computer interface (discussed in Chapter 11) and create a timed event with any available house and unit code.

- To run the fan under thermostat control, install a TempLinc temperature monitor in an area you want to cool with the fan. Configure the TempLinc temperature monitor to operate in the Cooling mode, and set it for the desired setpoint. Set the house/unit code on the TempLinc to the same house/unit code used by the X10 module connected to the fan. When the temperature exceeds the setpoint, TempLinc sends an On command, activating the fan. When the temperature drops to the setpoint, TempLinc sends an Off command, turning off the fan. For details, refer to the "Configuring TempLinc" section earlier in this chapter. Figure 7.12 illustrates how TempLinc and the whole-house fan work together.

---

**USING TEMPLINC FOR HEATING AND COOLING**

For more information on using TempLinc with plug-in X10 appliance modules, go to www.smarthome.com/SOLUTION75.HTML.

---

**FIGURE 7.12**

How TempLinc controls a whole-house fan.

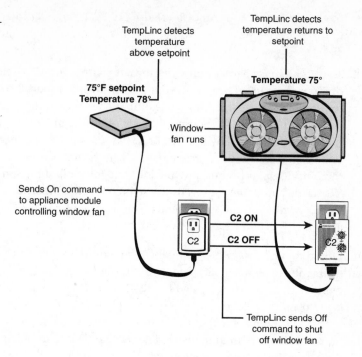

TempLinc detects temperature above setpoint

TempLinc detects temperature returns to setpoint

Temperature 75°

**75°F setpoint Temperature 78°**

Window fan runs

Sends On command to appliance module controlling window fan

C2 ON

C2 OFF

C2

C2

TempLinc sends Off command to shut off window fan

# Installing X10 Control for Space Heaters

If you always use a space heater in the same place, you could replace the existing wall outlet with an X10 wall outlet as shown in Chapter 5. However, you'll probably find it more convenient to use a plug-in X10 appliance module, which you can move around along with the space heater.

A typical cube-type space heater uses 1500 watts, which converts to about 13 amps. (To check the amp requirements for any device rated in watts: wattage divided by voltage equals amps.) Therefore, a 15-amp X10 appliance module is sufficient. If you use a space heater that requires more than 15 amps, you will need to use a 20-amp X10 wall outlet such as the Leviton #6296 instead of a plug-in appliance module. Note that a 20-amp X10 wall outlet has a single AC connector, rather than a pair of AC connectors as with 15-amp versions.

After you've connected the space heater to the X10 or X10–compatible appliance module or wall outlet, you can operate it in one of three ways:

- To run the space heater interactively, use any X10 or X10–compatible remote or tabletop controller to send an On command to the space heater module's house and unit code; this turns on the heater. To turn it off, send an Off command to the same house and unit code.

- To run the space heater at particular times, you can use a Mini Timer (refer to Chapter 6 for details); remember to use a unit code of 1–8 for the space heater's module or outlet. You can also use an X10 PLC-computer interface (discussed in Chapter 11) and create a timed event with any available house and unit code.

■ To run the space heater under thermostat control, install a TempLinc temperature monitor in an area you want to heat with the space heater. Configure the TempLinc to operate in the Heating mode, and set the TempLinc for the desired setpoint. Set the house/unit code on the TempLinc to the same house/unit code used by the X10 or X10–compatible appliance module or outlet connected to the space heater. When the temperature falls below the setpoint, TempLinc sends an On command, activating the space heater. When the temperature exceeds the setpoint, TempLinc sends an Off command, turning off the space heater. For details, refer to the "Configuring TempLinc" section earlier in this chapter.

Keep in mind that although the TempLinc temperature monitoring module can report temperatures between –60° F and 131° F, the PowerLinc II module component that provides X10 interfacing is rated for 32°–120° F. Thus, if you want to use TempLinc to operate a space heater to prevent pipes from freezing in a basement or crawlspace, you should *not* install the TempLinc's PowerLinc II module component in that location. Instead, plug the PowerLinc II module into an AC outlet in a finished space near the area you want to monitor, mount the TempLinc temperature monitoring module in the crawlspace near the pipes you want to protect, and use an extension cable to connect the components. Smarthome sells the #1132E 12-foot extension cable for about $10; use it in place of the normal cables supplied with TempLinc. Figure 7.13 illustrates a typical installation.

**FIGURE 7.13**

How TempLinc controls a space heater installed in a basement or crawlspace.

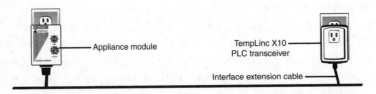

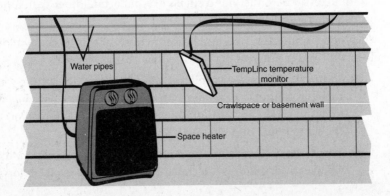

## Installing X10 Controls for Fans and Air Conditioners

Just as you can control whole-house fans and space heaters with X10 PLC, you can apply the same methods to control window, stand-mounted, or tabletop fans and even window air conditioners. Just use a plug-in X10 or X10–appliance module or wired-in electrical outlet and plug your fan or AC unit into it.

- To run the fan or AC unit interactively, use any X10 or X10–compatible remote or tabletop controller to send an On command to the house and unit code used by the fan or AC unit; this turns on the fan or AC unit. To turn it off, send an Off command to the module's house and unit code.

- To run the fan or AC unit at particular times, you can use a Mini Timer (refer to Chapter 6 for details); remember to use a unit code of 1–8. You can also use an X10 PLC-computer interface (discussed in Chapter 11) and create a timed event using any available house and unit code.

- To run the fan or AC unit under thermostat control, install a TempLinc temperature monitor in an area you want to cool. Configure the TempLinc to operate in the Cooling mode, and set the TempLinc for the desired setpoint. Set the house/unit code on the TempLinc to the same house/unit code used by the X10 appliance module or outlet connected to the fan or AC unit. When the temperature moves above the setpoint, TempLinc sends an On command, activating the fan or AC unit. When the temperature falls below the setpoint, TempLinc sends an Off command, turning off the fan or AC unit. For details, refer to the "Configuring TempLinc" section earlier in this chapter.

# Troubleshooting X10 HVAC Control

Problems with using X10 commands and devices to control your HVAC system or individual heating/cooling devices fall into these categories:

- Incorrect house/unit code combinations
- Incorrect mode selection
- Incorrect decode table selection

To solve problems with house/unit code combinations, try the following:

- Whenever possible, choose a house code that is not in use by other X10 devices or scenes for a TempLinc, TXB16, or other HVAC temperature monitoring or thermostat device. As you learned in earlier parts of this chapter, most of these devices use all the unit codes in a given house code for setting temperature, operating mode, or reporting temperature.

- If you need to reset a unit's house/unit code, follow the directions provided with the unit.

- Use a Maxi Controller or an X10 PLC-computer interface that can send house/unit codes as well as commands to program TempLinc, TXB16, or similar devices. You cannot use a mini-controller or Mini Timer because they don't use unit codes above 8, and you can't use a remote control that uses a separate On/Off button for each unit code.

To solve problems with mode selection, try these options:

- Reconfigure the device to use the correct mode. This might involve resending the house/unit code as well.
- Use the test procedures supplied with the device to check operation.

To solve problems with decode table selection (TXB16 and similar HVAC control devices):

- Make sure to send the command that selects the correct decode table before you send a command. Don't assume that the unit is already configured for the decode table you want to use.
- If you are unable to change decode tables, check the configuration of the *control device* (a device that uses the wires that ran to the thermostat in the original installation). For example, the TXB16 can be forced to use decode table B with SW1-4.
- Send the commands with a different type of device than you normally use. For example, if you normally use a Maxi Controller, use an X10 PLC-computer interface.
- Recheck the house code setting. If the house code on the Maxi Controller is not the same as the house code used by your HVAC control device, your commands will be ignored or will be picked up by another device set to that house code.

# THE ABSOLUTE MINIMUM

- X10 can be used to monitor and control temperatures in your home.

- The TempLinc temperature monitor from Smarthome can be used to monitor and report temperatures in both Fahrenheit and Celsius scales and provide thermostat functions.

- TempLinc is programmed with a Maxi Controller rather than with house/unit code dials.

- Some X10 home automation programs can interpret TempLinc temperature reports, but you can also translate the house code and preset dim level reported by TempLinc to determine the reported temperature.

- An X10 thermostat setback device mounts beneath your existing thermostat on the wall.

- The thermostat setback device has a small heater that raises air temperature by 5°, 10°, or 15° F.

- Your thermostat can be left at the same temperature setting at all times, but when the setback device is activated from an X10 controller, the thermostat will not turn on the furnace as often, saving money.

- The Residential Control Systems, Inc. (RCS) TXB16 is a widely supported X10 HVAC control system.

- The TXB16 has two components: The Control Unit replaces the original thermostat's control function, and the TS16 Wall Display Unit provides control buttons and a visual display.

- The TXB16 can be controlled with X10 commands or through the TS16.

- The TXB16 Control Unit must be plugged into a wall outlet to provide 12V power and to send/receive X10 commands with its TW523 interface.

- The TXB16 can be configured to receive only heating/cooling commands, or to work in a two-way function that also reports status back to an X10 software program.

- By configuring a TempLinc module to work in Heating or Cooling mode and setting it to the same house/unit code as a wall switch or appliance module, you can use TempLinc to turn on whole-house fans, window fans, window air conditioners, and space heaters whenever the temperature exceeds the desired setpoint.

- You can use TempLinc with a 12-foot extension cable to enable you to monitor areas that might fall below freezing, such as unfinished basements and crawlspaces.

8

# USING X10 TO CONTROL EXTERIOR LANDSCAPING

When you're planning home automation projects, don't overlook the great outdoors. X10 can make your home exterior safer and more inviting at night, give you a hand in the garage, and make enjoying hot tubs and spas easier than ever before. This chapter shows you how to take X10 outdoors.

# Connecting Standard Exterior Lighting to X10

Exterior lighting makes your home safer and more inviting at night. Whether you prefer to turn on the lights automatically when night falls or control that magic moment yourself, you can use X10 to make it happen. You can use X10 to control porch lights, floodlights, patio and deck lights, and garage lights, whether they use an On/Off switch or plug into standard AC outlets.

The following sections show you to automate your exterior lights to fit your needs.

## Controlling Porch Lights with X10

Before you start installing X10 light switches to control your porch lighting, take some time to plan your project with questions like these:

■ **How many light fixtures do you have on each porch?**—If you will be using an X10-compatible home automation program to control incandescent porch lighting, a basic light switch will be sufficient. However, if you don't want to use an X10-compatible home automation program to control porch lighting, consider scene-capable dimmer switches. You can start the evening with the lamps at a low level, raise them to full brightness when twilight is over, and dim them gradually to lights out by storing scenes in the switch's scene memory and activating each one with a separate X10 address.

■ **Do you want to control all porch lights as a group or individually?**—If you want to control the porch lights as a group, you can set them to the same address (house and unit code) as each other; you can assign them a house code different than other X10 devices in your system with unique unit codes and use the All Lights On command; you can set them to any desired address and control them through a home automation program.

■ **Can the porch lights be triggered with more than one switch in the house, such as an entryway switch and a switch in the living room?**—If so, your porch lights are connected in a three-way installation and you must use switches compatible with three-way lighting.

■ **What type of lighting does your porch use?**—If your porch uses lighting other than incandescent, you need to use appliance-type switches (also known as relay switches) instead of standard X10 light switches (which are made for incandescent lighting).

### Programming and Controlling Your Porch Lights

Depending on the type of porch lights and light switches you install and the controllers you use, you can choose from some of the following options to control them:

- Interactive or timed on/off
- Scenes
- Randomized on/off

Table 8.1 provides you with a checklist of the controllers you can use for the triggering effects you want. Keep in mind that dimming effects are not possible with nonincandescent lighting.

## TABLE 8.1 Controllers and Porch Lighting Effects

| Desired Effect | Computer Controller | Mini Timer | Maxi Controller | Wireless Remote | Photocell Sensor |
|---|---|---|---|---|---|
| Lights on at sunset | Yes | No | No | No | Yes |
| Gradual brightening at sunset | Yes | No | No | No | Yes |
| Activating one preset scene | Yes | 1 | Yes | 1 | 1 |
| Activating multiple preset scenes | Yes | 1 | Yes | 1 | No |
| Gradual brightening at preset time | Yes | 1 | No | No | 1 |
| Gradual dimming at preset time | Yes | 1 | No | No | No |
| Randomized on/off | Yes | Yes | No | No | No |

*1 Requires light switch with stored-scene capability.*

To learn about programming stored scene light switches and using Mini Timers, refer to Chapter 6, "Using Timers and Advanced Remotes for X10." To learn about programming and using X10-compatible computer interfaces, see Chapter 11, "Accessing X10 Home Control via Your Home Computer." For more information about using photocell sensors, see the "Installing Photocell Sensors for Outdoor Lighting" section later in this chapter.

## Controlling Patio, Pool, and Deck Lights with X10

X10 can also be used to control patio, swimming pool, and deck lights. Depending on the lighting technology used, you might have to use relay switches (which support fluorescent, low-voltage, and other types of nonincandescent lighting) instead of standard light switches. Use the following sections to help you choose the right switches for your exterior lighting types and requirements.

**MAKE SURE THAT YOU CONNECT TO THE CORRECT CIRCUIT**

If you have a separate electrical service for your garage, your patio, pool, or deck lights might be connected to that service rather than to your home service. You might need to plug a wireless transceiver or a tabletop controller into your garage to control exterior lights rather than using your home's X10 controllers. If the garage is connected to a separate phase on the same circuit as your home, use a coupler/repeater.

## Light Switches for Incandescent Lights

If your porch or other exterior lighting uses incandescent bulbs, you can use a basic two-wire light switch such as the X10 WS467. This switch can be dimmed through an X10 controller or transceiver. Some two-wire switches, such as X10's WS12A and Smarthome SwitchLinc RX Plus Dimmer and RX PLC Dimmer, also have built-in dimming controls. To learn how to install a two-wire light switch, refer to "Installing and Using X10 Light Switches" and "Installing an X10 Two-Wire Wall Switch" in Chapter 4.

**SO MANY SWITCHES, SO LITTLE TIME!**

Visit the X10 Smart Switches page at Smarthome www.smarthome.com/x10_smart_switches1.html to compare the features of various X10-compatible light switches for incandescent and nonincandescent lighting from vendors such as X10, Smarthome, Leviton, and HomePro.

If you want to dim your incandescent porch lights to different preset levels without using an X10-compatible home automation program and computer interface, you need to install a light switch that can store lighting scenes in memory, such as the two-wire SwitchLinc RX Plus Dimmer (#2386) or the three-wire Smarthome SwitchLinc Plus and SwitchLinc two-way dimmer or the HomePro dimmer switches. Each scene includes a preset dimming level, and you can also program the ramp rate (rate at which lamps brighten or dim) into the switch's memory.

To learn how to install a SwitchLinc or similar dimmer switch that uses a neutral wire, refer to the "Installing and Using X10 Light Switches" and "Installing a Smarthome Two-Way Dimmer Switch" sections in Chapter 4.

If your porch lights can be controlled from two or more switches, you must install a three-way X10-compatible switch at the master switch location and matching companion (slave) switches at the other locations, as shown in Figures 8.1 and 8.2. Use Figure 8.1 as a general guide to Smarthome and similar three-way switches that use a neutral (white) wire. Use Figure 8.2 as a general guide to X10 and similar three-way switches that do not use a neutral wire. Be sure to follow the detailed instructions provided with the switches.

**FIGURE 8.1**

A typical instal-
lation of a
Smarthome dim-
mer switch and
companion
switches to con-
trol a porch
light.

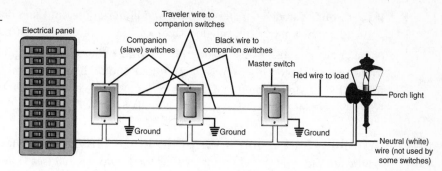

Note that the companion switch in Figure 8.2 does not have code wheels for house and unit codes; it is strictly used for local control.

**FIGURE 8.2**

A typical instal-
lation of an X10
three-way light
switch and com-
panion switch to
control a porch
light.

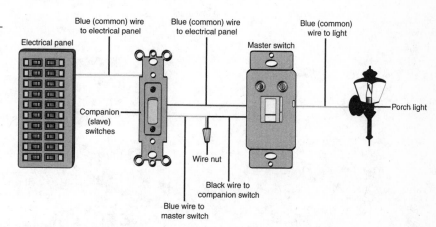

## Light Switches for Nonincandescent Lights

If your porch or other exterior lighting uses nonincandescent lamps, you must install a three-wire switch designed to support nonincandescent lights and appliances, such as the Leviton DHC #6291, X10 XPS3, HomePro RD-210, and the Smarthome SwitchLinc Relay series.

To learn how to install a three-wire switch, see the "Installing X10-Compatible Wall Switches for Use with Appliances" section in Chapter 5, "Using X10 to Control Appliances."

# Installing Photocell Sensors for Outdoor Lighting

Although you can control your porch lights with an X10-compatible computer program and interface or with a Mini Timer, you might prefer to install a photocell sensor to operate your porch, patio, deck, or pool lights. A photocell sensor can turn on lights in response to actual lighting conditions, such as cloudy conditions or a solar eclipse, instead of using the calculated times of sunrise and sunset as computer control does or a specific time the way that a Mini Timer does.

If your front and back porches get dark and light at different times on a given day, you can use two photocells, one for each porch, to individually control lighting.

Some photocell sensors are wired in place, while others combine a plug-in mini controller with a photocell sensor. To learn about photocell sensors combined with floodlights or wireless motion detectors configured to work as dusk-to-dawn lighting controls, see Chapter 9, "Using X10 to Provide Security."

## Installing and Using a Wired-in-Place Photocell Sensor

A wired-in-place photocell sensor such as the Leviton #6308 (see Figure 8.3) enables you to control a group of up to four porch or other exterior or interior lights using the same house code.

**FIGURE 8.3**

The Leviton #6308 photocell sensor.

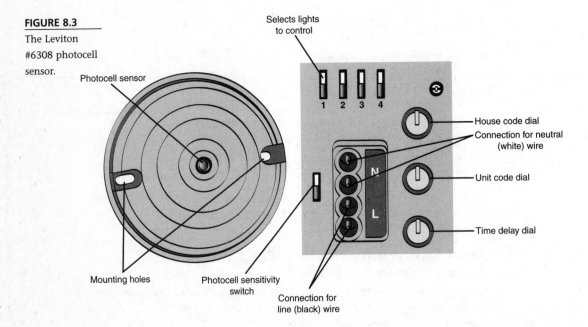

This type of sensor needs to be installed into an existing or retrofitted round or GEM electric wall box.

You should install the sensor in a location that does not receive direct sunlight, which could fool the sensor.

When you configure it, follow these guidelines:

- If you want to use the sensor to control other lights, use the same house code that is used by the modules connected to those lights.

- The unit code you select for the sensor is used as the starting point for other lights you want to control. The sensor, by default, controls the next four unit codes using the same house code as the sensor. For example, if you set the sensor's unit code at 4, the sensor can control unit codes 5–8. Switch 1 equals unit code 5 (4 + 1 = 5), switch 2 equals unit code 6 (4 + 2 = 6), and so forth.

■ To prevent the sensor from controlling a particular unit code in the sequence, slide the switch for that unit code to Off. For example, if you set the sensor's unit code to 4 but unit code 6 is used by a module you do not want to control, slide switch 2 to the Off position.

■ Use the Delay dial to specify how long to keep the lights or other modules triggered by the photocell on. You can select a delay up to 7.5 hours. Select 0 to use the photocell sensor as a trigger for dusk-to-dawn lighting.

■ Use the Dark/Dusk slider switch to adjust the sensitivity of the sensor. If you want the lights to come on before the area is fully dark, slide the switch to Dusk. When the switch is set to Dark, the sensor will not trigger lights or other modules until it is fully dark.

## Installing and Using a Plug-in Mini Controller with Photocell

The X10 SD533 Sundowner (see Figure 8.4) combines the features of a plug-in mini tabletop controller (Dim, Bright, All Lights On, All Units Off) with a photocell light sensor that can trigger lights at dusk. Therefore, you can use it to perform both jobs, particularly if you can place the controller in a location where it can be used to sense outside lighting levels.

### caution

If you don't have a wall box in a suitable location, you will need to install one or have one installed and have line and neutral wires run to it from an existing or new circuit.

Keep in mind that this sensor uses the same 120-volt AC power that AC wall sockets use. It can kill you if you don't take suitable precautions, including

• Shut off the power to the circuit containing the light switch you are working on.

• Tag the circuit breaker that is shut off as Out of Service to ensure that nobody turns it on while you are working on the light switch.

• Use a voltage tester to check the wiring into the light switch to ensure that power is off (refer to Figure 5.9 in Chapter 5, "Using X10 to Control Appliances").

If you are not comfortable working with electricity, work with a friend who is experienced with AC wiring, or hire a licensed electrician to install this sensor.

The photocell is on the front of the controller. The selection switch on the top of the controller is used to select unit codes 1–4 or 5–8 (as with other mini controllers, this unit cannot control unit codes 9–16). The House Code dial is at the upper right of the top of the controller, whereas the sensitivity dial (LIGHT->DARK) and in-out switches used to control lights with the photocell are located on the underside of the unit.

The photocell sensor in the Sundowner automatically turns on lights or other modules set to the same house code and unit codes 1–4 or 5–8 when the unit senses it's dark; you can control which unit codes are controlled with the photocell by adjusting the In/Out switches on the bottom of the unit. You should make sure that you use those unit codes only for lights you want to control with the Sundowner.

If the Sundowner turns on the lights when it is still bright outside, adjust the sensitivity control toward LIGHT; if the Sundowner turns on the lights well after dark, adjust the sensitivity control toward DARK. Place the Sundowner so that its photocell is not facing a light it controls.

## Using X10 in Your Garage

X10 has many uses in your garage. In addition to controlling built-in or plug-in lights, you can use X10 to

- Trigger lights in your home when the garage doors are opened
- Prevent unauthorized use of electric outlets
- Lock-out a garage door opener; plug your garage door opener into an appliance module and turn off the module when you go on vacation

## Controlling Garage Lights with X10

If your garage lights fixtures are wired in, you can use the appropriate type of X10 or X10-compatible switch to control them:

- Light switches for incandescent lighting such as accent lights on the front of the garage. Refer to the "Light Switches for Incandescent Lights" section earlier in this chapter for an overview of your options.

- Relay switches for nonincandescent lighting. Refer to the "Light Switches for Nonincandescent Lights" section earlier in this chapter for an overview of your options.

To control plug-in fluorescent lights over a work table or workbench, you can use

- Plug-in three-prong (grounded) appliance modules such the X10 AM466 (see Figure 8.5) or Smarthome ApplianceLinc series 2002SHL or 2002STW (see Figure 8.6)

- X10 or X10-compatible receptacles

You can also use appliance modules to control incandescent lights in your garage if you don't need to dim them.

**FIGURE 8.5**

The X10 AM466 appliance module works with three-prong (grounded) or two-prong appliances, fluorescent lights, and power tools up to 15 amps.

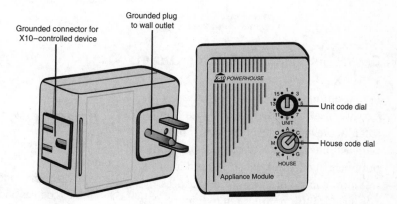

Grounded connector for X10–controlled device

Grounded plug to wall outlet

X-10 POWERHOUSE

Unit code dial

House code dial

Appliance Module

The Smarthome ApplianceLinc 2002-series module shown in Figure 8.6 provides a pass-through connector that is not X10-controlled. Use this type of module to enable an electrical outlet to provide full-time power for a device such as a battery charger while providing X10-compatible control for a fluorescent light or portable power tool up to 15 amps. The 2002SHL module is a one-way module, and the 2002STW module supports two-way operation and stored scenes.

**IN THE GARAGE, GROUNDED MODULES RULE!**

Although most home appliances require only two-prong outlets, many power tools and other appliances used in the garage require three-prong (grounded) outlets. Three-prong modules don't cost much more than two-prong outlets and you can always plug a two-prong appliance or lamp into a three-prong module.

**FIGURE 8.6**

The Smarthome ApplianceLinc 2002STW and 2002SLH modules provide an always-on pass-through connector.

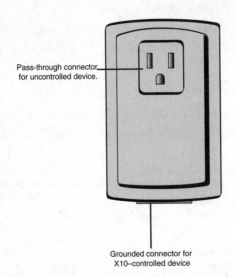

Pass-through connector for uncontrolled device.

Grounded connector for X10–controlled device

## Controlling Garage Electric Outlets with X10

If your garage doubles as a workshop, you can also use X10 to help make your garage safer by preventing local control of devices plugged into X10 or X10-compatible modules or outlets. By default, most X10 modules permit local control of lamps or appliances. Local control (sometimes referred to as *sense control*) means that the user can use the lamp or appliance's own On/Off switch to turn on the appliance even though the lamp or appliance is connected to an X10 module. To prevent a lamp or appliance from being used without permission, plug it into a module or outlet that does not permit local control. Modules or outlets that do not permit local control work only when the module or outlet receives an ON command from an X10 or X10-compatible controller.

**caution**

Set the modules and outlets in your garage for a separate house code from the modules and outlets in your home. Use a tabletop controller you can unplug and store to keep your electrical outlets under your control.

Keep in mind that you can always turn off a lamp or other device plugged into a module or outlet that does not permit local control using the device's own On/Off switch.

The Smarthome appliance modules shown in Figure 8.6 can be configured to prevent local control. These modules are programmed with an X10 or X10-compatible tabletop controller or wireless remote. For example, to program this type of module to use address B1 with local control enabled, send the command B1 ON. To program this type of module to use address B1 with local control disabled, send the command B1 OFF to program the module.

If you prefer a wired-in solution as a replacement for an existing wall outlet, use the Leviton #6280 15-amp duplex outlet shown in Figure 8.7 or the Leviton #6926 20-amp single outlet (not shown). Compared to a plug-in module, these outlets have two advantages:

- An unauthorized user can't bypass the module by unplugging it because the module is wired in.

- The outlet can be used to control other outlets connected to the same load (blue) wire (if available).

**FIGURE 8.7**

The Leviton #6280 X10-compatible outlet controls other downstream outlets connected to the same load (blue) wire.

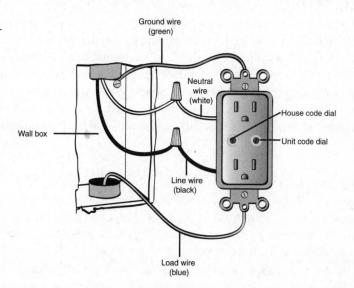

Ground wire (green)

Neutral wire (white)

House code dial

Wall box

Unit code dial

Line wire (black)

Load wire (blue)

For step-by-step installation instructions for X10 or X10-compatible appliance outlets, see the "Installing X10 Electrical Outlets" section in Chapter 5.

# Connecting Low-Voltage Accent or Holiday Lights to X10

If you use low-voltage walkway or accent lights as part of your landscaping, you have a couple of options for controlling them:

- Plug an X10 appliance (*not* a lamp) module into the AC outlet used by the transformer that powers the low-voltage lights and plug the transformer into that module.

- Replace the outlet used by the transformer with an X10 or X10-compatible electric outlet.

If you decide to use a plug-in module, you need to make sure that the outlet has a weatherproof enclosure or that you take other steps to prevent damage to the module. Some users report successfully covering the X10 appliance module with a plastic sandwich bag and using nylon tie strips to hold it in place.

If you prefer a more permanent solution, you can replace your outdoor electrical outlet with an X10 or X10-compatible outlet as described in the "Installing X10 Electrical Outlets" section in Chapter 5. In recent and new construction, outdoor electrical outlets are connected to indoor outlets that have ground fault circuit interrupter *(GFCI)* protection against electric shock. When you replace your existing outdoor outlet with an X10 or X10-compatible electric outlet, the new outlet will also be protected against electric shock if it is connected to a GFCI-equipped electric outlet.

---

**WINNING THE GFCI VERSUS X10 BATTLE**

In some cases, GFCI-equipped electrical outlets absorb so much of the X10 signal that the X10 module or outlet downstream from the GFCI-equipped outlet does not receive signals properly. To improve signal strength, add an amplified coupler-repeater to your X10 installation. See Appendix B, "Troubleshooting X10," for details.

Some GFCI-equipped electrical outlets are so sensitive that X10 signals can trip them. To solve this problem, connect your X10 controller, PC interface, or transceiver to a different outlet, preferably one on the opposite phase of the circuit to the GFCI-equipped outlet.

---

If you want your walkway or accent lights to be activated automatically by a photocell sensor, be sure to set the module or outlet controlling them for the same house code as the sensor and in an appropriate range of unit codes. For example, if you use a wired-in photocell sensor such as the Leviton #6308, you need to set the unit code for the accent lights to a value that is one to four unit codes higher than the photocell sensor. If the photocell sensor is set to use unit code 7, the module controlling walkway or accent lights could use unit codes 8–11. However, if you use an X10 Sundowner or similar device with a fixed range of unit codes, you must use unit codes 1–4 or 5–8, depending on the unit code range selected on the unit.

**UNIQUE UNIT CODES NOT ALWAYS NECESSARY**

If you want to turn on more than four lights with a photocell sensor that controls only four modules, assign some lights to the same unit code. However, make sure that you use the same unit code only for lights you will always want turned on or off at the same time.

Although strings of outdoor holiday lights don't use a transformer, you should use the same methods to connect and configure outdoor holiday lights as you use for low-voltage accent and walkway lights. Keep in mind that if you use holiday decorations that include a motor, such as an animated reindeer, you need to use an appliance module or outlet.

# Controlling Spas, Hot Tubs, and Pool Filters with X10

To make sure your spa, hot tub, or pool is ready for occupancy when you arrive, add it to your X10 home automation system and turn it on before you arrive. Because the motors in these and similar devices run on a 220-volt AC circuit, you need to replace the existing On/Off switch with a 220–volt-rated X10 or X10-compatible relay switch such as the X10 Pro XPS2 rather than a typical 110-volt relay switch.

Figure 8.8 shows how a 220-volt relay switch is wired.

**FIGURE 8.8**

The X10 Pro XPS2 220-volt relay switch handles motors up to 2 horse-power.

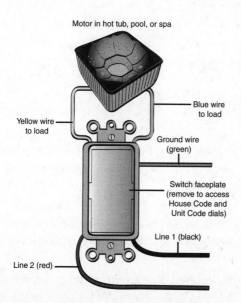

Motor in hot tub, pool, or spa

Blue wire to load

Yellow wire to load

Ground wire (green)

Switch faceplate (remove to access House Code and Unit Code dials)

Line 1 (black)

Line 2 (red)

Note that 220/230-volt circuits use a two-pole circuit breaker rather than a single circuit breaker as with a 110/115-volt circuit. See Figure 8.9 for a comparison.

**FIGURE 8.9**

A 110/115-volt (single-pole) circuit breaker (top) compared to a 220/230-volt (double-pole) circuit breaker (bottom).

Make **absolutely certain** you have turned off the correct circuit breaker before you remove your existing switch. As shown in Chapters 4 and 5, you should use a voltage sensor to make certain that you have disconnected power to the switch before you proceed with the installation or hire an electrician to perform the installation for you.

# Troubleshooting X10 Exterior Controls

If you're having problems with X10 modules running exterior lights or outlets, start by checking the house codes and unit codes, as you would with any X10 installation.

If you want to use the same tabletop controller or wireless remote to control interior and exterior lights, they must use the same house code or you must switch the controller between house codes.

If you are able to trigger some lights with a photocell sensor, but not others, your modules or outlets might not be set for an appropriate unit number. Review the instructions for your photocell sensor to determine which unit numbers can be controlled with your sensor.

If you are not able to control your garage or other exterior lights from within the house with X10, but you can plug in the controller into an exterior or garage outlet and control them, your garage or exterior lights are on a different circuit than your house wiring. Check to see if you have a separate electrical service for the garage. If you do, you can use a wireless transceiver and remote plugged into an outlet in the garage to control garage or other lights connected to the garage's service from within your house. If the garage uses the same electrical service as the house, use a signal bridge or coupler as described in Appendix B. For additional troubleshooting tips, see Appendix B.

# THE ABSOLUTE MINIMUM

- You can control porch, patio, deck, walkway, and other types of exterior lighting with X10.

- You can use photocell triggers, timers, or remotes to control exterior lights.

- To turn on exterior lights at sunset, use an X10 computer program and interface module.

- To turn on exterior lights at dark (regardless of actual sunset time), use a photocell sensor.

- The main advantage of using a timer to control exterior lights is to give a lived-in look to your home when you're away.

- You can use standard X10 light switches for incandescent porch or patio lights, but nonincandescent lights require relay switches.

- If your porch, garage, or other exterior lights can be controlled from two or more light switches in your home, you must replace the master switch with an X10-compatible three-way switch and the other switches with matching companion switches.

- You can use photocell sensors that are wired in, plug-in, battery-powered, or combined with floodlights to automate dusk-to-dawn exterior lighting.

- Some photocell sensors can be configured to turn off exterior lights after a user-specified delay, enabling you to enjoy your evening out without worrying about turning off the lights after you come in.

- Because many tools used in the garage are three-prong (grounded), you should use three-prong X10 modules or X10 outlets if you want to control devices in the garage with X10.

- If you replace an electrical outlet connected to a GFCI-protected circuit with an X10-compatible electrical outlet, you might need to use an amplified coupler-repeater to provide adequate signal strength to the outlet.

- You can automate spas and other 220/230-volt exterior devices by replacing the existing switch with an X10 or X10-compatible 220/230-volt relay switch.

**9**

# USING X10 TO PROVIDE SECURITY

Your X10 home automation system can do more for you than turn on your lights and run your appliances: It can keep your home and your family safe. In this chapter, you learn how to use X10 and X10-compatible devices to detect motion, sense opened doors and windows, and monitor doorways and other areas of your home. You'll also learn how to use X10 and X10-compatible modules as part of a comprehensive home security system.

# Methods of Securing Your Home

You can use many methods to help make your home more secure using X10-compatible hardware. These include

- Video cameras
- Motion detectors
- Door and window sensors
- Callback systems
- Remote access and control systems

This chapter focuses on video cameras, motion detectors, door and window sensors, and callback systems. Chapter 10, "Accessing X10 Home Control via Telephone," provides more information on X10-based telephone control and callback systems. Chapters 11, "Accessing X10 Home Control via Your Home Computer," and 12, "Accessing X10 Home Control via Your Home Network and the Internet," focus on computer, home network, and web control of X10 automation systems.

# Installing X10-Compatible Video Cameras

One of the easiest ways to improve home security with X10 is to install one or more X10 video cameras in your home. To name just a few possible uses, you can use X10 video cameras to

- See who's at the door
- Keep an eye on the baby
- Watch the kids in the backyard

Although X10.com is most famous for X10-compatible video cameras (a couple of years ago its pop-up ads were all over the Internet), X10.com is not the only supplier of video cameras that work with X10 home automation systems. However, its cameras are some of the most economical available, and are easy to set up in a single- or multiple-camera configuration.

In this example, let's look at the components in a typical X10.com kit: the XX16A instant-on XCam2 and its companion receiver, the VR36A (see Figure 9.1).

Both the camera and the receiver feature small rectangular antennas that must be aimed at each other for high-quality reception.

---

**MASTERING MULTIPLE CAMERAS**

If you get a multiple-camera kit or add additional cameras later, you will need to adjust the position of the receiver so that it picks up the best possible signal from each camera. For greatest flexibility, get a kit that includes the *CR12A*—a special remote control that can control XCam2 and similar cameras, standard X10 devices, and the matching wireless transceiver.

---

**FIGURE 9.1**

X10.com's
XX16A XCam2
(left) and VR36A
receiver (right).
Camera and
receiver supplied
courtesy of X10
Wireless
Technology, Inc.

**FIGURE 9.1**

X10.com's XX16A XCam2 (left) and VR36A receiver (right). Camera and receiver supplied courtesy of X10 Wireless Technology, Inc.

## Installation Preparations

Before you install the camera, consider the following issues:

- **Camera placement**—Decide where you want to place the camera. Keep in mind that this camera, like most X10 cameras, needs an AC (alternating current) power source, unless you want to use an extra-cost optional battery pack for maximum flexibility.

- **Potential sources of interference**— The camera and receiver use the 2.4GHz frequency band also used by most Wi-Fi wireless ethernet hardware and by the most common category of cordless telephones.

**caution**

I used an 802.11g Wi-Fi network adapter in the same room as the camera without any problems, but your experience might vary. You can select one of four channels on the camera and receiver to help minimize or eliminate interference.

- **Receiver location**—The maximum distance between the camera and the receiver is 100 feet, but brick or masonry construction or metal doors could considerably reduce the signal strength. The receiver must also be plugged into an AC power source and into a TV or VCR.

- **Light levels**—A color camera requires considerably more light than a black-and-white camera. If you want to use a camera to watch a dimly lit area outside your home, consider using a combination floodlight/camera such as the X10.com FloodCam, or use a low-light black-and-white camera such as the X10.com NightWatch wireless or NightWatch2 wired camera indoors or out.

- **Camera location**—If the camera must be mounted outdoors, you should use a weather-resistant camera such as the X10.com FloodCam.

■ **Angle of coverage**—The standard XCam2 and FloodCam cover a 60°
angle. Use the X10.com WideEye camera to double the viewing angle to
120°. If you need to view a wider area with a single camera, you can use a
Ninja Pan 'n Tilt mechanism. For details, see the "Moving the Camera" section later in this chapter.

## Configuring the Camera

The XCam2 camera and its power supply have separate settings. The camera has a
sliding switch for selecting channels beneath a rectangular rubber plug (see Figure
9.2). By default, the camera is preset to Channel A. You must use the same channel
on the camera(s) and receiver to ensure proper signal reception.

**FIGURE 9.2**

Major features of
the XCam2.

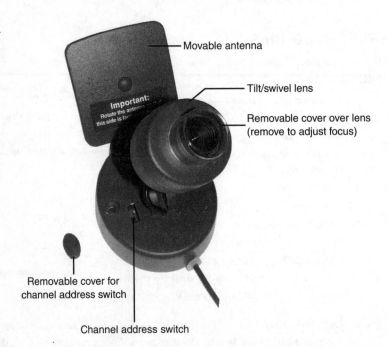

Movable antenna

Tilt/swivel lens

Removable cover over lens
(remove to adjust focus)

Removable cover for
channel address switch

Channel address switch

The addressable power supply has the familiar house code (red) and unit code
(black) dials (see Figure 9.3). The camera comes on automatically when you plug
in the power supply. However, if you have two or more cameras, you can use the
CR12A or CR13A camera-compatible remote controls to switch between cameras by
using the On/Off buttons or Scan buttons on the remote.

**FIGURE 9.3**

The XCam2's
addressable
power supply.

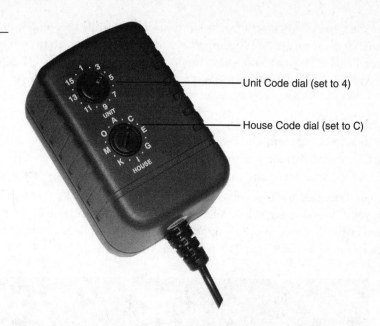

Unit Code dial (set to 4)

House Code dial (set to C)

## Configuring the Receiver

The receiver does not have house or unit code dials; it receives signals from the camera(s) on the channel (A–D) it is configured to use. A sliding switch on the bottom of the receiver (see Figure 9.4) is used to select the channel.

**FIGURE 9.4**

Bottom view of
the VR36A
receiver.

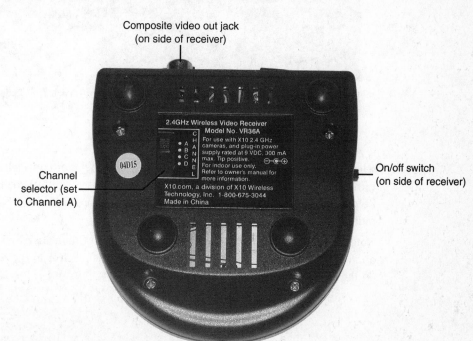

Composite video out jack
(on side of receiver)

Channel
selector (set
to Channel A)

On/off switch
(on side of receiver)

Use the On/Off switch on the receiver to turn it off while you plug it in to an AC outlet and connect the RCA composite data cable to the video in connection on your TV or VCR. You can display the signal on your TV or record it. After the receiver has been connected to an AC outlet and to the TV or VCR, turn it on.

## Using the Camera

As soon as the camera and receiver are plugged into an AC outlet and are set to the same channel, the camera starts sending live video to the receiver. How you view the video varies according to the method used to connect your receiver.

If you connected the receiver to the Video In jack on your TV (see Figure 9.5), turn on your TV and select Video, Aux, or a similar option on your TV's remote or front panel control. There might be a mode button, or you might need to cycle through the channels; consult your TV's instructions for details.

**FIGURE 9.5**

Connecting the receiver to the Video In jack on a typical VCR.

If you connected the receiver to the Video In jack on your VCR, turn on your TV, select the channel used for the VCR (typically channel 3 or channel 4), and then turn on the VCR. If you want to record live video, insert a blank tape and press the Record button(s) on your VCR or remote control. Consult your VCR's instruction manual for details.

Note that some wireless video cameras also transmit audio. To hear or record audio, be sure to connect the Audio Out jack on the receiver to the Audio In jack on the VCR or TV (refer to Figure 9.5).

## Using Multiple Cameras

If multiple cameras use the addressable power supply (as you saw in Figure 9.3), you can switch between them if you have the CR12A or CR13A remote and a compatible wireless transceiver, such as the TM751. The CR12A is often bundled with multiple camera kits. Both remotes are designed to work with an X10 wireless transceiver such as the TM751. The CR12A works with cameras in groups of four. The cameras must be grouped together as described in Table 9.1. All cameras in a group must use the same house code and a unit code in the range listed.

**TABLE 9.1   Allowable Unit Code Groupings for XCam2 Cameras**

| House Code | House/Unit Code for Group 1 | House/Unit Code for Group 2 | House/Unit Code for Group 3 | House/Unit Code for Group 4 |
|---|---|---|---|---|
| (same code A–P)* | A1 A2 A3 A4 | A5 A6 A7 A8 | A9 A10 A11 A12 | A13 A14 A15 A16 |

*\* This example uses house code A.*

To switch between cameras with the CR12A, use the On button that corresponds to each camera. For example, to switch between camera 1 and camera 4, press 4 On; camera 1 turns off and camera 4 turns on. You can also use the scan buttons on the CR12A remote (see Figure 9.6) to switch to each camera in sequence.

**FIGURE 9.6**

The CR12A remote (right) controls up to 16 cameras wirelessly through a transceiver module (left).

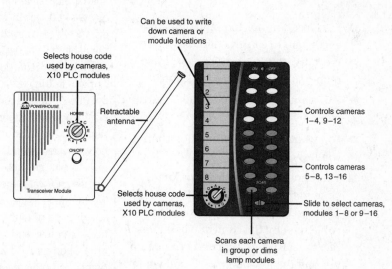

Can be used to write down camera or module locations

Selects house code used by cameras, X10 PLC modules

Retractable antenna

Controls cameras 1–4, 9–12

Controls cameras 5–8, 13–16

Selects house code used by cameras, X10 PLC modules

Slide to select cameras, modules 1–8 or 9–16

Scans each camera in group or dims lamp modules

### SINGLE CAMERA ON/OFF

If you want to control cameras without a CR12A or CR13A remote, or if your video camera does not include an addressable power supply, connect each camera's power supply to a standard X10 appliance module. Turn on the camera you want to view with a wireless remote/transceiver or a wired Mini Controller or Maxi Controller. To switch to another camera, you must turn off the first one and turn on the second one.

By default, the CR12A controls cameras on unit codes 1–4; unit codes 5–8 and codes 9–16 are reserved for normal X10 modules. If you control a dimmable lamp with unit codes 5–8 or 9–16, the scan buttons at the bottom of the control are used to dim or brighten the lamp as with the HR12A remote. If your cameras are installed on codes 5–8, 9–12, or 13–16 instead (refer to Table 9.1), you can use the other unit codes for standard X10 modules. If you have more than four cameras, I recommend using the CR13A remote, which makes controlling a larger number of cameras easier than with the CR12A.

Your X10 wireless cameras can also be used with computer- or Internet-based controllers. Use an X10-USB video capture adapter to connect the camera(s) to your PC. You can also use webcams made for PCs. However, webcams cannot be used with your TV or VCR. See Chapters 11 and 12 for details.

## When Wired Cameras Are Better

You also can use wired cameras that can be controlled via X10 remotes, such as the CR12A and CR13A. Use a wired camera in these circumstances:

- Your location has too much interference—due to construction (brick, masonry, steel)—or other causes for high-quality wireless video signals.

- You want to pick up audio as well as video.

- You want a lower-cost solution than a wireless camera.

- The camera will be located relatively close to the video receiver (TV or VCR). The exact distance depends on the cable used by the camera. For example, the X10.com Anaconda color camera and the low-light black-and-white NightWatch2 use 60-foot wire, whereas the XCam Anywhere color camera uses 15-foot wire. To determine whether you

can use one of these cameras, you need to determine the wire distance (not straight-line distance) between your camera and your video receiver.

**caution**

The *wire distance* for any wired device is the distance it takes to route the cable for the device from the device (a video camera, in this case) to the receiver. If you can run the cable through walls, the wire distance might be similar to the straight-line distance between device and receiver. If you plan to run the cable around doorframes and walls, the wire distance will be much longer than the straight-line distance. Measure your home carefully and determine what installation method you plan to use *before* you order a wired video camera.

## Moving the Camera

If you want to use a single camera to cover an angle of view wider than the camera supports, you need to use a camera that supports a pan-and-tilt mechanism. X10.com's wireless cameras can be used with the Ninja Pan 'n Tilt robotic camera mount (VK74A) and its companion Ninja ScanPad controller (CR14A). The Ninja (see Figure 9.7) can be panned through a 240° arc and a 130° tilt. The Ninja includes an addressable power supply similar to that used with XCam2. Wireless cameras are plugged into the Ninja base, and the base powers the camera as well as the pan-and-tilt mechanism.

**FIGURE 9.7**

The Ninja Pan 'n Tilt camera mount with an X10.com wireless camera and ScanPad remote. Photo supplied courtesy of X10 Wireless Technology, Inc.

The ScanPad remote sends signals directly to the Ninja base to move the camera interactively or move the camera to one of four preset positions.

## One Camera or More—Determining the Best Camera Strategy

How many security cameras do you need? Camera vendors offer multicamera bundles, suggesting that you need three or four, but do you? It depends on what you need to keep an eye on.

If you're mainly concerned about front or back entrance security, a single camera will probably suffice. However, if you want to watch your children at play, you'll want to have at least one camera in the playroom, one facing the back yard or other outdoor play area, and one facing the street.

If you're on the fence about the number of cameras you need, calculate the costs of buying a single camera and remote now and adding cameras later versus buying a multicamera bundle. Multicamera bundles can save you a lot of money, but might include additional remotes or modules you don't need. Shop carefully to get the bundle that's right for your situation.

If you're mainly concerned about using video security at night, consider a combination wireless video camera with floodlights such as X10.com's FloodCam.

## Recording for Additional Security

So far, this chapter has discussed using X10 security cameras in an interactive manner. If you connect your camera(s) to a VCR, you can simply press the Record button to make a recording of suspicious activity as it happens. However, if you want to record suspicious activity when you're away, it's time to use additional X10 devices to make your recording intelligent.

If you're using a security camera in an area that normally sees no activity, such as a window or back door, you can use an X10-compatible motion sensor and an X10-compatible home electronics controller to record activity.

### Using X10.com's VCR Motion Control Kit

X10.com bundles an outdoor X10 motion sensor and a VCR controller as the major components in its VCR Motion Control kit (see Figure 9.8).

**FIGURE 9.8**

X10.com's VCR Commander II (left) and EagleEye motion sensor (right) can be used to automate video recording from a security camera. Photo supplied courtesy of X10 Wireless Technology, Inc.

The VCR Commander II (UX23A) features an integrated wireless X10 receiver designed to pick up commands from up to four wireless motion sensors such as the EagleEye (MS14A) or ActiveEye (MS16A). After you've plugged in the VCR Commander II unit, pressed PLAY on the unit, and then pressed HOUSE on the motion sensor, the VCR Commander II will receive commands from the motion sensor. The Home and Away modes supported by the VCR Commander II enable you to disable the motion detector when you're home (Home mode) and re-enable it (Away mode) when you leave.

The less-expensive VCR Commander (UX21A) works with only one motion sensor. To configure the UX21A or UX23A to control your VCR, you use the VCR's remote to teach the VCR Commander or Commander II your unit's RECORD and STOP commands. You use an infrared *(IR)* emitter cable provided with the VCR Commander/Commander II to transmit these commands to the VCR.

When the motion sensor detects motion, it sends a signal to the VCR Commander/Commander II, which then sends the RECORD signal to the VCR. After five minutes have passed, the VCR Commander/Commander II shuts off the VCR.

For more information on the EagleEye and similar motion sensors, see the "Using X10 Motion Detectors to Improve Security" section later in this chapter.

## Using Smarthome's X10 to IR Linc

For additional flexibility, such as using a set-top DVD recorder instead of a VCR, or recording for more (or less) time or to switch on a TV automatically instead of recording, you can use Smarthome's X10 to IR Linc (#1623) to trigger your audio/visual device.

The X10 to IR Linc (see Figure 9.9) is a fully programmable X10 device. Use a Maxi Controller or an X10-compatible home automation program that can send X10 codes to configure the IR Linc. The X10 to IR Linc connects to an AC wall outlet with the included PowerLinc II adapter.

**FIGURE 9.9**

Smarthome's X10 to IR Linc.

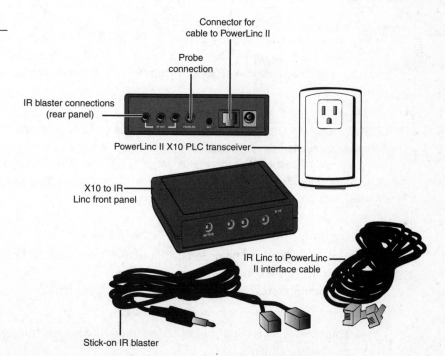

Connector for cable to PowerLinc II

Probe connection

IR blaster connections (rear panel)

PowerLinc II X10 PLC transceiver

X10 to IR Linc front panel

IR Linc to PowerLinc II interface cable

Stick-on IR blaster

The X10 to IR Linc can be used with one of several optional probes that detect whether a TV is turned on, an audio/visual device is turned on, or a video signal is being received. It has two built-in IR emitters and features ports for three optional external emitters (one external emitter is included).

You use your audio/visual device's remote control to teach the X10 to IR Linc commands that are stored in the device's memory. As each command is learned, you send the X10 control signal with a Maxi Controller (refer to Chapter 6, "Using Timers and Advanced Remotes for X10") or equivalent device that is associated with that command. These commands are listed in Table 9.2, along with how they are used by the X10 to IR Linc.

**TABLE 9.2**   X10 to IR Linc Function Codes

| Normal X10 Command | X10 to IR Linc Usage |
| --- | --- |
| All Lights On | Turn on the device |
| All Units Off | Turn off the device |
| On | Send a single command |
| Off | Send a single command |
| Bright | Use for functions such as volume up or channel up |
| Dim | Use for functions such as volume down or channel down |
| Repeated House/Unit Code | Send a single command |

To help understand how to program the X10 to IR Linc, let's assume that you want to teach the device to start VCR recording when code A2 On is received. This code could be sent by a motion detector or by any other X10 or X10-compatible transmitter.

---

**CREATE A LIST OF THE COMMANDS YOU WANT BEFORE YOU START**

Although you can remove an individual command from the X10 to IR Linc's memory, there's no way to print out the commands. Make a list of the commands you want to store in advance. A template you can use is located at the back of the instruction manual provided with the X10 to IR Linc.

---

1. Disconnect any probes connected to the IR Linc.
2. Make sure that you have plugged in a Maxi Controller and have configured it for the house code (A, in this example) you want to use for the command(s) you want to store in the IR Linc's memory.
3. Press and hold the Set button on the IR Linc's rear panel.
4. Point the VCR's remote control at one of the IR blasters (transceivers) on the front of the IR Linc.

5. Release the Set button after one second. Make sure that the red Active indicator light is blinking on the IR Linc's front panel. This indicates that the IR Linc is ready to receive a command from the VCR's remote control.

6. Press and hold the Record button on the VCR within five seconds of releasing the Set button.

7. Release the Record button as soon as the Active light on the IR Linc goes out. This indicates that the Record command has been received.

8. The green Probe indicator light on the IR Linc's front panel will begin to blink. This indicates that the IR Linc is ready to receive an X10 command.

9. To store A2 On as the code used to trigger Record, make sure that the Maxi Controller's house code is set to A, press the 2 button on the controller's keypad, and then press the On button. Perform these tasks within 15 seconds of step 7.

10. To verify that the X10 code has been received, make sure that the green Probe indicator light stays solid green for a few seconds and then turns off.

**caution**

IR Linc responds to the first X10 code it receives during the learning process (steps 8–10). To prevent other X10 codes from being received, disconnect any X10-computer interfaces (see Chapter 11) and Mini Timers (refer to Chapter 6) during the setup process. Also, if you use a wireless X10 transceiver and remote control (refer to Chapter 2, "Getting Started with X10 Home Automation"), make sure that these devices are not used.

If you have two-way X10 modules or light switches set to transmit codes that might be activated during the setup process, don't use them. If you're unable to avoid using them, disable the transmit option by sending the appropriate codes with your Maxi Controller or PC interface. Consult Chapters 6 and 11 for details.

The X10 to IR Linc can store a sequence of commands as a macro, enabling you to trigger multiple devices or functions with a single command. One such macro might go through the following steps:

1. Turn on the VCR

2. Turn on the TV

3. Switch the TV to the VCR monitoring channel (channel 3)

4. Record

5. Stop recording

6. Turn off the VCR

7. Turn off the TV

You start the process of creating a macro by deciding which X10 code will be used to trigger the macro, such as A12 On or another unused code. Next, store each command as described earlier in this section. However, during step 9, send the same code (such as A12 On) for each command. When the IR Linc receives this code from a transceiver, Maxi Controller, motion detector, or other source, it will send each command in order.

To make the IR Linc "smarter," connect one of the optional probes to the unit. For example, to determine whether a TV is turned on, you could use the TV detector probe (#8012). If a probe determines that the TV is turned on, the IR Linc can skip the macro step that turns on the TV. For information about this and other probes, see the Smarthome website at www.smarthome.com.

After you've configured the IR Linc to be triggered by a particular house or unit code, you need to set up the remote or other device, such as a motion detector, that will start the recording process.

# Using X10 Motion Detectors to Improve Security

As you can see from the previous sections, motion detectors can be valuable tools in improving security. You can use a motion detector to

- Turn on lights in a dim hallway or porch to make video recording sharper and clearer
- Trigger video recording when somebody or something enters an area
- Turn on porch lights at dusk and turn them off at dawn

However, motion detectors aren't just for security. If you've been telling family members "Turn off the lights when you leave a room," but nobody's listening, you can also use a motion detector to turn off the lights automatically. You can also use a motion detector to trigger fans or air conditioning units on or off to help keep your family cool and save money.

A motion detector can be configured to send a specified house/unit On code when it detects motion; most can also send an Off code after a user-specified interval has passed. Most motion detectors can also be used to turn on lights at dusk and off at dawn.

## Preparations for Setup

Before you put a motion detector in place, decide the following:

- **Where do you want to locate the detector?**—Many motion detectors, such as the X10.com MS14A and MS16A, are designed to work at least six feet from ground level. If you use battery-powered motion detectors, make sure that you locate them where they can be easily reached for battery replacement. If you prefer a motion detector that is AC-powered, you can get a floodlight with built-in X10-compatible motion detection/dusk-to-dawn triggers, such as the Leviton X10 motion detector (Leviton DHC #6417) or the Smarthome X10 motion detector floodlight (#4080XT).

■ **How long do you want the delay between motion sensing and light shutoff to be?**—With most motion sensors, you can adjust the delay between when motion is no longer sensed and the lights go out. Be sure to select a device that offers a long enough delay for your needs. For example, a short delay is suitable for an area with a lot of movement, such as an entryway. However, if you want to use a motion detector in a home office or bedroom, a longer delay is better. Some devices feature adjustable delays up to 256 minutes (more than 4 hours).

■ **How long is the range you need to support?**—Battery-powered motion detectors tend to have shorter ranges (up to 20 feet) than those that use AC power (40 feet or longer). Determine the distance from the location you want to use for the motion detector before you purchase one.

■ **What is the unit's on/off capability?**—Some motion detectors send only On signals, not Off signals. If you want to turn off lights after an interval, look for motion detectors that support both on and off functions.

■ **What on/off house/unit codes do you want the motion detector to send?**—Some motion detectors use the traditional house and unit code dials to set addresses, whereas others use memory. The ones that use memory can be a bit trickier to set up.

■ **Do you want the motion detector to control lights for dusk-to-dawn lighting?**—Some motion detectors can be configured to use the next sequential house/unit code after the code used for motion detection as a trigger for dusk-to-dawn lighting. Be prepared to adjust the house/unit codes used by porch or other exterior lights to match the code used by the motion detector.

## Using a Battery-Powered Motion Detector

X10.com sells several similar motion detectors (also referred to as *occupancy sensors*) such as the MS13A/MS14A (HawkEye) and MS15A/MS16A (ActiveEye) series. The MS13A (recently discontinued) and the MS15A are indoor-only units, whereas the MS14A and MS16A can be used indoors or outdoors. All four are easy-to-install battery-powered devices, and are sometimes sold by other vendors under different model numbers. All of them are wireless devices that communicate with other X10 or X10-compatible modules through a wireless transceiver such as the one you saw in Figure 9.6.

Compared to the MS14A, the MS15A and MS16A offer additional features and some difference in setup. See the "Additional Features of the MS16A" section later in this chapter for details.

Before you can configure any battery-powered motion detector, you must insert batteries. The MS14A uses two AAA batteries that fit into the battery compartment on the front of the unit (see Figure 9.10).

**FIGURE 9.10**

The MS14A wireless motion sensor sends wireless X10 signals to an X10 wireless transceiver. Remove the battery compartment cover to configure the unit.

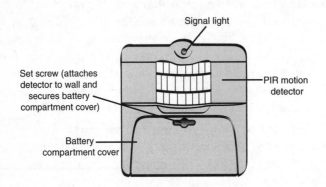

Signal light

Set screw (attaches detector to wall and secures battery compartment cover)

PIR motion detector

Battery compartment cover

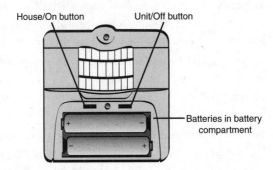

House/On button

Unit/Off button

Batteries in battery compartment

**PIR IS PASSIVE INFRARED**

Almost all one-piece motion detectors use passive infrared to detect motion. The motion detector actually detects temperature changes caused by a human being, animal, or object moving through the detector's field of vision. It's not as fancy as the laser beams you see at the movies, but it works. However, don't put a motion detector directly above or below a heating or cooling vent or near another heat source (such as an incandescent light). If you do, you'll have a lot of false alarms.

There are two buttons above the battery compartment:

■ House/On

■ Unit/Off

These buttons are used to program the operation of the motion detector. The red light above the detector photocell is used with the control buttons to indicate programming steps and the device's configuration.

By default, the MS14A sends codes to house code A and unit code 1 when it detects movement, day or night. These codes are transmitted to a wireless X10 transceiver such as the TM751 (refer to Figure 9.6). To test the motion detector, perform these steps:

1. Set the transceiver to house code A.
2. Plug a lamp into the transceiver (if it works as unit code 1) or plug the lamp into a lamp module set to house code A, unit code 1.
3. Turn on the lamp with an X10 remote or Maxi Controller.
4. Turn off the lamp with an X10 remote or Maxi Controller.
5. Press the House/On button on the motion detector to turn on the lamp.
6. Press the Unit/Off button on the motion detector to turn off the lamp.

To test the photocell, place the detector at a location about six feet off the ground and wait for a minute or two. Then walk past the detector. The lamp using code A1 should turn on (the motion detector sends the command A1 On). It will turn off after one minute without detected motion (the motion detector sends the command A1 Off).

## Changing the Default House/Unit Codes on the MS14A

If you want to use the motion detector to trigger a lamp or other device on a different house or unit code:

■ Make sure that you have a wireless transceiver configured to the house code you want to use; for example, house code B.

■ Note the unit code of the lamp or other device that you want to trigger with the motion detector; for example, unit code 3.

Follow these steps to change the house code from the default A to B:

1. Remove the battery compartment cover.
2. Press and hold the House/On button to switch to setup mode. The red light on the top of the detector will flash, and then blink once to indicate the stored house code (one blink = A).
3. Release the House/On button and immediately press it the number of times equal to the house code you want to set. In this case, press twice for B. You'd press three times for C, and so forth.
4. On the last press of the key, hold the House/On button down for three seconds.
5. After the red light has blinked twice to confirm the new house code setting (B), release the House/On button. The unit is now ready to detect motion and transmit to house code B.

Follow these steps to change the default unit code from 1 to 3:

1. Remove the battery compartment cover.

2. Press and hold the Unit/Off button to switch to setup mode. The red light on the top of the detector will flash, and then blink once to indicate the stored unit code (one blink = 1).

3. Release the Unit/Off button and immediately press it the number of times equal to the unit code you want to set. In this case, press three times for 3. You'd press two times for 2, four times for 4, and so forth.

4. On the last press of the key, hold the Unit/Off button down for three seconds.

5. After the red light has blinked three times to confirm the new unit code setting (3), release the Unit/Off button. The unit is now ready to detect motion and transmit to unit code 3 and the house code configured in the previous set of instructions.

---

**GET A SINGLE, SMARTER WIRELESS TRANSCEIVER**

If you want to use several wireless devices, such as motion detectors and remotes, you might need to use more than one house code. You could use a separate transceiver for each house code, but a better idea is to upgrade to a unit that can receive all house codes. Some examples include the Leviton RF 256 (model #HCPRF), which can be used with a companion six-way universal/X10 remote (model #HCCUR), the X10.com CM15A ActiveHome Pro computer interface, and the single Leviton RF 256 device transceiver base (#HCPRF). This wireless transceiver can receive any house code from A through P and any unit code from 1 through 16. It also has a companion six-in-one universal/X10 remote (#HCCUR). This wireless transceiver is available from Smarthome and other X10 vendors.

---

## Changing the Default Time Delay on the MS14A

You can also adjust the delay time before the detector turns off the light. The MS14A is preprogrammed to wait for one minute after the last activity has been detected before turning off the lights.

1. Press the House/On button once.

2. After the red light has flashed (within six seconds), press and hold the Unit/Off button.

3. The green light inside the photocell turns on.

4. Three seconds later, the red light begins to blink the current delay (see Table 9.3).

5. Release the Unit/Off button.

**TABLE 9.3** Delay Times Used by the MS14A Motion Detector

| Number of Blinks | Delay Time (Minutes) | Delay Time (Hours/Minutes) |
|---|---|---|
| 1 | 1 minute | — |
| 2 | 2 minutes | — |
| 3 | 4 minutes | — |
| 4 | 8 minutes | — |
| 5 | 16 minutes | — |
| 6 | 32 minutes | — |
| 7 | 64 minutes | 1 hour, 4 minutes |
| 8 | 128 minutes | 2 hours, 8 minutes |
| 9 | 256 minutes | 4 hours, 16 minutes |

Perform the following steps to view and change the current setting:

1. Press the House/On button once.

2. After the red light has flashed (within six seconds), press and hold the Unit/Off button.

3. The green light inside the photocell turns on.

4. Three seconds later, the red light begins to blink the current delay (refer to Table 9.3).

5. Release the Unit/Off button.

6. Immediately press the Unit/Off button the number of times needed to set the desired delay. That number should be the same number as the number of blinks shown in Table 9.3. For example, to set a delay of eight minutes, press the Unit Off button four times.

7. On the last press needed for the desired delay, hold down the Unit/Off button for three seconds.

8. The red light blinks to indicate the delay as shown in Table 9.3. For example, if you selected eight minutes, the red light will blink four times.

9. When the green light goes out, release the Unit/Off button.

## Using the MS14A for Motion Detection and Lighting

The MS14A can be fastened into place with screws or with a double-sided adhesive pad (both are supplied with the unit). Place it six feet or more above the floor, in a location where you can access the front panel to change batteries or adjust programming.

To use the MS14A to turn on a light (for energy saving or to help provide enough light for a security camera to work):

1. Configure the MS14A to send the house/unit code for the lamp module or light switch in the room. Refer to the "Changing the Default House/Unit Codes on the MS14A" section earlier in this chapter for details.

2. Configure the MS14A time delay desired. Refer to the "Changing the Default Time Delay on the MS14A" section earlier in this chapter for details.

3. Make sure that the lamp module or light switch is set to the house/unit code used by the MS14A.

When the MS14A detects motion, it will send the On code to the lamp or light switch's house/unit code stored in its memory. When no motion is detected within the specified time delay, the motion detector sends the lamp module or light switch an Off code. Figure 9.11 illustrates a typical situation.

**FIGURE 9.11**

Using a motion detector to turn on a light in the room when it is occupied, and to turn off the light in the room when it is not occupied.

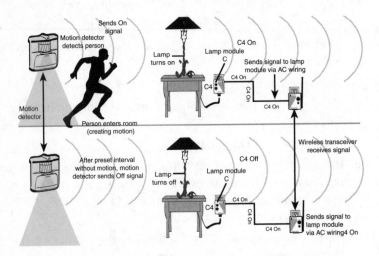

---

**WHEN MORE THAN ONE'S WHAT YOU NEED**

A single motion detector will do the job if there's only one way in or out of a room. However, if the room you want to control has more than one entrance or exit, you must select the position of the sensor very carefully or install a second motion sensor.

---

To turn on and turn off any other device—such as a fan, an air conditioner, a VCR, and so forth—with the motion detector, configure the motion detector to send the house/unit code for the module or switch that controls the device.

## Configuring the MS14A to Work at Night

The MS14A motion detector and similar models can be configured to trigger dusk-to-dawn lighting or to detect motion only at night. By default, this motion sensor sends an On code one unit code higher than its normal configuration at dusk, and sends a corresponding Off code at dawn. For example, if you have configured the motion sensor to send house/unit code B2 normally, it will send B3 at night.

To use this feature, do the following:

- Position the motion sensor where it will receive plenty of light during the day, but not be fooled by artificial light at night.

- Configure the motion sensor to the desired house/unit code setting for triggering a lamp or other device in normal mode.

- Configure the modules controlling interior or exterior lights that you want to use only at night to the same house code as the motion sensor, but one unit code higher than the module the motion sensor turns on when motion is detected. For example, if the motion sensor is configured to turn on a lamp using unit code 3, set the module(s) connected to the lights you want to use for dusk-to-dawn lighting to unit code 4. See Figure 9.12.

**FIGURE 9.12**

Using a motion detector to trigger dusk-to-dawn lights as well as motion-based lights.

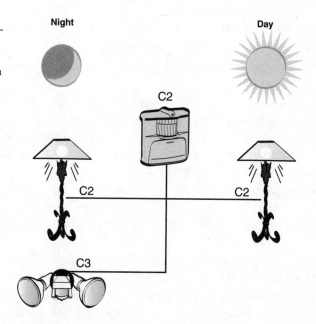

- Configure the MS14A to transmit only at night (its default is to transmit whenever it sees motion). Follow this procedure to determine the current setting for the motion sensor:

  1. Press the Unit/Off button once. The red light will flash.
  2. Within six seconds, press and hold the House/On button. The green light inside the photocell will turns on.

3. The red light blinks once if the motion sensor is set to detect motion at all times. The red light blinks twice if the motion sensor is set to detect motion only when it's dark outside.

To change the current setting:

1. Press the Unit/Off button once. The red light will flash.

2. Within six seconds, press and hold the House/On button. The green light inside the photocell will turn on.

3. After the motion sensor has reported its dusk/dawn setting (one blink for all times, two blinks for dark), release and immediately press the House/On button once (operates at all times) or twice (operates at night only). Hold down the button for three seconds on your last press.

4. After the red light has reported the setting (one blink for all times, two blinks for dark), release the House/On button.

---

**TRIGGERING MULTIPLE LIGHTS**

To trigger multiple lights with the motion sensor, you can

- Configure two or more lights to use the same house/unit code. This is the least flexible method.

- Create one or more scenes using intelligent lamp modules or light switches (consult Chapters 6 and 11 for details) and configure the motion sensor to send the house/unit code for the scene you have created. By creating different scenes (each scene uses a unit house/unit code), you can vary the lighting by reconfiguring the motion sensor.

- Use a two-way light switch or lamp module controlled by the motion sensor to send a house/unit On code to another module or switch or to send a code to trigger a scene.

---

## Additional Features of the MS16A

The X10 MS16A ActiveEye Motion Sensor features similar setup options to the MS14A, as well as an analog dial on the top of the unit. The analog dial is used to set variable delay rates from one minute up to 60 minutes. Table 9.4 shows how the MS16A motion sensor reports the delay setting.

**TABLE 9.4** Delay Times Used by the MS16A Motion Sensor

| Number of Blinks | Delay Time (Minutes) | Delay Time (Hours/Minutes) |
| --- | --- | --- |
| 1 | * | * |
| 2 | 2 minutes | — |
| 3 | 4 minutes | — |
| 4 | 8 minutes | — |
| 5 | 16 minutes | — |
| 6 | 32 minutes | — |
| 7 | 64 minutes | 1 hour, 4 minutes |
| 8 | 128 minutes | 2 hours, 8 minutes |
| 9 | 256 minutes | 4 hours, 16 minutes |

*\* Analog setting; the delay is set using the dial on top of the unit.*

## Using Other Types of Motion Sensors

If you're primarily concerned about detecting motion outside for triggering floodlights, you can purchase motion detectors with integrated floodlights, such as X10's PR511 detector with floodlight (see Figure 9.13). The Leviton X10 Motion Detector 6417 has a similar appearance, but differs in its operation.

**FIGURE 9.13**
A floodlight with integrated X10 motion detector.

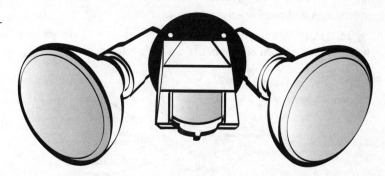

The PR511 supports a pair of 150-watt floodlight bulbs and has a motion detection range of up to 40 feet and an angle of 110°; the range, light sensitivity and time delay can be adjusted with dials. It uses the classic X10 house and unit (start) code dials to configure its starting address. Slider switches are used to configure additional addresses for lights controlled by the sensor and to specify which lights are turned on for dusk-to-dawn settings. The unit can be also be configured to work as a strictly dusk-to-dawn light. The Leviton 6417 has a similar control panel, but it lacks the dusk-to-dawn lighting features of the PR511. See Figure 9.14 for a comparison of the two unit's control panels.

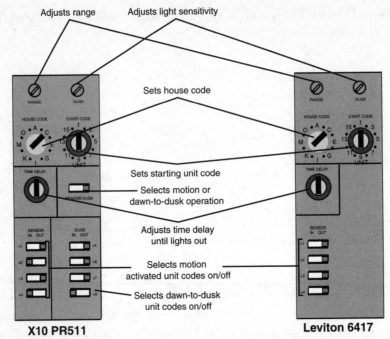

**X10 PR511**

**Leviton 6417**

The Leviton (Decora Home Controls) 6417 is designed especially for multiple installations: each unit polls other Leviton 6417 units on the same house/unit code, and
when one is trigged, all turn on. The Leviton 6417 lacks dawn-to-dusk features,
however. It is designed strictly as a motion detector.

Both units must be connected to AC wiring. Figure 9.15 shows how the motion
detector and floodlight components are connected to your home's AC wiring.

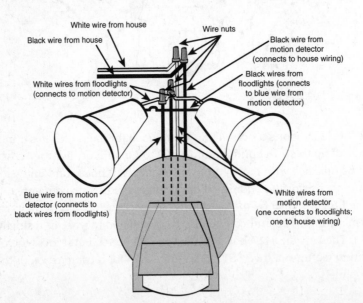

## Configuring the PR511 and Leviton 6417 for Motion Detection

After installation and testing (see the instruction manuals for each unit for details), the X10 PR511 and Leviton 6417 are configured in the same way:

1. Adjust the Dusk control (refer to Figure 9.14) to the halfway point for normal use.

2. Adjust the Range control (refer to Figure 9.14) to MAX unless small animals or other movements that are not threats trigger the floodlights; in such cases, reduce the range setting a bit until you are no longer troubled with false alarms.

3. Adjust the time delay (default 6 seconds) to a more appropriate value. For example, if you want to allow guests enough time to walk from their cars to your home, try 5 minutes. Other values include 30 seconds, 2 minutes, 15 minutes, or the maximum of 30 minutes.

## Configuring the PR511 and Leviton 6417 to Trigger Additional Lights

You can trigger up to four additional lighting or other X10 or X10-compatible modules with either unit in its motion-control mode. To configure this option

1. Select the house code used by the other modules you want to control.

2. Select a start (unit) code for the floodlight. This code will be used to trigger the floodlight from a remote or a separate motion detector. The other modules you want to control must be set to values that are one, two, three, or four unit codes higher than the start code you selected.

3. Adjust the sliders to turn on (In) or ignore (Out) the modules in the numeric range above the start code selected in step 2.

4. When the floodlight is activated by motion, On codes are sent to each house code set to In (step 3). See Figure 9.16.

Remember that the PR511 unit itself must be configured for sensor operation in order for its integrated floodlights to respond to motion (the Leviton 6417 operates only in sensor mode). However, the other devices selected with the sensor switches are triggered by motion, regardless of the selection of Sensor or Dusk (to dawn) mode.

The PR511 can also turn on up to four modules in a dusk-to-dawn arrangement by using sliders similar to those used for motion control. The difference is that the code numbers are +5, +6, +7, and +8 more than the start code. Figure 9.16 illustrates typical configurations for both units.

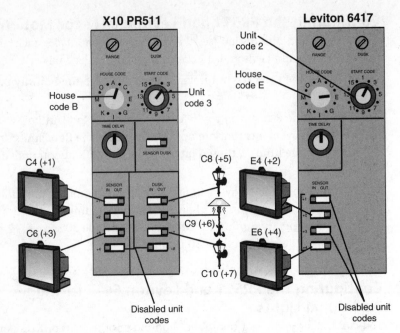

**FIGURE 9.16**

Possible configu-
rations for a
PR511 (left) and
Leviton 6417
(right).

# Installing Comprehensive X10-Compatible Security Systems

X10 and X10-compatible light switches and modules can be incorporated into security systems. Unlike other types of X10-compatible devices discussed in this chapter,
the door and window sensors and motion detectors in these security systems do *not*
transmit or receive X10 codes. Instead, each device uses wireless radio signals that
are assigned to a security zone in a security controller. Typical security controllers
can control up to 16 devices.

The major components of a typical X10 compatible wireless security system include

- **A security console**—This device receives signals from security components
  such as door and window sensors and motion detectors, and also includes an
  integrated siren, automated phone dialer, and a control for an X10 security
  light.

- **A security remote**—A wireless remote control that can arm and disarm the
  security system, trigger the security system, and control up to four X10 or
  X10-compatible modules and an X10 or X10-compatible security light.

- **One or more keychain remotes**—A small wireless remote that can arm
  and disarm the security system, trigger the security system, and control an
  X10 security light.

- **One or more door/window sensors**—A magnetic switch that is triggered when the door or window is opened, sending a wireless signal to the security console.

- **One or more motion detectors**—A PIR motion detector that sends a wireless signal to the security console when triggered.

- **One or more X10 or X10-compatible lamp modules**—One module is used to control the security lamp; others are used for additional lamps controlled by the security remote or any conventional X10 remote. The console takes the place of a wireless transceiver.

- **One or more sirens**—The siren is triggered when a door/window sensor or motion detector sends a signal, by the Panic button on the security remote, or through an X10 signal from a regular remote.

Depending on the security system you purchase, some of these components might be optional and can be added later. Figure 9.17 shows how the different parts of an X10-compatible alarm system work together.

**FIGURE 9.17**

How X10 modules integrate with a wireless security system.

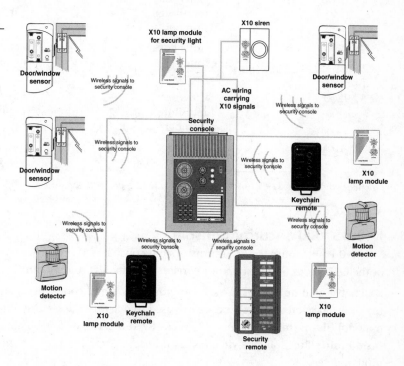

## Security System Consoles

The console of the security system you choose is the most important component in the system because it determines the major features of your security system. As you will see in the following sections, console features vary a great deal from system to system.

Table 9.5 compares the security system consoles discussed in the following sections. Use it as you shop for an X10-compatible security system.

**TABLE 9.5**    Comparing Wireless Security System Consoles

| Vendor | System Model Number | Number of Monitored Zones | Callback Features | X10 Module Support | Types of Remotes Supported |
|---|---|---|---|---|---|
| X10 | DS7000 | 16 | Calls back four numbers | Yes | Security remotes, wireless remotes |
|  | DC8700 | 16 | Calls monitored number* | Yes | Security remotes, wireless remotes |
|  | PA5800 | — | Calls back four numbers | — | Emergency call pendant |
|  | PA9200 | — | Calls monitored number* | — | Emergency call pendant, Big Red button |
| Radio Shack | 49–1000 | 32 | Calls back six numbers | Yes | Security remotes, wireless remotes |

*\* The monitoring service is $19.95/month, provided by ORCA, and sold separately.*

### X10 DS7000 Security Console

The X10 Powerhouse PS561 security system console (see Figure 9.18) is used as part of the DS7000 and other popular wireless security kits sold by many vendors.

X10 house and unit codes are set using the traditional code wheels on the front of the unit. The house and unit code are used to activate the security light and the optional alarm (refer to Figure 9.17). The Record, Arm, and Bypass buttons and the Install/Run1/Run2 slider switch are used to set up wireless remotes, sensors, and motion detectors.

## SMART UNIT CODE SELECTION FOR MORE VERSATILITY

The house/unit code dial on the console enables you to select any X10 or X10-compatible lamp module that is set to the same value as your security light. The security light can also be turned on and off from key-chain and security remotes. A security remote can also control lights and devices on unit codes 1–4. So, to provide the most flexibility, use a unit code other than 1–4 for your security light code.

Because security components are wireless, the console should be placed in a central location in your home that also has touch tone telephone access and AC power. A nine-volt alkaline battery is used to back up security settings. The console has a built-in alarm.

### caution

Although more and more homeowners are dumping traditional telephone systems and replacing them with cellular phones, don't do it if you plan to install a security system and want it to call you in the event of an emergency. The call-out features of these systems depend on standard touch tone telephone (land line) service.

**FIGURE 9.18**

The PS561, a typical security system console that can also control X10 devices.

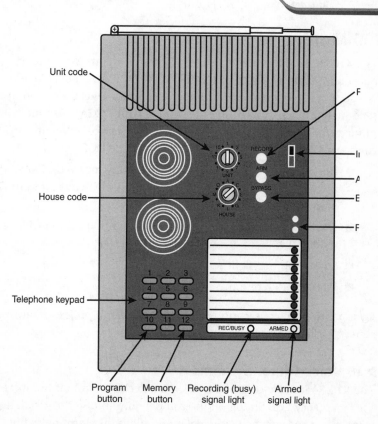

Unit code

House code

Telephone keypad

Program button

Memory button

Recording (busy) signal light

Armed signal light

You can add keychain or tabletop wireless remotes (Figure 9.19 shows a typical keychain remote), door and window sensors, and alarms to your system. Most kits include one or more of each type of component, but you can buy larger kits or add additional components separately. The security console can blink lights connected to X10-compatible light switches or modules when a security breach takes place.

**FIGURE 9.19**

A typical security keychain remote. Use the Arm button to program the device into the security console's memory.

# X10 DC8700 Monitored Security System

The X10 DC8700 Monitored Security System supports the same types of door/window and motion sensors and alarms as the DC7000 model discussed in the previous section. However, it also includes support for ORCA monitoring services (sold separately). When you register the console with ORCA, it downloads the support numbers necessary to contact the monitoring service automatically. You can also configure the following features not found in the DC7000:

- House/unit codes controlled automatically for lived-in look when set to Away mode—this feature makes the console act like a Mini Timer in Security mode.
- Daylight parameters for lived-in look lighting control when set to Away mode.
- Support for daylight saving time.
- Panic dialing on/off.

Consider this type of security system if you prefer a professionally monitored home security system or one with more features.

## X10 Voice Dialer Systems

The X10 PA5800 Voice Dialer is designed to call up to four numbers when you press the Emergency Call button on the call pendant. It also flashes all lights using the same house code as the Voice Dialer and plays an alarm noise until stopped. It is designed to provide help for elderly or bedfast individuals who might not be able to pick up a telephone and make a call in the event of a problem. It also supports X10 wireless remotes to make controlling lights and appliances easier.

Figure 9.20 illustrates the PA-5800 console and call pendant.

**FIGURE 9.20**

The X10 PA-5800 calls up to four numbers and also controls X10 devices.

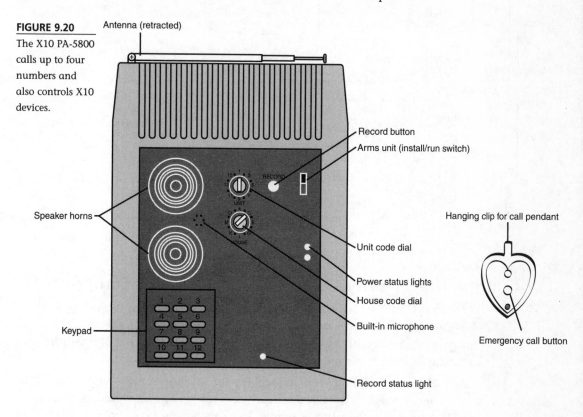

If you would prefer a voice-call system designed to call a monitored number and don't need X10 module support, consider the X10 PA9200 Monitored Personal Assistance System. It includes a single heart-shaped emergency call pendant and three Big Red Emergency button call devices that can be placed in various rooms.

## Radio Shack Plug 'n Power Wireless Home Security System

The Radio Shack Plug 'n Power Wireless Home Security System model 49-1000 supports up to 30 wireless security zones, 2 wired-in sensors, up to 16 keychain remotes, and up to 4 Plug 'n Power or other X10-compatible modules. It features an LCD display to make configuration easy. It can call back up to six numbers in case of emergency.

You can also call into the console and listen to status reports or control X10-compatible modules with touch of tone commands or through the unit's own keypad. Figure 9.21 illustrates major features this security system.

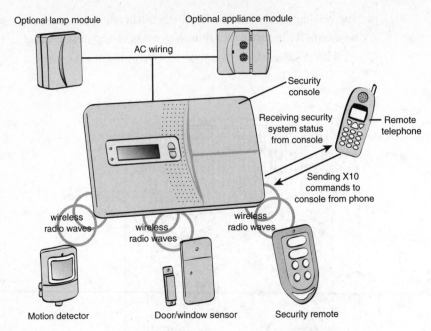

**FIGURE 9.21**

The Radio Shack Plug 'n Power Wireless Home Security System can also control up to four X10-compatible modules via its touchpad or remotely via telephone.

Optional lamp module

Optional appliance module

AC wiring

Security console

Receiving security system status from console

Remote telephone

Sending X10 commands to console from phone

wireless radio waves

wireless radio waves

wireless radio waves

Motion detector

Door/window sensor

Security remote

## Configuring the Security Console to Use Security Components

After you've installed the security console included in your security system, you have to teach the console to recognize each component. The process that follows is based on the process used by the X10 DS7000 security system, but other systems use a similar procedure (see the instructions for each component for details):

1. If the remote or other component has an X10 house code dial, set the dial to the same house code as the security console and the modules you want to control with the security console. This enables you to control lights as well as the security system with a keychain or other remote control. Note that some remotes do not use a house code dial.

2. Move the sliding switch on the security console to Install (refer to Figure 9.18).

3. Depending on the device, press its Arm or Test button (see Figures 9.22 and 9.23 for examples) and make sure that the security console beeps once (indicating that the signal has been picked up). If you are arming a door/window sensor, motion detector, or another device that uses a security zone, the next available light on the list of zones on the front of the console lights up. For example, the first motion detector or door/window sensor you install lights up #1, the next one lights up #2, and so on.

4. Slide the switch on the security console to Run 1 or Run 2 as specified in the directions for the device.

5. Test the device as specified in its instructions.

6. Write down the name and zone number assigned to the device. After all devices have been identified, you can transfer this information to the label on the front of the security console.

Some devices have a Code button (a small recessed button you'll need to push with a ballpoint pen or bent paperclip) to randomly assign a different code to the device if it is not recognized in step 3 or if the instructions for the device call for its use. If you need to use the Code button, repeat steps 3–5.

## Installing and Configuring Door and Window Sensors

Door and window sensors are used by most security systems to detect unauthorized entry. Door and window sensors are two-piece magnetic units, similar to the model shown in Figure 9.22.

**FIGURE 9.22**

A typical door or window sensor after installation but before battery installation.

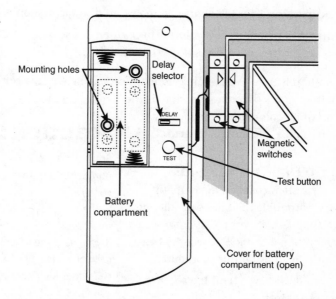

Mounting holes

Delay selector

DELAY

TEST

Magnetic switches

Test button

Battery compartment

Cover for battery compartment (open)

The sensor is wired to one part of the magnetic switch, and the other part of the switch is attached to the door or the window with screws or double-sided tape. Window switches can be mounted along the side (Figure 9.22 illustrates this position) or the bottom of a window frame. Some sensors use a nine-volt alkaline battery, whereas others, such as the sensor shown in Figure 9.22, use a pair of AA batteries.

The sensor is configured with a sliding delay switch (use MIN for windows and MAX for doors) on the front of the unit. The switches supplied with the sensor are the normally closed *(N.C.)* variety, which trigger an alarm when the door or window is opened or if a burglar cuts the wire between the sensor and the switch. Some sensors also support the normally open *(N.O.)* option. These sensors typically have a selector switch in the battery compartment for choosing the N.C. or N.O. mode.

To configure the security console to recognize each sensor, consult the detailed instructions with the sensor. The general procedure is given in the "Configuring the Security Console to Use Security Components" section earlier in this chapter.

## Installing and Configuring Motion Detectors

A security system's motion detectors report to the security console, rather than triggering lights or other X10 or X10-compatible devices as with X10-based motion detectors. The motion detectors use the same type of passive infrared detection used by X10-based motion detectors, so they should be installed at a height of five to six feet above floor level.

The motion detectors included in these security kits can be set to two levels of sensitivity:

- Select position 1 for instant triggering when a single motion is detected.

- If there are too many false alarms in position 1, use position 2, which triggers only if two movements have been detected.

The Code button is used to generate a random code, whereas the Test button fulfills the same function as the Arm button when configuring the security console to recognize the motion detector.

## Setting Up Dial-Out Features

Most security system consoles that support X10 or X10-compatible modules can call one or more telephone numbers in case of a security breach at home. The PS561 security console is programmed using this procedure:

1. Set the sliding switch on the security console to Install.

2. Press the Prog (program) button.

3. Use the keypad to enter the telephone number you want it to call first. Enter the number the same way you would if you were making the call yourself.

4. Press MEM, and then press 1 to record this as the first number.

**caution**

Enter the telephone number into the security console's dialer memory in the same way you'd make a call. For example, if you want the security system to call your office first and it's a local call, enter just the seven digits (for example, 555-1212). However, if you want the system to call a number that requires an area code (such as some cell phones), enter the area code plus number (for example, 999-555-1212). For a long-distance call, enter the prefix, area code, and phone number (for example, 1-999-555-1212).

5. Follow steps 2–3 to enter a second number (or the first number again if you want to use only a single call-out number).

6. Press MEM, and then press 2 to record this as the second number.

7. Follow steps 2–3 to enter a third number (or the first number again if you want to use only a single call-out number).

8. Press MEM, and then press 3 to record this as the third number.

9. Follow steps 2–3 to enter a fourth number (or the first number again if you want to use only a single call-out number).

10. Press MEM, and then press 4 to record this as the fourth (last) number.

Similar procedures are used to program numbers into the memory of personal dialers.

---

**WHO YOU GONNA CALL? NOT 911!**

Do *not* call 911 or another police or sheriff's department number with your security console. This is against the law in most locations (and for a very good reason: Your console can't answer any questions about what's happening at your house). Instead, program your security console to call yourself at work, call a neighbor, or call relatives and friends. Your best choice for call #1 is a neighbor you trust who can go to your home and make sure that there's a real problem, not just the kids sneaking in after school without their keys or security remotes. Make sure that you talk to everyone you want to call and make sure that it's okay to sign them up as members of your unofficial security force.

---

Don't forget to record a message when you set up your security console. To record a message with this security console, do the following:

1. Select Install.

2. Press Record and make sure that the Busy light turns on.

3. Speak into the front of the console (it contains a built-in microphone) with a message of no more than 15 seconds. Vendors recommend a message such as "There is a burglary in process at [*address*]. Press 0 to listen in."

4. The Busy light shuts off after 15 seconds.

5. To hear your message, plug an earphone into the Earphone jack and set the console to Run.

6. To repeat the message, move the slider switch to Install, and then to Run.

## How the Security Sensor Reports Problems

The popular PS561 security console shown in Figure 9.18 has a signal light for each of the first eight security zones. It uses various light patterns to identify security breaches or other problems with the security zones it monitors (each zone corresponds with a motion or door/window sensor) as listed in Table 9.6.

**TABLE 9.6**   PS561 Security Console Zone Signal Lights

| Signal Light | Meaning | Action to Take |
|---|---|---|
| Steady on | Door or window is open | Varies |
| Steady off | Door or window is closed | None |
| Slow flashing | Battery in sensor is low | Replace battery |
| Fast flashing | Device has been bypassed after reporting a problem or door/window is open | Check device; check door or window |

The console has two other lights. When the Battery light is on, the backup battery in the console is low and should be replaced. When the Armed light is on, the console is armed and ready to be activated.

The Radio Shack 49-1000 model uses its LCD text display to display status messages. These include

- **HOME CONTROL**—The console can be used as a tabletop controller.
- **ARMED HOME**—The console is armed and set for Home mode (motion detectors will be ignored).
- **ARMED AWAY**—The console is armed and set for Away mode (motion detectors will not be ignored).
- **PROBLEM X**—The sensor or motion detector in zone X has not reported in the last four hours.
- **TAMPER X**—The cover of the door/window sensor in zone X is open.

If you call in via telephone for status messages, the Radio Shack 49-1000 model speaks the current system status:

- **"Armed home"**
- **"Armed away"**
- **"Disarmed"**
- **"Panic alarm"**
- **"Alarm in zone X"** (X is replaced with the actual zone number.)

## Testing the Security System

After you've armed the system, you should test it. To test the system, set the slider switch on the security console to Run 1 or Run 2 and open a monitored door or window. A loud (95dB) alarm built into the console turns on, X10 or X10-compatible lamps or light switches modules on the same house code as the console blink on and off, and the auto-dialer calls each number in sequence. If your alarm system has an external X10 or X10-compatible alarm, it will also sound.

---

**THIS IS A TEST—DO YOUR CALLBACK PARTNERS KNOW?**

To avoid panicking the people you've asked to be your callback partners, call them before you test your system and alert them that the call they're about to receive from your unit is a test. Ask them to call you back after they've received the message. When they call you back, remind them that the next time your system calls, they should check out your home.

---

## Arming and Disarming Your Security System

You can arm or disarm your security system in a variety of ways, depending on the system and the remote controls you use. For systems based on the PS561 security console, you have the following options:

■ **Instant mode**—This is the arming mode used by the keychain remote (refer to Figure 9.19) at all times and by the handheld remote (see Figure 9.23) if set to Min. The system is triggered by any opening of a monitored door or window. The keychain remote can also disarm the system, turn on and turn off lights controlled by the house code used by the security console, and trigger a panic alarm when the Arm/Disarm buttons are pressed at the same time.

■ **Delay mode**—This is the arming mode used by the handheld remote (see Figure 9.23) when set to Max. Pressing the Arm button on the security console always uses this setting. In this mode, you press Arm as you leave the house and the system arms itself after one minute. When you enter through a monitored door, you have 30 seconds to disarm the system before it calls out or sounds the alarm.

■ **Arm Away**—This arming mode can also be set by the handheld remote. When this mode is selected, both door/window sensors and motion sensors are armed. Use this mode when you're away from home.

■ **Arm Home**—Select this mode with the handheld remote to ignore motion sensors, but leave door and window sensors armed. This is a perfect setting to use at night while you're home.

## Controlling X10 Devices Through Your Security Console

As you learned in earlier sections, the house and unit code selection on the security console is used to select the X10 lamp module used for the security light. Make sure that you have an X10 lamp module set to this house/unit code combination.

When the alarm is tripped, the security light will flash on and off and the siren in the security console and any additional sirens will sound until the system has been disarmed.

**FIGURE 9.23**

A handheld security remote.

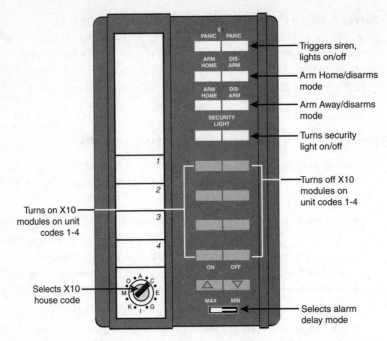

PANIC    PANIC — Triggers siren, lights on/off

ARM HOME    DIS-ARM — Arm Home/disarms mode

ARM HOME    DIS-ARM — Arm Away/disarms mode

SECURITY LIGHT — Turns security light on/off

Turns off X10 modules on unit codes 1-4

Turns on X10 modules on unit codes 1-4

ON    OFF

Selects X10 house code

MAX    MIN — Selects alarm delay mode

If you have a security remote similar to the one in Figure 9.23, you can also control X10 or X10-compatible lights or other modules on unit codes 1–4. The security console acts as a wireless receiver for X10 signals as well as security signals from the security remotes.

Therefore, if your wireless security console is set to house code D and unit code 6, the X10 or X10-compatible module controlling the lamp or light fixture you use for the security light should also be set to house code D and unit code 6. A handheld security remote can also control modules set to house code D and unit codes 1–4. Other unit codes using the same house code as the security system are ignored by the security system. They can be controlled by standard X10 or X10-compatible controllers.

Use Table 9.7 to help you plan the interaction of your wireless security system with X10 or X10-compatible devices. Table 9.8 is a sample worksheet after it has been completed.

**Table 9.7**   X10-Based Security System Planner

| Selected House Code for Security Light | Selected Unit Code for Security Light | Location of Security Light* | Device on Unit Code 1^ | Device on Unit Code 2^ | Device on Unit Code 3^ | Device on Unit Code 4^ |
|---|---|---|---|---|---|---|
| — | — | — | — | — | — | — |

*\* Be sure to set module or switch to the house code and unit code configured on the security console so that the security light will be activated.*

*^ This applies only if you have a handheld security remote. Make sure that each module or switch is using the same house code as the security light and the security console. Check the unit code as well.*

**Table 9.8**   Sample Completed X10 /Security System Planner

| Selected House Code for Security Light | Selected Unit Code for Security Light | Location of Security Light | Device on Unit Code 1 | Device on Unit Code 2 | Device on Unit Code 3 | Device on Unit Code 4 |
|---|---|---|---|---|---|---|
| D | 8 | Den | Kitchen light | Bedroom light | Hallway light | Porch light |

In the example shown in Table 9.8, the den light will be used as the security light. I recommend that the security light be located in the area of the home with the most valuable items. If your den has high-ticket home entertainment and electronic items or doubles as your home office, it's a logical place to protect with the security light. It's essential to ensure that the house and unit codes you choose for the security light are the same as the codes you program into your security console!

If you have a handheld security remote (refer to Figure 9.23), you can also control X10 or X10-compatible modules on unit codes 1–4. I suggest that you choose other lights in critical areas such as those found in Table 9.8. Keep in mind that although the security light can use any unit code, the security remote can only control devices on unit codes 1–4.

# Troubleshooting X10 Security Systems

Follow these basic principles to solve problems with the elements of your security system:

- **Check settings**—Although this chapter covers the configuration processes used by the most popular X10-compatible security hardware, many variations are possible. Be particularly careful when working with devices that don't use code dials but require you to push, release, and hold down buttons in varying combinations to set or view the configuration.

- **Check battery power**—Most components covered in this chapter rely on alkaline batteries. Although most security consoles monitor battery life for monitored devices, other types of home security devices, such as standalone X10-compatible motion detectors, do not. Use fresh high-quality batteries when you install the devices, and never substitute cheaper super heavy-duty batteries.

- **Double-check device and module house/unit code combinations**— As with most X10 devices, the security devices in this chapter can work with only a single X10 house code. If some lights or other devices are not triggered when you expect them to be, you might have the house code set incorrectly on the modules, light switches, security console, or motion detector.

- **Keep motion detectors out of direct sunlight**—Whether battery-powered or AC-powered, these devices use infrared detection. Direct sunlight prevents them from working properly.

- **Adjust motion detectors if movement is not detected or spurious alarms are triggered**—If the motion detector doesn't have range or sensitivity settings, adjust its location. For units with those adjustments, make small changes and test each change to determine whether it's satisfactory.

- **Check phone numbers for accuracy**—Call the numbers you want to program into your security console's call-out memory to make sure that they work. If you want to call a person (yourself or anyone else) in a large corporation where touch-tones or a live operator are used to route calls, make sure that you use the direct number.

For additional troubleshooting tips, see Appendix B, "Troubleshooting X10."

# THE ABSOLUTE MINIMUM

- Kits containing one or more video cameras can provide real-time security coverage of interior rooms, doorways, and yards.

- Wireless cameras typically use the same 2.4GHz frequency band as Wi-Fi home networks, but you can select from several channels to avoid interference.

- By using a special remote control, you can switch between video cameras that have addressable (house/unit code) power supplies, and you can also tilt and swivel cameras using an optional powered base.

- You can use motion sensors to turn on a VCR for security video recording as needed.

- Motion detectors can be used to turn on VCRs, turn on and turn off lights, and control other devices as needed for security or energy-saving considerations.

- Most motion detectors used by X10 are battery-powered.

- You can purchase floodlights with integrated X10 motion detectors, and floodlights with integrated wireless video cameras.

- Wireless security systems can be used to flash a selected X10 light on and off during a break-in.

- Wireless security systems typically include door/window sensors, motion detectors, keychain and handheld remotes, and a security console that controls the system.

- The security remote is used to arm and disarm the console. The console must be taught to recognize each device. The console also acts as a wireless receiver for security devices and remotes, and transfers commands to the X10 or X10-compatible modules it controls.

- The security console can also dial out with a recorded message to family, friends, and neighbors when the system is tripped.

- Typical consoles can support at least four different telephone numbers and a recorded message.

- Some security systems can be used with professional monitoring services.

- Instead of a full security system, you can get a callout or monitored system for use by elderly or bedfast patients who don't need X10 module control or motion or door/window sensors.

- The handheld security remote doubles as a control for up to four X10 modules as well as the security system.

- The keychain remote controls only the security system.

- Batteries are used to power most parts of a wireless security system, so the use of fresh alkaline batteries and periodic checks of battery power are highly recommended.

# PART IV

# REMOTE ACCESS TO YOUR X10 HOME CONTROL SYSTEM

10

# ACCESSING X10 HOME CONTROL VIA TELEPHONE

If you want to use X10 to operate your home remotely, you can use your touch-tone telephone keypad or your voice as your remote control. You can also receive calls from your home warning you of problems caused by power failure, fire, flood, low temperatures, and similar problems. To learn how your telephone can act as a gateway to home control and to home protection, read on.

# X10 and Home Telephone Systems

As you learned in Chapter 9, "Using X10 to Provide Security," X10-based systems can be used to alert you to break-ins at your home. As this chapter shows, X10 can also be used as part of telephone-based remote control of your home.

X10 signaling can be used to control modules through house and unit codes via touch-tone telephones or to control modules as well as groups of modules and pre-defined macros and procedures through touch-tone and voice commands. However, X10 is not suitable for warning you of power failure or similar nonsecurity problems at home because it relies on AC power lines to carry information. Therefore, this chapter also deals with a popular self-contained family of devices for home monitoring, the Sensaphone 1100 series, which can be used along with X10-compatible telephone-based home control systems.

# Installing and Using a Touch Tone Controller

If you want to pick up the phone at your office, your vacation home, or anywhere else to control your home with X10, you need to install an interface between your X10 home automation system and your telephone line. The interface translates touch-tone codes from your remote telephone into X10 codes and transmits those codes over your home's AC wiring to X10 and X10-compatible modules. A touch-tone interface doubles as a tabletop controller, enabling you to use a single device for local and remote control of your X10 home automation system.

The most common X10 telephone controller is the X10 TR16A Touch Tone Controller (see Figure 10.1). The Touch Tone Controller plugs into any AC outlet and into a normal RJ-11 telephone line; use the two-wire splitter (included) if you want a regular telephone or answering machine to share the same wall jack.

## Configuring the TR16A Touch Tone Controller

Flip open the front panel of the TR16A to access the configuration panel (see Figure 10.1).

The three dials across the top right are used to set the security code. By default, each security code wheel is set to Off. However, you should use the code dials to set a unique security code from 0–999. The security code will be used as a PIN number when you call into the Touch Tone Controller.

There's a blank chart on the inside of the lid (not shown), which you can use to identify the modules that the Touch Tone Controller will control.

**FIGURE 10.1**

The configuration panel for the TR16A Touch Tone Controller.

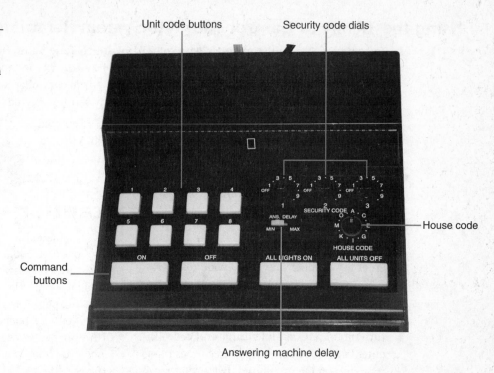

Unit code buttons

Security code dials

Command buttons

House code

Answering machine delay

### RINGING, DINGING, FLASHING

If you have trouble hearing the phone ring, you can use a lamp or other module set to a unit code corresponding to the last (right-side) digit you use for the security code. For example, if you set the right-side dial to 7, set a lamp module to 7 on the same house code controlled by the Touch Tone Controller. When the phone rings, the lamp connected to the phone will blink (see Figure 10.2). If you prefer, you could also use an alarm, a fan, or another device that can be turned on and off to inform you of an incoming call.

Turn the House Code dial to the house code used by the modules you want to control remotely (A–P).

Select MAX on the Answer Delay slider (labeled *Answering Machine* on some versions) if you use an answering machine and want to use the Touch Tone Controller. In this mode, you can enter touch-tone codes with your phone even after your answering machine picks up. MIN (labeled *Normal* on some versions) should be used if you don't have an answering machine.

**caution**

The TR16A can control modules with unit codes from 1–10 via touch-tone telephone. However, it can only be used as a tabletop controller with unit codes 1–8.

## Using the TR16A to Control Your X10 System Remotely

To control X10 modules remotely with the TR16A Touch Tone Controller, call your home from any touch-tone telephone. If you don't have an answering machine running on the same line, you will hear three beeps after the controller answers (which takes 15–35 seconds, depending on the Answer Delay setting selected on the TR16A).

Enter the security code you set on the unit. After you've entered your security code, you will hear three beeps, indicating the TR16A is ready to accept commands. If you use an answering machine, wait until it answers, and then enter your security code (the TR16A will not prompt you). Listen for the three-beep response from the TR16A.

To control modules with unit codes from 1–9, enter the number on your keypad; use 0 for the module using unit code 10, followed by * for On or # for Off. For example, to turn on an X10 module using unit code 3, enter 3*. To turn off an X10 module using unit code 10, enter 0#. The TR16A beeps three times after receiving an On command, twice after receiving an Off command, and once if you press an invalid key.

**caution**

Don't use the Touch Tone Controller if you use an answering service provided by your telephone company. The service answers your phone before the TR16A can pick up the line, preventing you from controlling your X10 system.

To control two or more modules with a single command, enter the unit code for each module, and then press * (On) or # (Off). For example, to turn off unit codes 3, 7, and 10, enter 370#. To turn on unit codes 1, 2, and 8, enter 128*. The Touch Tone Controller hangs up the line after 30 seconds of inactivity.

Figure 10.2 illustrates a typical session with the Touch Tone Controller.

## Using the Touch Tone Controller as a Tabletop X10 Controller

The Touch Tone Controller features the following keys for local control of X10 modules (refer to Figure 10.1):

- Number keys from 1–8, corresponding to unit codes 1–8
- On, Off, All Lights On, All Units Off command keys

To control one or more modules, press the number key(s) corresponding to the unit code(s) you want to control, and then press the On or Off key. For example, if you press 2, 4, 5, On, modules on those unit codes are turned on. If you press 1, 2, 8, Off, modules on those unit codes are turned off.

**FIGURE 10.2**

Calling in to control home automation devices via the Touch Tone Controller.

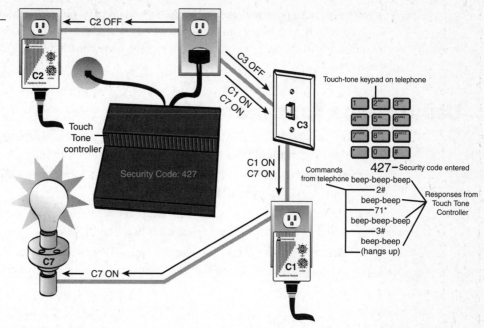

To turn on all X10 lamp modules and light switches using the same house code as the TR16A, press All Lights On. To turn off all X10 modules (including appliance modules) and switches using the same house code as the TR16A, press All Units Off.

## Limitations of the Touch Tone Controller

Although the Touch Tone Controller provides basic tabletop and remote telephone control of your X10 home automation system, it has some limitations:

> **caution**
>
> Note that the Touch Tone Controller doesn't support Bright or Dim commands; you will still have to use a tabletop or wireless remote and transceiver to control these lighting options.

- Although the Touch Tone Controller provides feedback in touch-tone mode when it receives a command, you cannot monitor two-way modules to determine whether they received the command.

- The Touch Tone Controller does not support extended X10 codes such as Preset Dim, used by some types of dimmable lamp modules as well as thermostats and other specialized devices. You can use On and Off commands only.

- You cannot control modules with unit codes beyond 10 in Touch-Tone mode or modules with unit codes beyond 8 in Tabletop Controller mode.

If you need more powerful remote access to your X10 home automation system, voice-activated control, or the ability to receive telephone warnings of climate-control failures at your home remotely, consider the other options discussed in this chapter.

# Using Home Automated Living

Home Automated Living (HAL) offers three different products featuring telephone voice-enabled control of your home via your personal computer:

- **HALbasic**—Supports up to eight X10 devices, eight macros, eight scenes, four scheduled events, and one if/then rule
- **HALdeluxe**—Supports up to 256 X10 devices with larger numbers of scenes, scheduled events, if/then rules; adds timer control
- **HAL2000**—All HALdeluxe features, plus HVAC systems, home theater systems, custom interfaces, onscreen displays, security, and weather station integration

All three versions support voice control via remote telephone, extension phones in your home, and microphones connected to your PC. For other differences, see the Home Automated Living website.

---

**COMPARING HAL VERSIONS**

For a more detailed comparison of HAL versions, visit the Home Automated Living: Features List page at www.automatedliving.com/products_features.html.

For a detailed listing of the X10, X10-compatible and other home automation devices supported by each version of HAL, visit the Home Automated Living: Compatible Interfaces List at www.automatedliving.com/products_interfaces.html.

---

HAL controls your X10 home automation system via your home computer, but it also includes voice or touch-tone telephone control. The following sections discuss how to configure HAL to enable you to control your home via your telephone line and PC and how to use HAL with X10 modules. HAL has many more features for both telephone and computer control than we have space to discuss here; be sure to see the Home Automated Living website at www.automatedliving.com/ for more information.

Note that HAL *must* be used with an always-on desktop PC. Although HAL is much more powerful than the Touch Tone Controller, it is not a standalone system.

HALbasic offers very limited home automation. For most users of X10 and X10-compatible home automation modules, the mid-range HALdeluxe is the version of HAL that will be most useful. Consider HAL2000 if you have an X10-compatible or other controllable thermostat such as the RCS TX-15B, infrared home automation devices, or home controller/sensor products from vendors such as JDS Stargate, Smart Homes, HAI Omni, and others.

## HAL's PCI Voice Portal Modem

HAL's capability to accept voice commands depends upon the installation of a compatible voice modem in your desktop PC. Although standard voice/data/fax modems might work with some of HAL's features, the safest way to configure your PC is with a modem specifically designed for use with HAL, or a modem tested to fully support all of HAL's functions.

Only two PCI-compatible modems are currently supported for use with HAL:

- Home Automated Living's own HAL Internal PCI Voice Portal (available from Home Automated Living's web store or bundled with some HAL kits)

- The now-discontinued Creative Labs Digicom DI5630-3H PCI modem (one of several similar models sold as "Creative Modem Blaster Flash 56 PCI")

Depending on how you buy HAL, you might receive a PCI Voice Portal with your software or have to buy it separately.

Although it is possible to disable HAL's use of the modem to enable you to connect to the Internet through a dial-up ISP and re-enable HAL control afterward, or to use two analog modems (HAL's and a regular modem) in your system, HAL works best if you use a broadband Internet connection (such as DSL or cable) and use its modem strictly for HAL-based control of your home automation system.

To install the modem, you must remove the cover of your desktop PC, locate an empty PCI expansion slot, and insert the card.

**caution**

If you're a novice at performing PC upgrades, take these precautions:

- Connect an antistatic wrist strap to a metal part of the chassis and make sure that the metal plate on the wrist strap is touching your wrist before you remove the modem from its package. This minimizes the chances of damaging electrostatic energy (static electricity) being discharged into your modem or other computer component.

- If you don't have a wrist strap, touch a metal part of the case before you open the case and again as soon as you open the case.

- Use a manual screwdriver instead of an electric one. An electric screwdriver can strip out screw holes.

For more about performing PC upgrades, read my book *TechTV's Upgrading Your PC, Second Edition* (New Riders, 2004).

---

**NOVICE UPGRADER? HERE'S HELP!**

If you've never installed an add-on card in your desktop PC before, check out the Modem Installation Guide at the Home Automated Living website: pwww.homeautomatedliving.com/docs/helpfiles/ModemInstallationGuide.doc.

This file is stored in Microsoft Word 2000 format, which means that it's readable by Word 2000 and later versions. If you can't open the file after you've download it, get the free Microsoft Word Viewer 2003 from the Microsoft Office website: http://office.microsoft.com. Check the Downloads section of the website.

---

You can configure HAL to work as a speakerphone by connecting a microphone to the MIC jack and a mono speaker to the SPKR jack on the rear of the PCI Voice Portal card. After the PCI Voice Portal card has been installed, connect a supported X10 or X10-compatible computer interface to your computer and install HAL from the software CD.

## Using HAL Setup to Configure Your System

During installation, the HAL Setup Wizard runs, enabling you to configure remote voice control, voice recognition, and X10 control as well as other features.

If you decide to configure HAL to use your existing X10 or X10-compatible modules during HAL setup, you must know the following:

- The location of each module (note that HAL refers to modules as *devices*)
- A descriptive name for each module
- The address (house/unit code) of each module
- The type of module
- The actions the module can perform (dimmable, On/Off, and so forth)

If you skipped any options or need to change settings later, you can use the HAL System Settings menu to enable or adjust settings as described in the following sections.

## Adjusting HAL's Telephone Settings

To adjust HAL's settings for accepting commands from a remote phone call, open the HAL System Settings menu and click Telephone. Make sure that the Telephone Enabled box is check-marked, that your voice modem (the HAL Voice Portal PCI or compatible) is listed in the Modem Communication Settings dialog, and that you note which key is listed for the Telephone Interaction Attention Tone (the key you press to notify HAL that you want to give commands). By default, the pound (#) key is used. Use the Telephone Volume Adjustment dialog to adjust the volume for the Output Remote Handset (for remote calls) or for the Input Local Handset (for house phones).

## Adjusting HAL's Voice Recognition Settings

Unlike X10's Touch Tone Controller, which responds only to touch tones, all versions of HAL also use verbal commands from a remote phone. Open the Voice Recognition dialog from the HAL System Settings menu to adjust settings.

Select the Remote Telephone Handset from the Parameter Set menu (you can also select microphone, attention word, and local telephone handset) to start. You can adjust remote telephone timeout (in seconds), voice recognition, confidence adjustment level, and sound sensitivity.

To configure individual voice recognition features such as Acceptance Threshold, Garbage Penalty, and others, click Advanced.

## Configuring HAL's X10 Module Support

To enable or adjust HAL's X10 module support after HAL is installed, click HAL Automation Setup, Devices. Existing *devices* (HAL's term for X10 and X10-compatible modules) are listed by location. Information includes module type, dim support, X10 address, verbal confirm (HAL asks for confirmation when you give a command), and action confirm (HAL uses text-to-speech to confirm the command has been acted upon).

If you prefer to control X10 modules by address only, you do *not* need to create modules in this section. However, if you prefer not to memorize which module is located in a particular area or performs a particular function, setting up your modules is highly recommended.

Click Report to print a list of devices (modules). To add a device, click Add to start the Device Wizard.

On the Location screen, provide the following:

- The location of each module.
- The device (lamp module, appliance module, and so on).
- Module type (only HAL2000 supports non-X10 modules).
- A descriptive name (created from the location and device type; it can be changed if desired).

Click Next to continue to the Address screen:

- Select the house code and unit code using the onscreen dials.

Click Next to continue to the Device Actions screen:

- Select Dimmable for incandescent lights that are controlled by lamp modules or dimmable switches; click Options to open a dialog for selecting basic and advanced dimming options and two-way support.

- Select Open/Unlock for controlling powered doors and locks; click Options to specify whether to use Always On (use with modules in momentary state) or not (use with modules in continuous state).
- The actions that the module can perform (dimmable, On/Off, and so forth).

Click Next to continue to the Confirm dialog:

- Check Confirm Verbal Commands if you want HAL to ask you to confirm the command before executing it.
- Check Confirm the Action if you want HAL to inform you that the action has been completed.

Click Next to continue to Assigning Groups. This dialog enables you to place the module in a group that can be controlled with a single command. A module can be associated with more than one group. For example, you could create an After Dark group and place lamp modules or switches that control the front and back porch lights and the hallway and entrance lights. The modules controlling hallway and entrance lights could also be part of an Indoor Light group, and the modules controlling front and back porch lights could also be part of a Security Lights group.

## Creating Macros, Scenes, and Modes

Open the HAL Automation screen to create tasks (macros), modes, and schedules.

Click Tasks to create a macro (a series of commands). One advantage of creating macros, even for simple tasks, instead of just giving the commands orally one after the other, is that you have the option of assigning them a three-digit code you can enter on a remote or home telephone connected to HAL. You can also assign a custom recognition phrase that you can speak to HAL to start the macro or use the name of the macro to activate it.

If you want to set your home automation devices to one set of options when you're at home, another when you're away for the day at work, and yet another when you're away on a trip, use modes instead of macros. A mode stores a series of actions, like a macro, but it's designed for putting your home into a particular state you want to use on a continuing basis. The mode name can be used to activate the mode remotely (see the next section for details), or you can use a three-digit code or a custom recognition phrase.

HALdeluxe and HAL2000 also support multiple if/then situations (rules); HALbasic supports only one. A trigger event such as Rear Entry Motion, rather than a remote command, is used to evaluate a rule. Such a rule might contain the following events:

IF rear entry motion sensor ON

AND time after sunset

THEN turn on back porch lights

IF statements are marked as TE (trigger events); AND statements are marked as SC (secondary conditions).

Rules can be restricted to operate during certain house modes only, dates, days of week, and device status. Although you cannot directly run a rule remotely, you can switch the house mode remotely. This enables you to safeguard your home if, for example, an evening out turns into an overnight or longer stay away from home. In such a case, you could call your home and have HAL switch the mode from the mode you normally use in the evening to a mode you use for vacations. Rules used only during the mode you use for vacations would then be activated.

## Using HAL to Control X10 Modules Remotely

Call in to your home, and HAL answers the phone and plays a greeting. Press the attention key (# is the default) during the greeting to put HAL into listening mode. The voice commands listed in this section also work if you're sitting at your computer using a microphone to talk to HAL.

You can use HAL to control X10 modules in several ways:

- By device (module) name
- By group name
- By macro name
- By recognition phrase
- By scene name
- By mode name
- By address (house/unit code)

The "Talking to HAL" chapter of the HAL manual provides numerous examples of command syntax. Here are a few examples based on this syntax.

To turn on a device (module) using the descriptive name (italics) created during X10 module definition:

>"Turn on the *hallway light*."

To turn off a device using its descriptive name:

>"Turn off the *front porch light*."

To turn on (or off) a group of devices:

>"Turn off the *porch lights*."

Other options (**boldface**) you can use in a command include

- Duration—"Turn on the *living room light* for **one hour**."
- Dimming—"**Dim** the *dining room light* to **50 percent**."

- Open/close/lock/unlock—"**Close** *living room draperies.*"
- Status—"What is the **status** of the *hallway light?*"
- Current mode—"What is the **house mode**?"
- Schedule—"In 10 **hours** turn off the *porch light.*"

You can also schedule module events orally (but not group events or dimming) to take place on the current day, the following day, every day, every other day, one or more days of the week at a particular time, on a particular date, on a particular day of the week, on weekdays only, or weekends only. Sunrise and sunset instead of fixed times can be used with some schedule commands.

If you have not defined a name for a new X10 device, you can also use the command "Open Console" and specify a particular X10 address:

- "Turn *B5* **On**."
- "Turn *C3* **Off**."

# Using HomeSeer Phone

HomeSeer home automation (see Chapter 11, "Accessing X10 Home Control via Your Home Computer," for details) is a powerful PC-based home automation system that supports X10 modules and other types of home automation hardware.

By adding HomeSeer Phone software and a compatible modem (if one is not present), you can control HomeSeer via a remote touch-tone phone or a phone within your home.

HomeSeer Phone supports the following voice modems:

- HomeSeer PCI modem
- Way2Call Hi-Phone Desktop modem (USB); includes HomeSeer Phone
- Any voice modem that uses the Rockwell/Conexant chipset (does not support using phones in your home to control HomeSeer Phone)

HomeSeer Phone uses AT commands (the standard command language used by modems) to control your modem.

HomeSeer Phone 2.0 includes a scripting language that enables the user to create new voice recognition commands, accept keypad input, and run VBScript.

The following sections discuss how to use HomeSeer Phone; for more details about HomeSeer, see Chapter 11.

## Using HomeSeer Phone to Control X10 Modules

HomeSeer Phone can control X10 modules by DMTF (touch-tone) commands, X10 addresses (house/unit code on/off), voice commands, and triggers to events.

When a HomeSeer event is created, a DMTF code (two, three, or four digits) can be assigned to it. When a user calls into a home controlled with HomeSeer and logs in, entering the keypad digits followed by # starts the event.

---

**ADDING DMTF CODES TO AN EXISTING EVENT**

If you install HomeSeer Phone after working with HomeSeer, edit the properties for any event you want to control via touch-tone. Enter the numeric code you want to use to trigger the event into the DTMF field.

---

HomeSeer events can also be created that use Phone as the trigger, including

- First ring
- Each ring
- Caller ID information
- Outside call is answered
- Message left or read
- Call ended

You can also adjust the number of rings before HomeSeer Phone picks up the call and change the default greeting.

To prompt HomeSeer to control an X10 module by its house and unit code, enter 3# after logging in. HomeSeer Phone asks for house and unit code and command (On or Off); provide the information requested.

To enable an event to be started with a voice command, edit the Event Properties sheet, click Trigger, and enter the word(s) you want to use to start the event. Select Enable from the Enable pull-down menu. If you want HomeSeer to confirm the command before starting it, check the Confirm box. For more details about creating an event, see the "Creating an Event with HomeSeer" section in Chapter 11.

# Keeping Your Home Safe with Sensaphone

If your main interest in telephone-based home automation is protecting your home from water leaks, freezing, and power failure, consider a self-contained home monitoring solution such as the Sensaphone 1100 series of monitoring devices. They are self-contained, so if your home loses AC power, you can still receive warnings via telephone. The Sensaphone Cottage Sitter series is based on the 1100 series and also provides remote control of temperature and X10 modules.

A self-contained home monitoring system is a better solution, especially for protecting a second home, vacation home, or vacation cabin. The Sensaphone 1100 series of monitoring devices is a popular monitoring solution.

# How Sensaphone Works

Sensaphone connects to your telephone line. It can share the line with answering machines and devices such as the X10 Touch Tone Controller; plug the devices into an RJ-11 line splitter if necessary. Sensaphone includes a built-in microphone, a built-in temperature monitor, and a built-in AC power sensor, and can be connected to up to four optional sensors (see Figure 10.3). Optional sensors include humidistat (measures humidity), water detector, magnetic reed switch (detects open doors and windows), infrared motion detector, smoke detector, and remote temperature sensor. Sensaphone plugs into an AC wall outlet, and uses six D-cell alkaline batteries to provide backup battery power.

**FIGURE 10.3**

Sensaphone 1104 connected to typical external sensors.

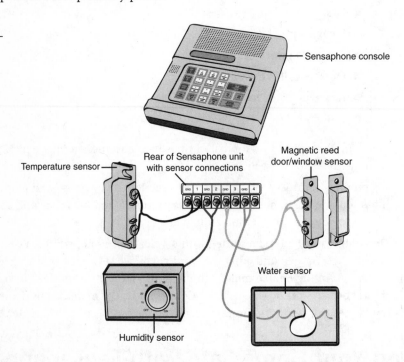

If a built-in monitor or external sensor detects a condition beyond normal boundaries, Sensaphone takes the following steps:

1. Sensaphone waits a user-defined length of time, called the *recognition time*, to establish whether the condition goes away.

2. If the condition continues beyond the recognition time set for the monitor or sensor, Sensaphone triggers an audible alarm unless the Mute feature is enabled.

3. Sensaphone waits the specified call delay time, and then calls the first number on its list.

4. If the first call is not acknowledged, Sensaphone waits the specified intercall time and calls the second number.

5. Step 4 repeats until the alarm is acknowledged or until the last number is called.

6. Steps 3–5 are repeated until the alarm is acknowledged or until the maximum number of calls (the Max Calls setting) is reached.

---

**HEARING SENSAPHONE FOR YOURSELF**

Visit the Sensaphone demo page at www.sensaphone.com/demo.html to learn how you can call up a working Sensaphone and hear a live report of monitored conditions.

---

## Configuring Sensaphone for Use

The telephone-style keypad on the front of the unit (see Figure 10.4) is used to program the unit. At a minimum, you need to program the following:

■ **ID number**—Generally the phone number of the location where Sensaphone is installed.

■ **Call-out numbers**—These are the numbers Sensaphone will call in the event its sensors detect a problem. Model 1104 can call up to four numbers, and Model 1108 can call up to eight numbers.

■ **The maximum (high) and minimum (low) temperature limits—** Sensaphone will call each call-out number in sequence if these limits are exceeded.

**FIGURE 10.4**

Sensaphone's keypad is used to program functions and callout numbers.

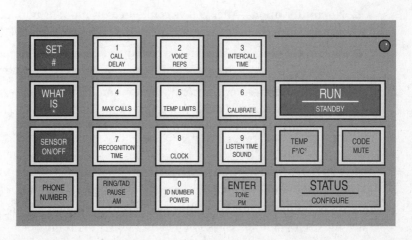

---

**SAVE MONEY WITH CALLING CARDS AND SENSAPHONE**
Sensaphone can store up to 32 digits per each phone number it can call. It supports calling card and dialaround calling, as well as calls to a beeper or pager. See the "Special Dialing" section in the Sensaphone instruction manual.

---

After you've programmed Sensaphone, you can store a four-digit security code to prevent unauthorized fiddling with the unit. If you enable the security code, you must provide it when prompted or you will not be able to access Sensaphone.

# Adding and Configuring Sensors

Sensaphone can use optional dry contact (open or closed) and temperature sensors.

Although Sensaphone contains a built-in temperature sensor, you might want to use a remote sensor as well to detect temperature extremes away from the unit.

By default, sensor 1 is configured as a temperature sensor, whereas sensors 2–4 are configured as dry contact–open. The rear of the Sensaphone unit has four or eight contacts for sensors, depending on the unit. Refer to Figure 10.3.

## General Sensor Adjustment

You can adjust the following options for all sensor inputs:

- **Enable/Disable**—By default, all sensors are enabled On.
- **Recognition time**—From zero seconds (immediate) to 272 minutes (almost five hours); the default is three seconds.

## Configuring Sensor Inputs

You can configure each external sensor input as

- **Normally open**—After you've configured an input as normally open, Sensaphone speaks the number of the input, followed by "OK."
- **Normally closed**—After you've configured an input as normally closed, Sensaphone speaks the number of the input, followed by "beep, OK."
- **Temperature**—After you configure an input as temperature, Sensaphone speaks the number of the input, followed by "temperature." Note that input 1 is already configured as a temperature sensor by default.

## Temperature Sensor Adjustments

You can adjust options including maximum temperature, minimum temperature, temperature calibration and Fahrenheit or Celsius units for the built-in or remote temperature sensors in the Sensaphone and Cottage Sitter units.

---

**CHOOSING TEMPERATURE SETTINGS WISELY**

When you set up maximum and minimum temperatures, choose temperatures that indicate a serious problem and are well away from established limits. For example, if you are monitoring a vacation home that has a thermostat normally set at 50° F, choose a minimum temperature that is several degrees lower, such as 40° F. If you choose a temperature within one or two degrees of your set point, such as 48° F in this example, many normal thermostats might not start heating until the temperatures falls two degrees below the set temperature, and you might get a false alarm call.

---

## Sound Alarm Monitoring Adjustments

Sensaphone will respond to loud sounds picked up by its built-in microphone. You can adjust the following options for the built-in microphone:

- **Sound alarm sensitivity**—From 1 (most sensitive) to 255 (least sensitive); the default is 32.
- **Recognition time**—From 2 to 59 seconds; the default is 8 seconds.
- **High sound alarm**—Enable/disable.

## AC Power Monitoring

By default, Sensaphone will respond to AC power failures. You can adjust the following options for AC power monitoring:

- **Enable/disable AC power monitoring**—Default is On (enabled).
- **Recognition time**—From 0 seconds to 272 minutes; the default is 5 minutes.

Sensaphone immediately calls the stored phone numbers as soon as a power failure lasts beyond the recognition time.

# Responding to a Sensaphone Alarm

When Sensaphone detects a condition that lasts long enough to trigger an alarm, you can acknowledge the alarm in one of three ways:

- Press any key on the Sensaphone.
- Enter 555 on your telephone's touch pad when Sensaphone calls you with an alarm.
- Call back the number where Sensaphone is located after hanging up.

# Receiving a Status Report Remotely

You don't need to wait for Sensaphone to call you with an alarm to find out what's happening at your vacation home. Call in, and after Sensaphone answers and you've logged in using your security code, Sensaphone provides the current time, lists the current temperature, status for other sensors, electricity and battery status, and sound level. After providing status, it opens the microphone for the defined listen-in time. After the status message has been repeated, Sensaphone says "Have a good day" and hangs up the phone.

If the temperature is too high or too low, Sensaphone says "High" or "Low" after providing the temperature. If other sensors have been triggered, the status report for that device will say "Exists."

Disabled sensors are reported as "Off." Battery problems are reported as "Low" (voltage between 8.2 and 7.2 volts) or "Replace Batteries" (voltage below 7.2 volts).

# Controlling Sensaphone Remotely

When you call into Sensaphone, you can also

- Enable or disable any input
- Enable or disable high sound alert alarm monitoring
- Enable or disable AC Power monitoring
- Turn on the listen-in option
- Play the status report

See the Sensaphone instruction manual for details.

# Typical Sensaphone Sessions

A transcript of typical Sensaphone status reports might read like the following. In these examples, sensor 1 is the default temperature sensor, whereas sensor 2 is an external temperature sensor detecting outside temperature, sensor 3 is a normally closed reed switch used to sense unauthorized door or window openings, and sensor 4 is a normally closed water sensor.

*All Status Normal Call*

Assuming that you set a security code, you will be prompted by Sensaphone:

"Enter Security Code"

After you've entered the security code, Sensaphone greets you with

"OK" (if you enter the wrong code, Sensaphone says "Error. Have a good day" and hangs up)

Next, Sensaphone says its ID (phone) number and the current time:

"Hello, this is telephone number 555-9999: the time is 11:35 p.m."

Then Sensaphone lists each sensor and its status:

- "Number 1, 51 degrees, OK"
- "Number 2, 35 degrees, OK"
- "Number 3, OK"
- "Number 4, OK"
- "The electricity is ON"
- "Battery Condition OK"
- "Sound Level, OK"
- "Listen to the sound level for 10 seconds"

Next, Sensaphone transmits live audio to you for the specified time (10 seconds in this example).

Following that, Sensaphone repeats the status message.

Finally, Sensaphone signs off:

"Have a good day"

*Call with Temperature Problem (Sensor 2) and Water Problem (Sensor 4)*

This call sounds like the earlier call, but the reports for sensors 2 and 4 are different:

- "Number 2, 15 degrees, LOW"
- "Number 4, EXISTS"

"EXISTS" means that the sensor has been tripped. In this case, the problem might be that a water pipe near an outside wall has frozen and ruptured.

"Warning message received by 555-8888"

555-8888, in this example, is your office phone number. The number listed by Sensaphone in a status report with problems is the last number dialed.

## Sensaphone Cottage Sitter

The standard Sensaphone 1104 (four inputs/four phone numbers) and Sensaphone 1108 (eight inputs/eight phone numbers) do *not* provide temperature control. If you want to control your vacation home's thermostat remotely, opt for the Cottage Sitter versions FGD-1104-CS or FGD-1108-CS. Sensaphone Cottage Sitters have all the features of the standard 1100-series Sensaphones, but they also support one or two thermostats with a separate three-wire connection at the rear of the unit (see Figure 10.5).

You can use two thermostats, one set for the normal home temperature, and one for the normal away temperature as shown in Figure 10.5, or you can use a specially designed setback thermostat. In either situation, you can call into Sensaphone and use your touch-tone keypad to send the On command to activate the thermostat set to the higher temperature (a perfect way to warm up your vacation home before you arrive). If you forgot to turn down the heat before you leave, call Sensaphone and use your touch-tone keypad to send the Off command to switch to the thermostat set to the lower temperature. You can also get the same status report that is provided by a standard Sensaphone.

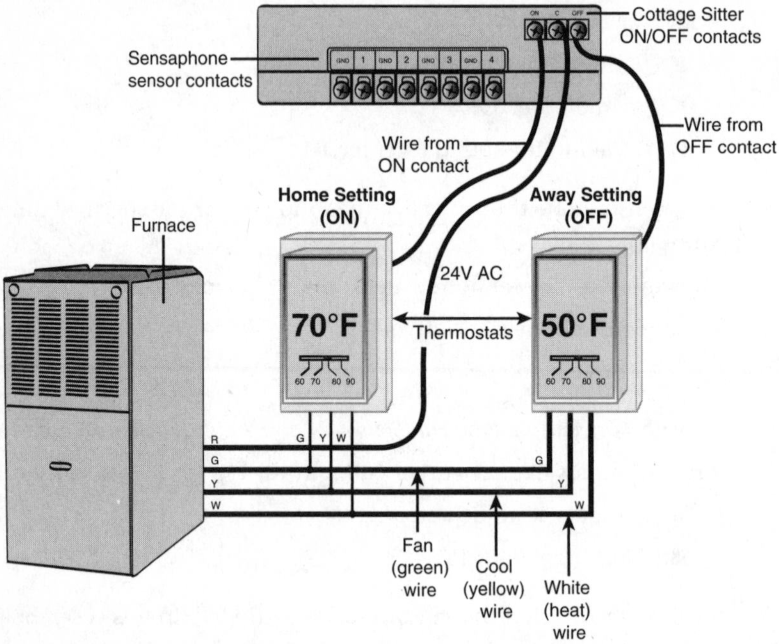

**FIGURE 10.5**

Sensaphone Cottage Sitter connected to home and away thermostats.

If you prefer not to connect your thermostat to the Cottage Sitter, you can also use the three-wire connector to send on/off commands to an X10 Powerflash (universal) module that can be connected to your thermostat or to the On/Off switch on a furnace.

# Troubleshooting Telephone Access to X10-Based Systems

Try the following solutions if you are having problems with telephone access to X10 modules or other parts of your home automation system:

■ **Can't control X10 modules**—If you use touch-tone commands to access the module directly (by address), make sure that the modules you want to control are using the correct house and unit code. If you use the Touch Tone Controller, you cannot control modules with unit codes higher than 10, and you cannot control modules that use a house code different from the one preset on the controller console. If you use voice activation such as with HAL or with HomeSeer Phone, make sure that you properly identify the module.

- **Can't start scenes or macros**—If the scene has been assigned an X10 address, refer to the previous tip. If the scene or macro was created with HAL or with HomeSeer Phone, make sure that the scene or macro has been assigned a name or a touch-tone (DMTF) code. If you cannot start the command by voice, enter the appropriate DMTF code.

- **Can't get past the login sequence**—If you use a security code or login sequence but the remote access device keeps rejecting it, you have probably forgotten the code or have not recorded it correctly. Follow the unit's instructions for setting a new access code or PIN.

- **Can't share the line with an answering machine**—Follow the unit's instructions for use with an answering machine. In some cases, you will not be prompted to enter your access code or PIN. Try the access code or PIN even if you are not prompted. If you continue to have problems, adjust the setting on your unit or try a different type of answering machine

---

**BE CLOSE TO HOME WHEN YOU TRY TELEPHONE ACCESS**

The easiest way to work the bugs out of your telephone access system is to use a cell phone and call in while you're at home! You can even sit at the keyboard of your PC or next to your console unit and reprogram access codes or other settings if you have problems. If you have your PC configured to accept voice commands (an option with HAL and HomeSeer Phone), disconnect the microphone from your PC or mute it using the audio mixer in Windows so that it won't pick up your commands.

---

# THE ABSOLUTE MINIMUM

- You can control X10 modules via touch-tone telephone or by voice.

- You can monitor your home's temperature, security, and other conditions with a self-contained callback device (Sensaphone).

- A Touch Tone Controller (X10 TR16A) enables you to control up to 10 X10 modules via a remote touch-tone telephone.

- The Touch Tone Controller can also be used as a tabletop controller for up to eight X10 modules.

- You can turn one module or a group of modules on and off with the Touch Tone Controller, but you cannot receive feedback from two-way modules or send Bright/Dim commands.

*continues*

- HAL (Home Automated Living) is a series of home automation products that permit voice-activated or touch-tone control of X10 and other types of home automation devices.

- HALdeluxe is recommended for use with X10 or X10-compatible modules, whereas HAL2000 is recommended for use with thermostats, whole house home automation products, and infrared devices such as home theater systems.

- You must install a HAL PCI Voice Portal modem if you don't already have a compatible modem.

- You can use a remote touch-tone telephone, a telephone connected directly to the HAL PCI Voice Portal modem, or a microphone connected to your PC to control HAL with voice commands.

- You can also use touch-tone (DMTF) commands to control modules by address or through tasks (macros).

- HomeSeer Phone is a voice-command add-on to HomeSeer (discussed in Chapter 12), which supports a wide variety of modems.

- You can add voice commands and DMTF (touch-tone) commands to existing HomeSeer events (macros) if you later upgrade to HomeSeer Phone.

- Sensaphone is a self-contained home monitoring system designed to monitor temperature, sounds, and other types of optional sensors.

- Sensaphone can be used along with the Touch Tone Controller and other telephone-line devices.

- Sensaphone provides status reports whenever you call in, or can be programmed to call you if temperatures, noise levels, or sensors are triggered.

- An adjustable delay feature helps prevent false alarms.

- The Cottage Sitter version of Sensaphone can turn on and turn off your HVAC system.

11

# ACCESSING X10 HOME CONTROL VIA YOUR HOME COMPUTER

If you have a home computer, it's probably already a big part of your home entertainment and home organization picture. Why not use it to control your home with X10? This chapter shows you how to use your computer to control X10 devices and make your home automation system smarter than ever before.

# Connecting Your Computer to Your X10 System

If you want to use your PC to control your X10 home automation system, you need hardware and software.

The hardware you'll need

- USB or serial (COM) port X10 controller
- Cable (usually provided with the controller)

The required software

- Various home automation programs compatible with X10 and with your X10 controller; the controller usually includes software, but third-party or enhanced titles might also be available

The USB and serial ports are usually located on the rear of a desktop or laptop computer. Figure 11.1 shows typical locations for these ports on the rear of a desktop computer.

**FIGURE 11.1**
USB and serial ports on a typical desktop computer.

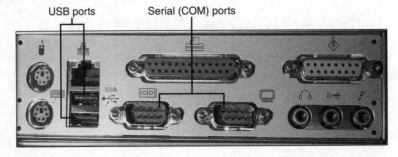

USB ports    Serial (COM) ports

## Serial Port

The first X10 interfaces for PCs used the venerable 9-pin serial (COM) port shown in Figure 11.1. The serial port continues to be used for some types of X10 computer interfaces, but its slow speed, lack of resource sharing with other ports, and the increasing numbers of PCs that lack a serial port suggest that this is not the most desirable way to interface your PC with X10.

Some major types of serial-port-to-X10 interfaces are the following:

- **FireCracker (CM17)**—A simple serial (COM) port pass-through device that emulates an X10 wireless remote. It is often sold in a bundle that includes an X10 wireless remote, wireless transceiver, and lamp module. Add FireCracker Fuse software to create timed events or the FireCracker Macro Recorder to create a series of commands you can play back whenever needed.
- **X10 Activehome Computer Interface (CM11A)**—Stores programs in battery-backed memory and includes home automation software.

- **PowerLinc II Serial**—A more powerful serial interface that can also be used in place of TW523 interfaces. The PowerLinc II Serial uses a module that plugs into an AC wall socket, rather than being wireless as is FireCracker. This interface includes X10 program development software.

## USB

A USB *(universal serial bus)* interface can be used by any computer running Windows 98, Second Edition or greater as well as Macintoshes. USB ports are designed to coexist with each other, and if you don't have enough USB ports on your system, you can add additional ports by connecting a USB hub to another system. Most recent desktop and laptop computers have anywhere from two to as many as eight USB ports, making USB the preferred interface type for long-term use.

Some major types of USB interfaces to X10 home automation systems are the following:

- **PowerLinc USB**—An entry-level USB interface that includes Smarthome Manager Essential home automation software; the computer must be kept on to run timed or macro-triggered events

- **PowerLinc Controller USB**—This interface features built-in memory and timer, enabling you to shut off the PC and still control devices with timers and macros; bundled with Smarthome Manager Essential or Smarthome Manager (full version) home automation software.

- **X10 ActiveHome Pro Controller CM15A**—This interface features built-in memory and timer, enabling you to shut off your PC and still control devices with timers and macros; includes an all-house-code RF transceiver; bundled with ActiveHome Pro home automation software.

## Important Features

When you select a PC interface for your X10 home automation system, look for these features:

- **Built-in timer and memory**—If your PC interface doesn't have these features, you must leave your PC on at all times to control your X10 devices. Keep in mind that if you plan to control your X10 home automation system via a home network or via the Internet, you don't need this feature.

- **USB interface**—USB plugs into virtually every computer built in the current decade, can plug into a USB hub, and doesn't require complex hardware configuration.

- **Bundled software features**—Some vendors provide stripped-down home automation software, which might control only a few devices, with their PC interface modules; other vendors provide full-featured products with more capabilities. If you decide to buy an interface bundled with an entry-level home automation program, find out how much it will cost to upgrade to the full version product.

- **Third-party software compatibility**—If you decide at a later point to change software, find out whether other software programs will support your interface.
- **Mac OS software support (if you use a Mac)**—Some interfaces can be used with Mac OS by purchasing additional home automation software, but some work with Windows only.

# Installing a Computer Interface for X10

The installation process for your computer interface will vary, depending on whether you are using a serial (COM) port or a USB port interface device. With either type of device, however, you normally install the software first (check the directions for your specific device to make sure). Be sure the computer you connect to the X10 interface has a working Internet connection. No matter what software you use, you will want to check for upgrades as soon as you install the program. Some programs require a working Internet connection so that the program can be registered. After the software has been installed, you typically then connect your interface to your PC. With a serial interface, connect the device to a serial port on the rear of your PC. If the cable has thumbscrews, be sure to fasten them securely (see Figure 11.2).

To connect a USB interface, connect the flat end (Type A connector) of the USB cable to a USB port on your PC (see Figure 11.2) or to a USB hub if you are out of USB ports. The other end of the cable (Type B) connects to the interface box that plugs into the wall.

**FIGURE 11.2**

Connecting a USB or serial cable from a typical X10 serial port interface to a desktop PC.

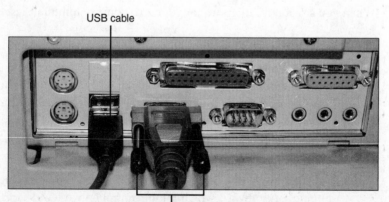

USB cable

Thumbscrews on serial cable

After the interface has been connected to the PC, plug the interface box into the AC wall socket (see Figure 11.3).

**FIGURE 11.3**
A typical USB
interface to X10
after being con-
nected to an AC
wall outlet.

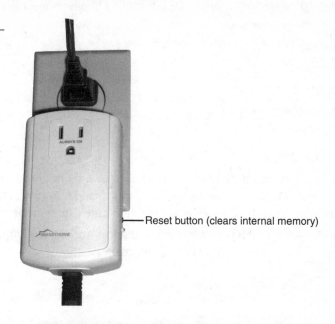

Reset button (clears internal memory)

If the unit requires batteries to maintain timers and programs, such as the X10 CM15A, insert batteries only after connecting the unit to the AC outlet and your computer's USB port.

After you've connected your computer-X10 interface to an AC power line and your computer, start the software provided with the unit. Note that the FireCracker interface transmits signals to an X10 wireless transceiver plugged into an AC outlet instead of a wired transceiver.

Make sure you have a listing of the X10 devices in your home automation system, their locations, their house/unit codes, and their capabilities. You can use the forms provided in earlier chapters to list this information.

# Using Smarthome Manager

Smarthome Manager Essential requires Windows 98SE, Me, 2000, or XP. It is bundled with the Smarthome PowerLinc Controller USB and other Smarthome X10-compatible computer controllers. You can upgrade to the full version of Smarthome Manager at any time, or you might be able to buy a bundle featuring the PowerLinc Controller USB and Smarthome Manager.

The full version of Smarthome Manager works the same way as Essential, but adds the capability to automatically detect some types of modules and create additional conditions within actions. In this chapter, I will use *Smarthome Manager* to refer to both versions except when I discuss features present only in the full version. When you start Smarthome Manager, it opens a Windows Explorer–like interface called *My House*, which features four objects:

- Locations
- All Devices
- Event Triggered Action
- Time Triggered Action

## Creating a New Location

Select the Locations icon to create a location, such as a room or section of your home. Click Add a New Location (see Figure 11.4) to add a location. A new location is named New Location by default; type over the name with your preferred name.

You can also right-click the Locations icon and select Add a Location. The location is used as part of the name of any action you create.

**FIGURE 11.4**
Adding a location with Smarthome Manager.

Click to add a new device

Click to add a new location

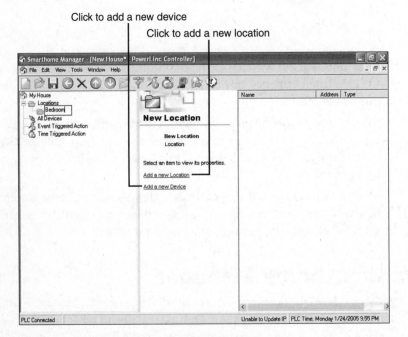

## Adding Devices to Smarthome Manager

After you've added a location, you can add a device to that location or add another location. Click Add a New Device or right-click All Devices and Select Add Device (refer to Figure 11.4) to bring up a device properties dialog (see Figure 11.5).

Specify the device type, house and unit codes, and provide a descriptive name. When you select a particular module, the properties menu changes to reflect the features of that module. For example, if you have a dimmer switch, you can select the ramp rate (how quickly the light fades on and off) and the default brightness level when you turn it on.

**FIGURE 11.5**

Configuring a Smarthome two-way dimmer switch.

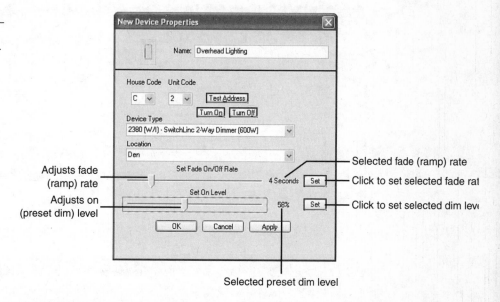

To add another device to the same location, click the location in the left window, and then click Add a New Device in the center pane. Each device is listed in the right-side pane (see Figure 11.6).

---

**TEST ADDRESS MAKES SETTING UP REMOTE DEVICES EASIER**

If you're setting up devices in various rooms, Test Address keeps sending on and off signals until you click Stop. This provides you with time to walk to the module's location to see whether you've properly identified the device.

---

## Controlling a Device Interactively with Smarthome Manager

To turn on a device that's off, double-click it in the right pane. If the device is already on, double-clicking it turns it off. For additional control options, right-click the device and select Control Device from the contextual menu. You can send the following commands:

- On
- Off
- Bright

- Dim
- Dimmer Level

**FIGURE 11.6**
Device listing
for the selected
location.

Selected location

Modules in selected location

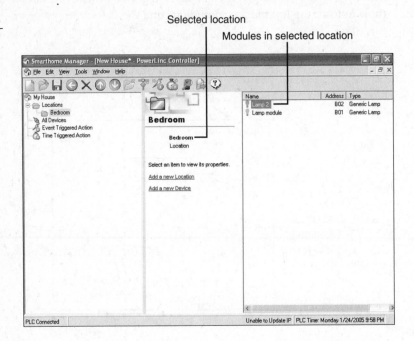

**Bedroom**

Bedroom
Location

Select an item to view its properties.

Add a new Location

Add a new Device

| Name | Address | Type |
|------|---------|------|
| Lamp 2 | B02 | Generic Lamp |
| Lamp module | B01 | Generic Lamp |

With some types of Smarthome modules, you can select Keypress to speed up operation. With two-way modules, select Status Request to see whether the module is on
or off, or to view its current settings.

## Creating a Timed Action

The real power of an X10 computer interface is its capability to create events that
can run automatically. With Smarthome Manager, you can create actions that are
triggered by time or by a particular event.

To create a timed action, click Time Triggered Action in the left pane. Then click
Add a New Timer in the center pane. The New Timer Properties dialog (see Figure
11.7) is displayed. Enter a descriptive name for the event, specify when the action
should occur, and click OK.

---

**SUNRISE AND SUNSET VARY—MAKE SURE THAT YOUR INTERFACE IS READY!**
If you specify sunrise or sunset as in Figure 11.7, you need to make sure that your system
knows when sunrise and sunset take place. Use the Set Sunrise/Sunset tool in the Tools
menu to specify your location and daylight saving time settings. See "Using the
Smarthome Manager Tools Menu" section later in this chapter for details.

---

**FIGURE 11.7**
Creating a new
timed event.

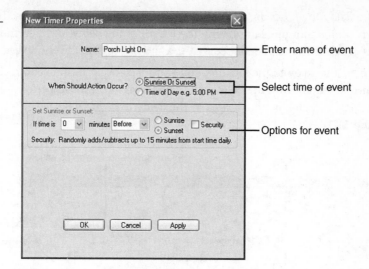

—— Enter name of event

—— Select time of event

—— Options for event

Your new timer is stored under the Time Triggered Action object in the left pane. Next, right-click the new timer object and select Add Event Step to open the Select Device Action dialog (see Figure 11.8).

**FIGURE 11.8**
Specifying an
action to take
during a timed
event.

Select the action you want to take from the listing, and then click OK. You can use the increment bright, increment dim, or repeat dim commands with any dimmable module, including entry-level lamp modules.

To add a step to an action, right-click the action, select Add Event Step, and select another device and another action. Repeat as desired. For example, you can create an action that turns on various interior lights at a specified time (or at sunset), as in Figure 11.9.

## Adding a Delay to an Action

It can be useful to add delays to an action. For example, you can create an elegant effect in your home if you turn on lights one by one at sunset or at a specified time. To add a delay to an action, right-click the action and select Add Delay. In the Enter Delay dialog that appears, specify the length of the delay in the form *minutes:seconds*. A delay object then appears at the end of the list of event objects.

To move the delay to the location you want it to occur in the action, click the green up-arrow button until the delay is in the correct location. To perform an action after the delay, drag the action desired to the delay to create a nested effect as in Figure 11.10.

**FIGURE 11.9**

A timed action that triggers multiple devices.

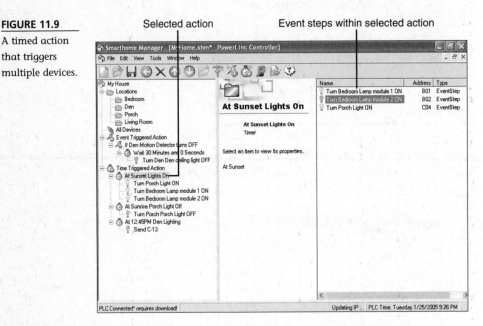

**FIGURE 11.10**

Placing delays between actions correctly (left) and incorrectly (right).

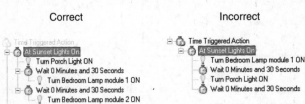

If you don't nest the desired actions after each delay, the delays will be ignored. A Warnings dialog (shown in Figure 11.11) will be displayed when you download the program to the controller (see the "Downloading Your Smarthome Configuration to the Controller" section later in this chapter for details). Click the links in the Warnings dialog to see examples of incorrect and correct program logic.

To add another delay, repeat these steps. When you are finished, your action might resemble the one shown in Figure 11.12, which has three steps, separated by two delays.

**FIGURE 11.11**
The Warnings dialog indicates problems with your action.

**FIGURE 11.12**
An action with multiple delays and devices controlled.

At Sunset Lights On action

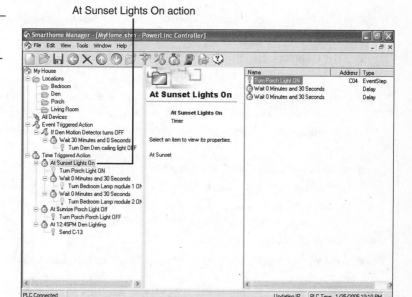

# Creating an Event-Triggered Action

If you want one X10 module to turn on others, you need to create an event-triggered action. For example, you can use an X10 motion detection module to turn on an X10 camera and a lamp in the same room, or use an X10 door or window sensor to trigger a call from an X10 telephone module to your remote location.

To create an event-triggered action, right-click the Event Triggered Action object in the left pane and select Add Trigger. This displays the Event Triggered Action dialog. Select the device you want to use as the trigger from the pull-down menu, and then select the device action you want to use as the trigger. Depending on the device, you can choose from on, off, bright, dim, or a preset dim level. Click OK after you've made your selections. This creates a conditional statement at the start of your action (If *this event* ...).

---

**USING THE RIGHT TRIGGER FOR YOUR ACTION**

Think carefully about the action you choose for your triggering device. If you want to save power in a room, for example, when the motion detector no longer senses activity in the room, Off would be the right choice to trigger turning off the light in the room. However, if you are using a motion detector for security, an action such as turning on a video camera or lights should be triggered by the motion detector being activated by movement in the room.

Don't be afraid to experiment. See the section "Saving Your Smarthome Configuration" to learn how to save your current configuration and any changes you make.

---

Next, right-click the conditional (If) action you just created and select one of the following options from the right-click menu:

- **Add trigger**—Use this only if you want to create an action that depends on two or more triggers taking place.

- **Add delay**—Use this to insert a pause between the start of the action and the next step. For example, if you want to use a motion detector to turn off a room light, add a delay of a few minutes to ensure that the room is really empty.

- **Add condition**—With the Essential version of Smarthome Manager, you can add a day of the week condition, which enables you to select which day or days this action applies to. Upgrade to the full version, and you can also set up other conditions, including device state, time of day, day of month, or month of year.

- **Add event step**—Select this option to control another X10 device.

Figure 11.13 shows an action that turns off the ceiling light in the den if the motion detector turns off and 30 minutes have elapsed.

**FIGURE 11.13**

An event-triggered action that includes a time delay.

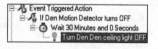

To create this action, I used the following procedure:

1. Right-click Event Triggered Action.
2. Select Add Trigger.

3. Select the trigger device (Motion Detector in Den) and state (Off) from dialog and click OK.

4. Right-click the new object If Den Motion Detector Turns OFF.

5. Select Add Delay.

6. Enter delay time (30 minutes) from dialog and click OK.

7. Right-click the object Wait 30 minutes and 0 seconds.

8. Select Add Event Step.

9. Select device (Den Ceiling Light) and action (Off); click OK to complete the action.

## Saving Your Smarthome Configuration

As soon as you set up your X10 modules, you should save your home automation configuration. Saving your configuration enables you to recall it in case of computer power failure. As you create actions to go with your modules, you can use different names to save different configurations. This enables you to create configurations suitable to different times of the year or different situations.

To save your current configuration:

1. Click File, Save As.

2. Enter a unique name for your configuration (see Figure 11.14).

3. Click Save.

**FIGURE 11.14**

Saving your current Smarthome configuration.

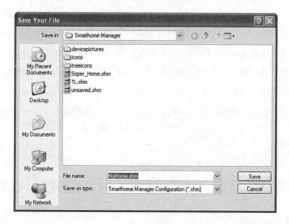

The name of your saved configuration is displayed at the top of the Smarthome Manager screen. When you change a saved configuration, the configuration name ends with an asterisk at the top of the Smarthome Manager screen. This serves as a visual reminder that you have made changes.

# Downloading Your Smarthome Configuration to the Controller

If you are using a controller with onboard memory and timers, such as the Smarthome Controller USB, you need to download your configuration before it can be used to run your home. To download the configuration, click File, Download or press the F12 key.

During the download process, a series of status messages is displayed, and a Download Complete dialog box appears when the download is completed. Click OK.

# Using the Smarthome Manager Tools Menu

The Tools menu provides a variety of utilities that you can use to make your home automation configuration easier.

- **Signal Test**—This test sends a stream of on/off signals to a house/unit code combination of your choice.

- **Advanced Controller**—This dialog (shown in Figure 11.15) enables you to send commands directly to a specified house/unit code send house/unit codes for programming, enables you to adjust various X10 parameters for more reliable operation, and provides a printable report of recent commands.

- **View All X10 Codes**—Displays codes assigned to switches and modules (see Figure 11.16). Note that this grid does *not* list codes used for scenes.

- **Set Time**—Sends the time you select (default is the current time) to the controller. To test a stored program using time-triggered actions, you can use this option to send a specified time to the controller.

- **Synchronize Time to PC**—Sets the controller to the current time stored on the PC.

- **Get Time**—Displays the time stored in the controller. Use this to verify that your controller has the correct time stored in its memory.

- **Set Sunrise/Sunset**—Displays a dialog where you can choose the nearest city

**caution**

If you're experimenting with different configurations, keep in mind that after the configuration has been downloaded into the controller, the controller will run your X10 devices until you download a different configuration—or until you disconnect the controller from the AC wall outlet or clear the controller's memory (refer to Figure 11.3).

**caution**

After you've used the Set Sunrise/Sunset dialog, make sure that your PC clock is correct, and then click Synchronize Time to PC.

and state to determine sunrise. Click Advanced to enter latitude, longitude, and time in relation to GMT (Greenwich Mean Time) if the city/state calculation of sunrise/sunset is incorrect, or if you don't find a city close enough to your location.

**FIGURE 11.15**

The Advanced Controller menu.

Sends house/unit codes

Report of recent activity

Switches back to standard control

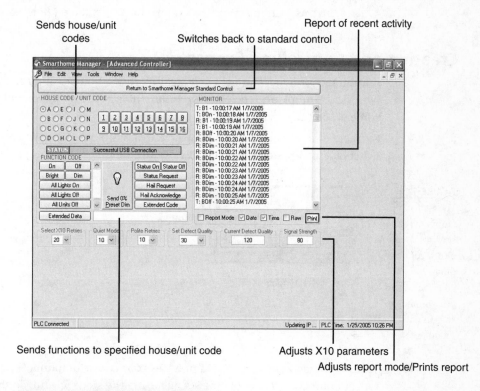

Sends functions to specified house/unit code

Adjusts X10 parameters

Adjusts report mode/Prints report

**FIGURE 11.16**

Use View All X10 Codes to see which codes have not yet been assigned to switches or modules in your home automation system.

■ **Connect to Power Line Controller (PLC)**—Use this option with serial (COM) port controllers to ensure that you are connected.

■ **Auto Detect Devices**—(Full version only) Automatically detects two-way devices.

■ **Options**—Changes various options for Smarthome Manager.

## Creating and Controlling Scenes

Smarthome Manager can help you create scenes if you use Smarthome's SwitchLinc/LampLinc/ToggleLinc programmable switches and modules in your X10 home automation system.

To create a new scene, click View, SwitchLinc/LampLinc Window. This displays the SwitchLinc/LampLinc dialog shown in Figure 11.17.

**FIGURE 11.17**

The SwitchLinc/ LampLinc dialog provides manual and wizard configuration for your Smarthome programmable switches and modules.

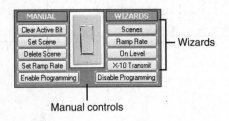

Manual controls

Wizards

The SwitchLinc/LampLinc dialog provides your choice of manual control or wizards for configuration. To create a new scene using the scene wizard, do the following:

1. Click the Scenes button (refer to Figure 11.17).

2. Click Add to Scene, and then click Next. The clear code is transmitted to the switch or module to prepare it for a new scene.

3. Adjust the lamp's brightness using the switch, an X10 remote, or Smarthome Manager's direct control (refer to the "Controlling a Device Interactively with Smarthome Manager" section earlier in this chapter) .

---

**DIMMER LEVEL TO THE RESCUE**

If you're working with a switch or module that's rooms away from your location, use the Dimmer Level option in the Control Device dialog to choose the brightness you want.

---

4. After you've adjusted the brightness manually, click Next.

5. Enter the desired scene address. You can use an unused unit code from the house code setting you normally use or choose any unused house/unit code address. Write down the house/unit code address, and click Next.

6. Smarthome Manager sends the scene setting to the switch or module. Click Finish to close the wizard.

## Making Other Adjustments to Smarthome Switches and Modules

Other wizards you can run from the SwitchLinc/LampLinc dialog include the following:

- **Ramp Rate**—Use this wizard to adjust the speed at which the switch or lamp module brightens or dims.

- **On Level**—Use this wizard to set the brightness level used when the switch or lamp module is turned on.

If you previously used an X10 Maxi Controller to configure your Smarthome programmable light switches and modules (see the "Configuring Programmable Modules" section in Chapter 6, "Using Timers and Advanced Remotes for X10," for details), you can save yourself some dial-turning and button-pushing by using the following manual options in the dialog:

- **Clear Active Bit**—Click this button instead of sending the clear command sequence O16, N16, M16, P16, M16.

- **Set Scene**—Click this button instead of sending the scene membership command sequence M16, N16, O16, P16.

- **Delete Scene**—Click this button instead of sending the remove command sequence O16, P16, M16, N16.

- **Set Ramp Rate**—Click this button instead of sending the scene fade-on rate command sequence N16, O16, P16, M16.

- **Disable Programming**—Click this button instead of sending the disable programming command sequence M16, O16, P16, N16, P16.

- **Enable Programming**—Click this button instead of sending the enable programming sequence N16, M16, O16, P16, P16.

- **X10 Transmit**—Open this dialog to select disable X10 transmit (available with two-way switches and modules) instead of sending the Disable PLC transmissions command sequence M16, N16, P16, O16, P16. You can also use this dialog to enable X10 transmit instead of sending the Enable PLC transmissions command sequence O16, M16, N16, P16, P16.

### Triggering a Scene

After you've created a scene, you can incorporate it into an action you create with Smarthome Manager. Use the following steps to do so:

1. Create the action as described in the section "Creating a Timed Action" earlier in this chapter or "Creating an Event-Triggered Action," also earlier in this chapter.

2. When you want to add a step that triggers a scene, right-click the preceding step and select Add Event Step.

3. From the Select Device Action menu, click the Click Here link to display advanced options (see Figure 11.18). Select the device containing the scene.

4. Enter the house and unit code of the scene you want to trigger. Click OK.

5. Add additional steps as desired.

**FIGURE 11.18**

Selecting a device and house/unit code combination to trigger a scene.

# Using HomeSeer

HomeSeer, which is available from HomeSeer Technologies (www.homeseer.com), supports X10 as well as many other home automation systems, including Z-Wave, Napco Gemini, Global Cache, On-Q System, Lightolier Compose, HAI Omni, and others. It does so through the use of ActiveX plug-ins developed by HomeSeer and third-party vendors. HomeSeer is an excellent choice to manage a multistandard home automation system.

HomeSeer also includes a web server, enabling you to access your home automation system remotely via a home network or the Internet. For more information about using the HomeSeer web server, see Chapter 11.

HomeSeer is available in two forms:

■ **HomeSeer SE** supports only Z-Wave hardware, and is sold as part of various Z-Wave kits by HomeSeer.

■ **HomeSeer** (full) is sold separately. As shipped, it's ready to work with X10, Z-Wave, and some other home automation controllers. You can add extra-cost optional plug-ins to support other home automation systems.

The following discussion is based on HomeSeer version 1.7.x; you can download a free 30-day trial of the latest version from the HomeSeer website.

# Starting HomeSeer with the HomeSeer Assistant Wizard

When you start HomeSeer, a setup wizard known as the *HomeSeer Assistant Wizard* appears . Unless you disable it, this wizard appears by default each time you start HomeSeer.

The wizard offers options to

- Configure HomeSeer's web server (see Chapter 12 for details)
- Enable Z-Wave control
- Set up X10 devices
- Import configuration data from X10.com's ActiveHome or IBM's Home Director home control programs
- Create a schedule for a device
- Check for updates
- Set up a microphone for voice recognition
- Set up your hardware interfaces to your home automation system

Because the wizard makes it easy to configure the various parts of a home automation system, I recommend you allow the wizard to run at startup until you have configured the hardware you plan to control with HomeSeer.

## Setting Up Your Hardware Interfaces

When you start HomeSeer for the first time, you should configure the hardware interface(s) that connect your PC to your home automation system. From the Hardware Assistant Wizard , select Tell HomeSeer about my hardware interfaces, and then click Next in this dialog and the following dialog to display the Interfaces tab of the Options menu (shown in Figure 11.19).

The X10 Interface section occupies the upper-left corner of the dialog. Click the down-arrow next to Device and select your X10 interface device from those listed. If your X10 device uses a serial (COM) port, be sure to select the correct COM port number. Click Options if you need to adjust other settings for your interface. Click OK when you're finished. Click Finish to close the wizard.

---

**KEEPING HOMESEER FRESH**

You should check for program updates the first time you run HomeSeer and frequently thereafter. See the next section, "Installing Program Updates," for details.

**FIGURE 11.19**

Click to select your X10 interface

The Interfaces
tab of the
Options menu is
used to select
interfaces for
X10, Z-Wave,
and other home
automation stan-
dards.

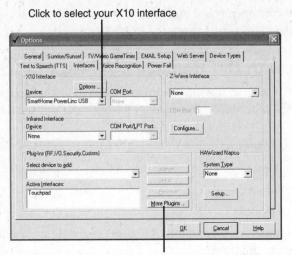

Click to check for additional plugins and HomeSeer updates

## Installing Program Updates

You can check for free and extra-cost program updates to HomeSeer in two ways:

- Select Check for Updates to HomeSeer using the Updater in the HomeSeer Assistant Wizard
- Click More Plugins from the Interfaces tab of the Options menu (refer to Figure 11.19), and then click Next.

To open this dialog after you've started HomeSeer, click View, Options, and click the Interfaces tab.

The Check for Application Updates dialog appears when you start the update process. From this dialog, you can enable HomeSeer to check for updates at startup or at a particular time of day, and to run a specified event when updates are available. Make any changes desired, click Next, and again click Next on the following page to continue.

The HomeSeer Updater displays updates, plug-ins, and scripts that you can install (see Figure 11.20). The Cost column indicates which updates are free and the cost of optional plug-ins and scripts. The list is color-coded. Click Configure to adjust how updates are displayed. To get more information about an update or plug-in, click the item to select it, and then click Package Description.

Click the box next to each update you want to install. To install selected updates, click Install Now. A progress window appears and displays installation details. Click Exit when the installation process is complete.

**FIGURE 11.20**

Selecting updates from the HomeSeer Updater.

Selected for installation

Not selected

Free updates

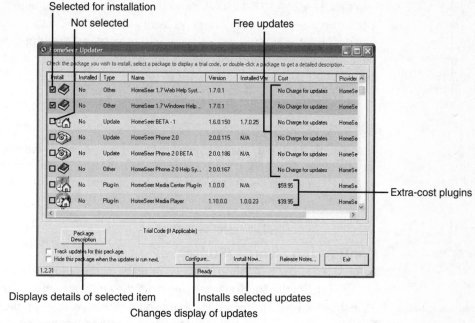

Displays details of selected item

Installs selected updates

Changes display of updates

Extra-cost plugins

## Specifying X10 Device Types

To specify the types of X10 devices in your home automation system when you start HomeSeer, click Tell HomeSeer About My X10 devices in the HomeSeer Assistant Wizard. If you have already started HomeSeer, click View, Options, Device Types. Either method opens the Device Types dialog shown in Figure 11.21.

**FIGURE 11.21**

Selecting and configuring a type of X10 device.

Attributes (options) for selected device type

Selected device type

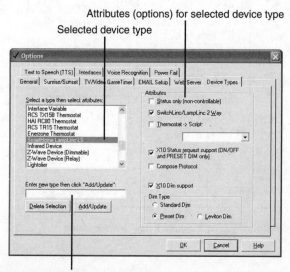

Enter name to create a new device type

Select the type of X10 device you have from the list of devices at left. The attributes menu at right automatically displays available attributes, such as dimming, two-way options, and so forth. Select additional attributes if they apply to your hardware. Click OK when finished. Repeat this process as needed until all the X10 modules and switches that you want to control with HomeSeer have been identified. You can also add an unspecified module type and customize its attributes.

---

**SPECIFY NOW, CONFIGURE LATER**

Don't confuse the Device Types dialog with the Add Device and Device Properties dialogs (see the section "Controlling Devices Interactively with HomeSeer" later in this chapter for details). Those dialogs are used to specify the location and house/unit code for each device.

---

## Configuring Sunrise/Sunset

If you want to create lighting, security, or other actions that are triggered by sunrise or sunset, select the Sunrise/Sunset tab from the Options menu. Choose a location from the Pick Location menu or specify your latitude and longitude. Click Calculate to display sunrise and sunset for the current date and location you specified (see Figure 11.22). Click OK to lock in your selection. HomeSeer uses this information for all actions that depend on sunrise/sunset timing.

**FIGURE 11.22**

Specifying sunrise/sunset times for your location.

Enter latitude and longitude of your location if it isn't listed in the database

Click to select a location

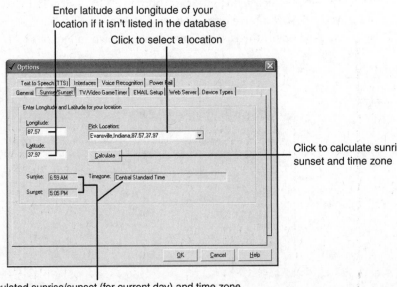

Click to calculate sunrise sunset and time zone

Calculated sunrise/sunset (for current day) and time zone

## Specifying Other Options

Other options you can specify within HomeSeer's Options menu include

- **TV/Video Game Timer**—Use this option to create one or more users for a TV or video game connected to a specified X10 plug-in module or wall outlet. Each user can be assigned a particular length of time to use the specified module on a daily or weekly basis (see Figure 11.23). To access the device connected to the module, the user must enter the house code and password specified by using a Maxi Controller.

**FIGURE 11.23**

Using the TV/Video Game Timer dialog. A Maxi Controller (inset) is used to enter the password house code and password.

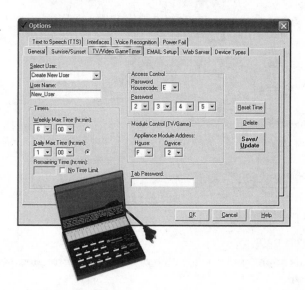

- **Text-to-Speech**—Use this dialog to enable HomeSeer to talk to you and to specify a voice.

- **Voice Recognition**—Use this dialog to enable HomeSeer to respond to voice commands.

- **Power Fail**—Use this dialog to enable HomeSeer to recover from a power failure and continue to control your home.

- **General**—Use this dialog to configure how HomeSeer starts, shuts down, logs events, edits scripts, and adjusts specified event times when security mode is enabled.

# Adding and Configuring Devices with HomeSeer

After HomeSeer has started, you've configured your hardware interface and X10 devices with the wizard, and you've closed the wizard, you should start to add specific devices to your home automation configuration. To add a device, click the Devices (light bulb) icon under the Views menu at the left side of the HomeSeer interface (refer to Figure 11.26). Then right-click within the list of Devices and select Add Device from the contextual menu to bring up the Device Properties dialog shown in Figure 11.24.

**FIGURE 11.24**

Setting up a two-way LampLinc module.

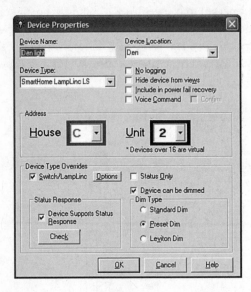

To set up a device, specify these items:

- The device name
- Device location (enter the location or select an existing location from the pull-down menu)
- Device type (based on the list you viewed or modified in the "Specifying X10 Device Types" section earlier in this chapter)
- Select options, such as voice command, logging, and others
- Specify the house (red) and unit (black) code for the device
- Configure the device's dimmer and other options

Click OK when you've finished. Repeat as needed until all the devices you want to control with HomeSeer have been identified.

To adjust properties for an existing device, right-click the device and select Device Properties. The same Device Properties dialog shown in Figure 11.24 will be displayed.

## Adjusting Specific Device Options

If the device you are installing has specific options that you can configure, the dialog enables you to make suitable changes. For example, if you are installing a Smarthome SwitchLinc, LampLinc, or similar modules, as in Figure 11.24, click the

Options button to specify the preset dim level and ramp rate and to enable or disable transmit (two-way operation) for modules supporting these features (see Figure 11.25).

**FIGURE 11.25**

Specifying preset dim and ramp rates for a SwitchLinc or LampLinc module.

Other types of devices have different options, such as a serial port setting for some types of thermostats, key definitions for infrared devices, and house code values beyond P. Click Help if you need assistance in setting up some types of devices; click OK when you've finished.

After you have configured some devices, the HomeSeer display resembles the one shown in Figure 11.26.

**FIGURE 11.26**

HomeSeer's Devices view.

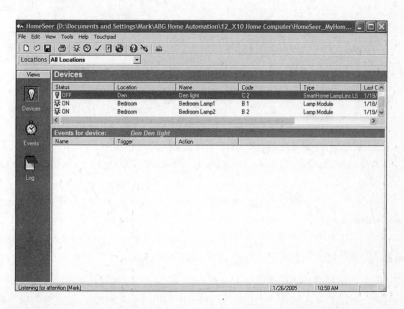

## Controlling Devices Interactively with HomeSeer

To send commands to any device defined in HomeSeer, right-click the Device and select Device Command from the contextual menu. Depending upon the device, you can select On, Off, Dim To, Thermostat, or Control.

If you select Dim To, you can select levels ranging from 0–100% in 10% increments. If the device is a thermostat, you can set the temperature, and turn on heating, cooling, or the fan.

## Creating an Event with HomeSeer

After you've configured your X10 devices in HomeSeer, you can create events. HomeSeer uses a single dialog to create all types of events, including those triggered by time, conditions, or other factors. To create an event, click the Events (alarm clock) icon in the Views menu to display existing events. Then right-click anywhere in the list of events and select Add Event to display the Event Properties dialog (shown in Figure 11.27).

**FIGURE 11.27**

Selecting a trigger for an event.

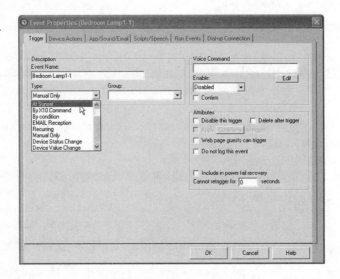

### Selecting a Trigger for an Event

You can choose any of the options shown in Table 11.1 as a trigger for an event.

Enter the name you want to use for the event, specify its type, and specify the group (optional). Depending on the trigger type you select, the dialog changes to reflect the options, as shown in Table 11.1.

## **TABLE 11.1**   HomeSeer Trigger Options

| Trigger Type | Trigger Options | Notes/Tips |
|---|---|---|
| Absolute time Time/Date | Time; any date or optional calendar; security option | Security option varies actual trigger by amount of minutes specified in General options tab |

**TABLE 11.1**   (continued)

| Trigger Type | Trigger Options | Notes/Tips |
| --- | --- | --- |
| At Sunrise | Before or after sunrise; security option | |
| At Sunset | Before or after sunset security option | |
| By X10 Command | House/unit code; one of the following: on, off, dim, all units off, all lights on, dim, bright, all lights off, extended, hailrequest, hail ack, preset dim, ext data, status on,status off, status request, any | |
| By Condition | Time is, date is, status of installed X10 modules | Status options include on, off, duration of time on or off, changed to on/off/dim/bright, value equals, others |
| EMAIL Reception | Mail received from specified address or any address | |
| Recurring | Repeats on user-specified schedule | Useful for testing a remote device; device keeps working until you can view it |
| Manual Only | Use with voice commands | Used with HomeSeer Phone option (see Chapter 10 for details). |
| Device Status Change | Any installed device specified device; status on/off; status changed to on/off/dim/any; status unknown | |
| Device Value Change | Greater than, less than, equal to, not equal to, set to, any value | Useful for controlling thermostats or when a script has been written assigning text values to certain conditions |

You can also specify whether to use voice commands to trigger the event, what attributes to assign to the event, days and times to run the event, and whether to enable the event as part of power fail recovery.

Select the option(s) desired and click OK to close the dialog, or click the tabs to view other options.

## Device Options

To select the devices you want to use in the action, click the Device Actions tab. Select the devices you want to use in the action from the Available Devices list and drag them to the Selected Device: section of the dialog (see Figure 11.28).

Double-click each device in the Selected Devices portion of the dialog to display the Device Command dialog (see Figure 11.29). Configure the device as desired. Figure 11.29 shows typical options for a lamp module.

**FIGURE 11.28**

Selecting the
devices to use in
the event.

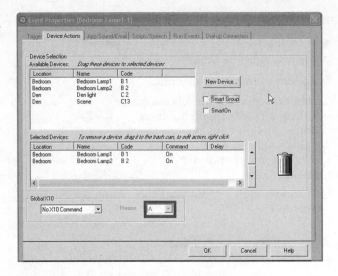

**FIGURE 11.29**

Configuring a
bedroom lamp
to dim to 16%
during an
action.

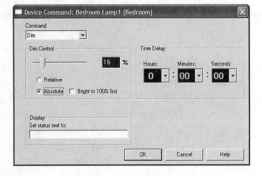

You can turn all lights on or off, all units off, turn on or turn off a lamp, set the
brightness level, and specify a time delay if desired.

## Specifying Other Options

Click the App/Sound/Email tab if you want to run an application as part of an
event, play a sound, or send an email (including an optional attachment) during
an event.

This tab offers many possibilities:

- Use the launch application option to start a slide show or a media player to
  set the mood for a romantic evening or to kick off a party
- Use the play sound option as part of a security or door-opening event to alert
  a visually impaired user to a potential problem

■ Use the EMAIL option along with a security event such as a motion detector, or a door or window trigger to send an alert to your office or school email address that there might be problems at home

---

### PREPARATIONS BEFORE YOU CAN USE APP/SOUND/EMAIL

If you want to use the App/Sound/Email tab to alert you to a problem, make sure that you do the following:

■ Convert any non-WAV audio (such as MP3 or WMA compressed digital audio files) into WAV. You can use the Sound Recorder applet in Windows or other audio recording programs to make the conversion.

■ Set up HomeSeer to use your email program.

Set up a test event that you can trigger manually to see whether these features are working correctly before you create an event to warn you of an actual problem.

---

Use the Scripts/Speech tab (shown in Figure 11.30) to select a script to run during an action or to add computer-generated speech to your action.

**FIGURE 11.30**

Adding a script
to warn of a
weather alert
and computer-
generated speech
to an event.

Configures a dial-up Internet connection for use by HomeSeer

Adds existing events to this event

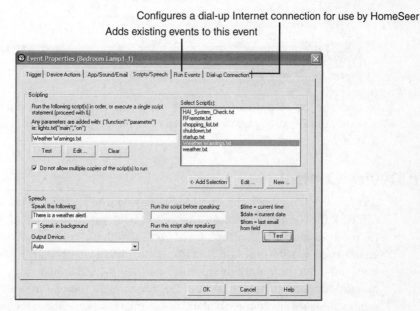

Click Run Events to chain existing events together into a single event. This is easier than re-creating an event.

Click Dial-Up Connection to configure HomeSeer's connection to the Internet if you don't use a broadband home network.

Click OK to complete the event.

## Viewing the Event Log

HomeSeer, as you have already seen, is a powerful and complex program. To review what you have done with it since installation or to determine whether there are any errors in a script you are using, click the Log (notebook) icon at the left side of the screen. The event log is displayed (as in Figure 11.31).

**FIGURE 11.31**

Viewing a section of the event log.

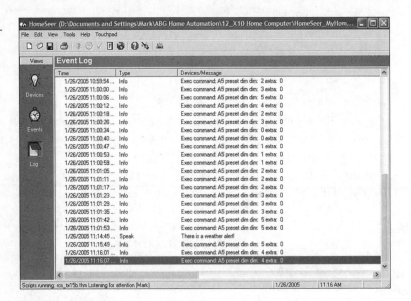

To clear the log, stop updates, or open the log in a new window, right-click anywhere in the Event Log window and select the appropriate option from the contextual menu.

## Using Device Control

Instead of drilling down through the device menu to control a particular device, you can click the Control Panel icon (the yellow light switch icon) at the top of the HomeSeer display to open the Device Control dialog. The Device Control dialog enables you to send commands to a specified device, to all lights (on/off), to all units (off only), or to only the specified address. With a light switch, you can use it to send standard, preset, or Leviton dim commands. You can also use this dialog to send address strings to a SwitchLinc or LampLinc module for scene programming as discussed in Chapter 6; click Address Only to send the address without a command.

## Using the Tools Menu

The Tools menu features a variety of utilities you can use to configure various parts of HomeSeer. These include the following:

- **Get Device Status**—Use this utility to determine the status of a two-way device
- **Security Mode**—Turns on security mode for events that are security enabled (refer to the "Selecting a Trigger for an Event" section earlier in this chapter)
- **Enable All Events**
- **Disable All Events**
- **Listen for Commands**—Enable this option if you use voice commands
- **MSAgent Properties**—Configures speech options for Genie and other agents
- **Assistant Wizard**—Opens HomeSeer Assistant Wizard
- **Voice Recognition Properties**—Use this utility to fine-tune the sensitivity and accuracy of HomeSeer's voice recognition engine
- **Voice Recognition Training**—Runs the Microsoft Speech Training Wizard, which optimizes voice recognition performance and accuracy
- **Reset Device Status**—Resets all devices to unknown; use if your devices do not properly report their status
- **Edit Startup Script**—Opens the Startup script in Notepad
- **Edit Shutdown Script**—Opens the Shutdown script in Notepad

> ## caution
>
> The scripting tools in HomeSeer (it supports VBScript and other programming languages) enable it to perform almost any home automation task, but be careful if you're not familiar with writing scripts (which are, essentially, short computer programs). Carefully study the help files and script examples provided as part of HomeSeer (use the Updater to download examples) before you modify a script. Modify existing scripts, save the changes with different names, and make sure that you understand how they work before you try creating a script from scratch.

# Using X10 ActiveHome Pro

X10's ActiveHome Pro is an enhanced version of the original X10 ActiveHome software. ActiveHome Pro is bundled with the X10 CM15A two-way X10 computer interface. The CM15A also acts as an all-house-code RF transceiver for use with X10 and

X10-compatible wireless remote controls. The CM15A uses four AAA batteries to back up its built-in memory and timer, enabling you to use it to run your home automation system without a PC.

ActiveHome Pro has built-in support for X10-brand and Leviton-brand modules, light switches, and other X10 devices. ActiveHome Pro can also be used with other X10-compatible modules and switches. ActiveHome Pro requires Windows 98SE, Windows Me, Windows 2000, or Windows XP. It supports interactive control of X10 modules, timers, and macros. Purchase the optional Smart Macros plugin to add conditional macros using If-Then and AND-OR-ELSE logic.

**caution**

During installation of the CM15A, make sure you follow the manufacturer's instructions to insert the batteries only after the module has been connected to an AC wall outlet and to your PC's USB ports. If you install the batteries first, Windows will detect the module as an "unknown device" and it will not work until you remove the batteries and install it correctly.

## Registering ActiveHome Pro

When you start ActiveHome Pro for the first time, you need to enter the registration code emailed to you by X10.com. Enter the code and click Register Now! When the registration code entry field changes to "Registered," click Close to use the program. If your installation uses plugins, they also need to be registered.

**EARLY UPDATES HELP MAKE AUTOMATION EASIER**

Check for updates as soon as you install ActiveHome Professional. Click Help, Check for Update. Install the updates as soon as you can to add more features and fix any program bugs that might be present. See "Updating ActiveHome Professional" later in this chapter, for details.

## Working with My Room

When you start ActiveHome Pro for the first time, you automatically open a sample home automation configuration called "My Room." My Room has four predefined components (refer to Figure 11.32):

- My Lamp (control for an X10 lamp module); A1
- My Appliance (control for an X10 appliance module); A2
- Sample Macro 1; A3 Off
- Sample Macro 2; A3 On

To learn how to use ActiveHome Pro, I recommend you modify these components to match a room in your current home automation configuration.

## Modifying My Room's Module Addresses

To change the house and unit code (X10 address) used by the lamp module, click the address field in My Lamp and type in the correct house/unit code. To change the X10 address used by the appliance module, click the address field in My Appliance and type in the correct house/unit code. Figure 11.32 shows the My Lamp and My Appliance controls after being changed to match the modules installed in my home.

**FIGURE 11.32**

My Home after changing the default X10 addresses for My Lamp and My Appliance to the correct X10 addresses for a room in my home.

## Modifying My Room's Name

To rename My Room to the name of an actual room in your house, right-click My Room in the Rooms menu in the left-hand window and select Rename Room. Enter the name of the room in the Rename Room dialog that appears and select a header color for the modules in this room. Click OK.

## Renaming and Editing a Module

To edit the name or other information for a module, right-click the module control and select Edit Module. In the Edit Module dialog (see Figure 11.33), enter a new name for the module, select the module type (lamp, appliance, sensor, retail, pro modules, security, other), select a specific model of module, the room where the module is located, and the X10 address (house/unit code). Click OK when finished.

**FIGURE 11.33**

Editing a
module.

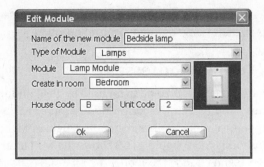

## Removing Modules from a Room

To remove a module from a room, right-click the module in the right-side menu
and select Delete Module. Click OK on the confirming dialog. Note that any timers
used by the module are also deleted.

Deleted modules are placed in ActiveHome Professional's own Recycle Bin, which is
located at the bottom of the left-hand menu. To learn how to retrieve deleted modules, see "Retrieving a Deleted Module," later in this chapter.

## Adding a Module to a Room

To add a module to a room, click the type of module you want to add from the
Modules section of the left-hand menu. Click the double-down arrow next to
Modules to display the list if it not visible. After you select the module type, a new
window opens on the bottom of the screen (see Figure 11.34).

**FIGURE 11.34**

Selecting a mod-
ule type from the
Modules menu.

Click to start downloading update

Click the module you want to add to the room and drag it to the room section of the dialog. Release the module, and an Edit Module dialog appears similar to the one shown in Figure 11.33. Enter the name you want to use to identify the module, enter the X10 address the module uses, edit any other settings necessary, and click OK.

After you have added the modules you want, close the Modules dialog at the bottom of the screen by clicking the X next to the Order Direct button.

---

**FAST ORDERING FOR X10-BRAND MODULES**

You can order X10-brand modules from the X10.com website by clicking the Order Direct button shown in Figure 11.34. An order page for the particular model at the X10.com website opens when you click the Order button on the control dialog for each module (refer to Figure 11.35).

---

## Controlling Modules Interactively

You can control modules interactively with ActiveHome Pro. Click the switch to turn on a lamp or appliance module. With a lamp module, drag the slider to the desired brightness. See Figure 11.35 for an example.

**FIGURE 11.35**

Turning on lamp modules to full brightness and 44% brightness.

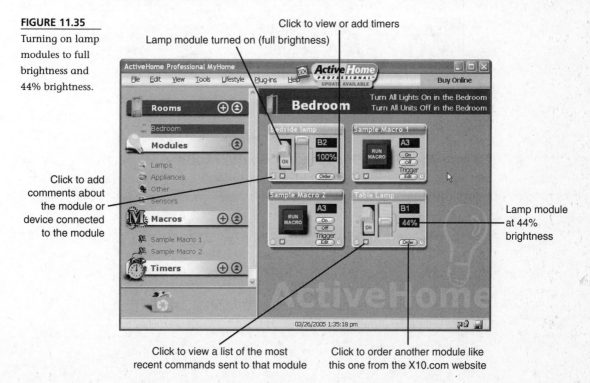

Click to view or add timers

Lamp module turned on (full brightness)

Click to add comments about the module or device connected to the module

Lamp module at 44% brightness

Click to view a list of the most recent commands sent to that module

Click to order another module like this one from the X10.com website

## Creating a Timed Event

To unleash the real power of computer control of X10 modules with ActiveHome Pro, add a timer to a module. A timer (comparable to a timed event in other home automation programs) turns on and turns off a module according to the time of day, dawn, or dusk. To view existing timers or set up a new timer, click the timer button (refer to Figure 11.35) to open the Timer Designer (see Figure 11.36).

**FIGURE 11.36**

Working with the Timer Designer in its default (simple) mode.

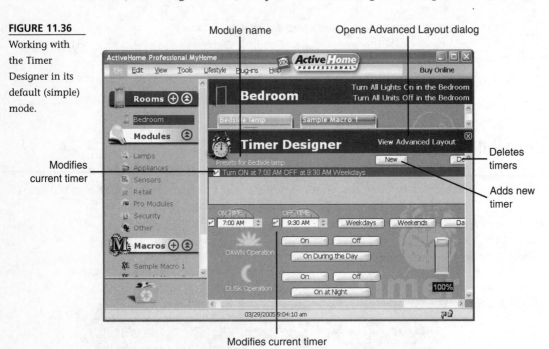

Module name
Opens Advanced Layout dialog

Modifies current timer

Deletes timers

Adds new timer

Modifies current timer

## Using the Timer Designer in Simple Mode

To modify an existing timer, highlight it at the top of the Timer Designer. From the default (simple) mode, you can

- Adjust on/off time
- Select dusk-to-dawn or dawn-to-dusk operation
- Turn module on at dawn or on at dusk
- Select dimming level for lamp modules
- Weekday, Weekend, or Daily operation
- Delete the timer

To set a particular time to turn on a module, make sure the time field is white. If the time field is grayed out, click the On button for Dawn or Dusk until the field is white. Enter the time, or scroll through time in five-minute increments with the up and down arrows.

To select dusk-to-dawn operation, click On at Night. To select dawn-to-dusk operation, click On During the Day. To turn a module on or off at dawn or dusk, click the On or Off button next to DAWN Operation or DUSK Operation.

To adjust the dimming level for a lamp module, drag the slider to the desired dimming level.

To specify daily operation of this timer, click Daily. To use the timer on Monday-Friday only, click Weekdays. To use the timer on Saturday and Sunday only, click Weekends.

To delete the highlighted timer, click Delete.

To add a new timer, click New. The same options are available for a new timer as for an existing timer.

Figure 11.37 shows the full Timer Designer in default (simple) mode after creating new timers for the bedside lamp.

**FIGURE 11.37**

Using the Timer Designer to create multiple timers for a single module.

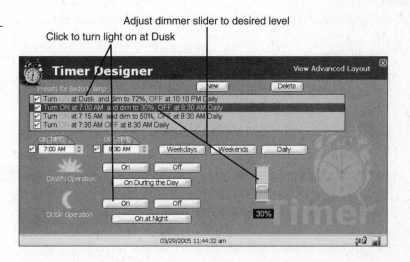

To set a particular time to turn on a module, make sure the time field is white. If the

## Using the Timer Designer's Advanced Mode

If you want to specify particular days of the week in a timer or adjust the start and ending times of a timer for improved security, click View Advanced Layout (refer to Figure 11.36) to open the dialog shown in Figure 11.38.

## Closing Timer Designer

When you are finished using the Timer Designer in either mode, click the X at the upper right-hand corner of the Timer Designer window to close the Timer Designer.

**FIGURE 11.38**

Using Advanced
Layout to create
a Sunday-only
timer.

Dawn timer delay options

Switches to simple layout mode

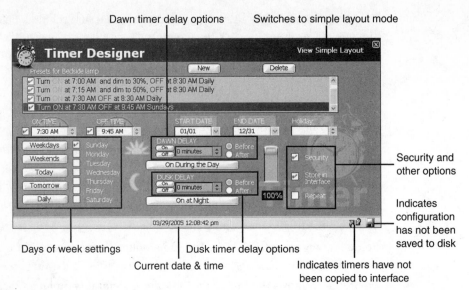

Security and
other options

Indicates
configuration
has not been
saved to disk

Days of week settings

Current date & time

Dusk timer delay options

Indicates timers have not
been copied to interface

## Adding a Room

To add a room to ActiveHome Pro, click the plus (+) sign next to Rooms in the left-hand menu. When the Add a Room dialog appears, enter the name of the room to create, select a header color for the modules in the room, and click OK to create the room. After you add a new room to your configuration, use the Modules menu to add modules to the room. See "Adding a Module to a Room" earlier in this chapter, for details.

## Storing Changes to Your Configuration

To save changes and additions to the default
ActiveHome Pro configuration under a different
name, click File, Save As. Enter the name you
want to use for the new configuration, and
click Save. By default, your configurations are
stored in the default ActiveHome Pro folder
unless you choose a different location. See
Figure 11.39.

## Updating ActiveHome Professional

By default, ActiveHome Professional checks
for updates automatically and displays an
"Update Available" button at the top of the
screen when an update is available. Click this
button to start the update process. You can
also check for updates through the Help menu.

**caution**

ActiveHome Pro must be
shut down during the
update process. It will
save over the existing
configuration. If you have
modified My Home and prefer to
save your changes to your own file-
name, save the changes as discussed in "Storing Changes to Your
Configuration."

**FIGURE 11.39**

Saving your
ActiveHome Pro
configuration.

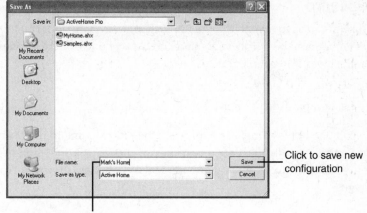

Click to save new
configuration

Enter name of new configuration

An update history dialog (see Figure 11.40) is displayed when you click the Update
Available button. Information about the latest update is listed at the top; scroll down
for earlier versions. Click Update to continue the process.

**FIGURE 11.40**

Viewing the
ActiveHome
Professional
update history.

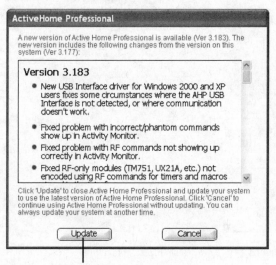

Click to download the latest update

On the Welcome dialog that follows, click Next to continue. Click OK on the
Application Shutdown dialog to shut down ActiveHome Professional. The Installing
dialog appears briefly, listing each file as it is downloaded to your system. If the download includes updates for the CM15A ActiveHome Pro USB interface, make sure it is
connected to your computer before you click OK on the X10 Hardware Setup dialog. To
complete the update process, click OK on the ActiveHome Pro Update dialog.
ActiveHome Pro restarts automatically.

# Creating a Macro

You can make your ActiveHome Pro system even more powerful by creating macros, which are a sequence of events that can involve one or more modules. ActiveHome Pro includes two sample macros:

- Sample Macro 1 is blank.
- Sample Macro 2 has three pauses built into it.

To edit one of the sample macros, click the macro name in the Macros section of the left-side menu. To create a new macro, click the plus (+) sign next to Macros in the left-side menu. In either case, the Macro Designer (shown in Figure 11.41) opens.

**FIGURE 11.41**

The ActiveHome Professional Macro Designer.

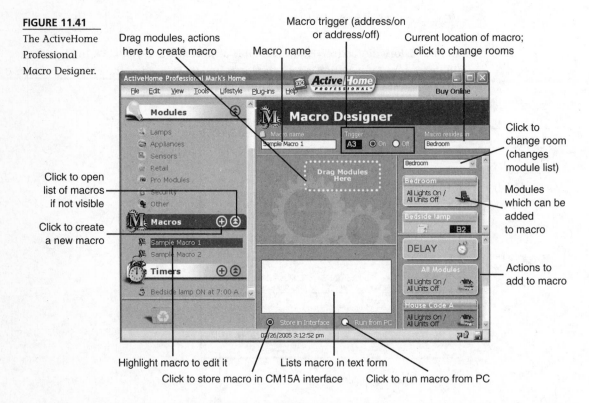

Drag modules, actions here to create macro

Macro trigger (address/on or address/off)

Macro name

Current location of macro; click to change rooms

Click to change room (changes module list)

Click to open list of macros if not visible

Modules which can be added to macro

Click to create a new macro

DELAY

Actions to add to macro

Highlight macro to edit it

Lists macro in text form

Click to store macro in CM15A interface

Click to run macro from PC

Add steps to the macro by dragging a module from the modules list or an action from the actions list shown in Figure 11.41. For example, to create the macro shown in Figure 11.42, I performed the following steps:

1. I dragged the Bedside Lamp module into place to create step 1.

2. I set the brightness slider to 61%.

3. I dragged the Delay action into place to create step 2.

4. The Delay time is 00:05:00 (5 minutes) by default. If I had wanted to change the default to a different time, I could have typed in the delay I wanted or clicked on the up/down arrow buttons in the Delay icon.

5. I dragged the Table Lamp module into place to create step 3. I did not adjust the brightness of this lamp.

**FIGURE 11.42**

A three-step macro that turns on one lamp, waits, and then turns on the other lamp.

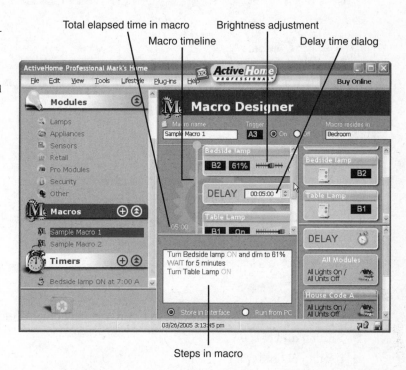

Total elapsed time in macro    Brightness adjustment

Macro timeline    Delay time dialog

Steps in macro

## Testing, Viewing Editing, and Deleting Macros

After you create your macro, you should test it. To test the macro, right-click on the macro in the Macros section of the left-side menu. Select Trigger Macro.

To edit a macro, right-click it and select Edit Macro or just click the macro name. To view all your macros in a compact form, right-click any macro and select Macro Summary View (see Figure 11.43).

To edit the steps in any macro from Macro Summary View, click the Edit button. To add a timer to any macro from Macro Summary View, click the Timer button.

To delete a macro, right-click the macro in the Macros listing and select Delete Macro. When the Delete this Module dialog appears, click OK to delete the macro. If you don't want to confirm the deletion each time, click the Don't Ask Again box in the Delete this Module dialog before you click OK.

**FIGURE 11.43**

Viewing macros in Macro Summary View.

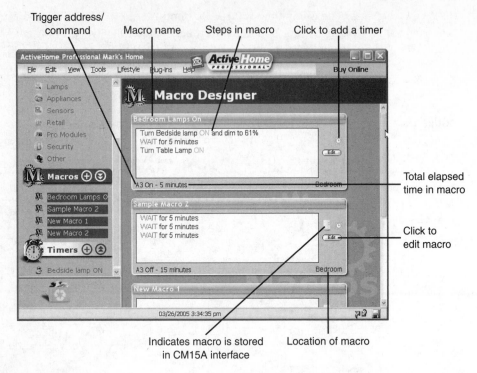

Trigger address/ command

Macro name

Steps in macro

Click to add a timer

Total elapsed time in macro

Click to edit macro

Indicates macro is stored in CM15A interface

Location of macro

## Using the Tools Menu

Use the Tools menu (see Figure 11.44) to perform a variety of tasks including

- Turning all lights on
- Turning all units off
- Working with the CM15A interface module (downloading, clearing the memory, setting up the module)
- Controlling lights, appliances, and units
- Monitoring activity
- Configuring preferences

### Downloading Your Configuration

The CM15A interface provided as part of ActiveHome Pro can store programs and run them without being connected to your computer. After you save your configuration (see "Storing Changes to Your Configuration" earlier in this chapter for details), click Tools in the top-level menu, and then click Download Timers and Macros. Click Yes on the Warning dialog that appears to continue. At the end of the process, a Message dialog indicating the timers and macros have been downloaded appears. Click OK to close the dialog.

**FIGURE 11.44**

Turning on bed-
room lights
using
ActiveHome
Professional's
Tools menu.

The first time you download your configuration to the CM15A, you will need to configure your hardware interface if you did not do so through the Hardware Interface
Configuration option in the Tools menu. When prompted, select the location, set up
the CM15A's RF transceiver, and select the house code you want to monitor. Click
Update Interface when done. See Figure 11.45.

**FIGURE 11.45**

The Hardware
Interface
Configuration
dialog.

Select location

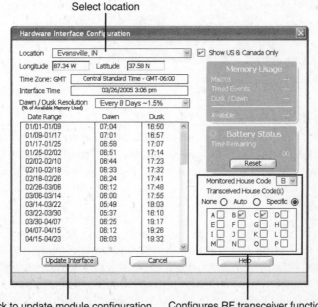

Click to update module configuration    Configures RF transceiver function

## Editing Preferences

To change the default settings used by ActiveHome Pro, select Preferences from the Tools menu. The Preferences menu is in two parts. The first part includes Action Warnings; for every action in this section that is checkmarked, you must confirm the action before it takes place. This default helps you to avoid deleting modules or other settings by mistake. Clear the checkmarks to skip the confirmation dialog. The second part of the preferences menu is used to configure other parts of the program. Figure 11.46 shows the entire preferences menu's list of defaults. (Note that you might need to scroll to see all of it on your PC.) Click Close when you have reviewed or edited the settings in the Preferences dialog.

**FIGURE 11.46**

The ActiveHome Professional Preferences menu.

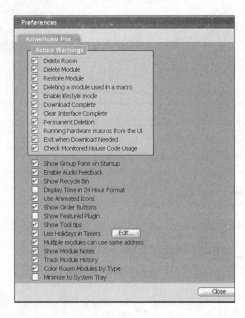

## Viewing the Activity Monitor

ActiveHome Professional stores all X10 commands you have sent to modules in its Activity Monitor. This includes commands given with remote controls, tabletop controllers, or X10-enabled wall switches. To see the contents of the Activity Monitor (Figure 11.47), press the F2 key or click Activity Monitor from the Tools menu.

# Using Lifestyle Mode

As an alternative to setting up macros and timers, you can use the Lifestyle Mode to automatically play back every X10 command sent by ActiveHome Professional in the last 24 hours. To activate Lifestyle Mode, click Lifestyle in the top-level menu and then click Enable Lifestyle. Click OK on the confirming dialog (see Figure 11.48).

**FIGURE 11.47**

The ActiveHome
Professional
Activity Monitor.

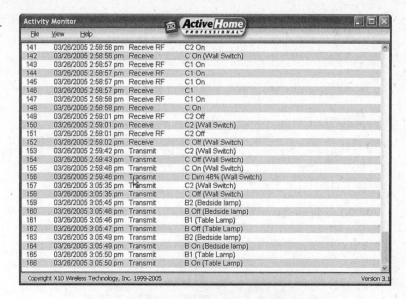

**FIGURE 11.47**

The ActiveHome
Professional
Activity Monitor.

**FIGURE 11.48**

Preparing to
enable Lifestyle
Mode.

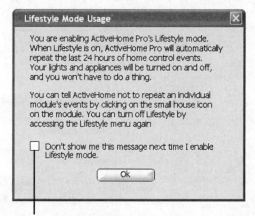

Click to turn off this confirmation dialog.

When ActiveHome Pro is running in Lifestyle Mode, an animated house icon appears in the lower right-hand corner of the program screen. To prevent a particular module from being controlled by Lifestyle Mode, click the small red house button on each module dialog. When the house turns blue, it is not controlled by Lifestyle Mode. See Figure 11.49.

To disable Lifestyle Mode, click Lifestyle, Lifestyle Mode again to uncheck it.

## Retrieving a Deleted Module

After you delete a module, you might need to retrieve it. To see deleted modules, click the Recycle Bin icon in the bottom left-hand corner of the ActiveHome Professional screen (see Figure 11.50). To retrieve a deleted module, drag the module to the room you want to use it in. Click OK on the Restore This Module dialog.

**FIGURE 11.49**

ActiveHome Professional running in Lifestyle Mode.

Click red house to disable Lifestyle Mode for that module

Checkmark indicates Lifestyle Mode is selected.

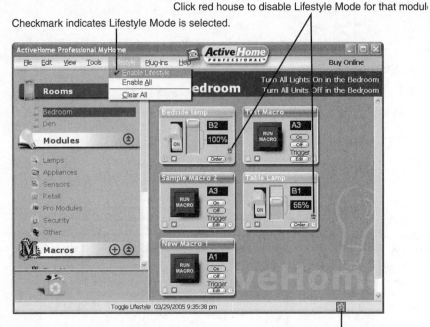

Indicates Lifestyle Mode is selected.

**FIGURE 11.50**

Restoring a deleted module.

Deleted modules

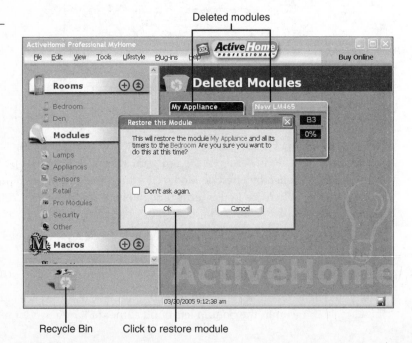

Recycle Bin       Click to restore module

To delete modules from the Recycle Bin, right-click it and select Empty Deleted Modules.

## Ordering SmartMacros and Other Plug-ins

To see which plug-ins are available for ActiveHome Pro, click the Plug-Ins menu and select Download Plug-Ins. This opens the ActiveHome Pro plug-ins page at www.activehomepro.com/plugins/index.html.

The SmartMacros plug-in adds conditional logic to macros, the ability to trigger macros with various types of X10 hardware, timers, and macros, and an Advanced Mode that adds IF/AND/OR/ELSE logic and other features. SmartMacros are created using drag-and-drop editing.

The iWitness plugin enables you to view and control X10 security cameras with ActiveHome Pro.

For pricing, order information, and screen shots, see the ActiveHome Pro plug-ins page.

## Creating Reports and Printing Labels

Use the File, Reports menu to create three types of reports about your SmartHome system:

- The General report opens a web page listing each room in your home, each module, and each macro.
- The Macros report opens a web page listing each macro and the commands it contains.
- The Status report opens a web page listing information for the CM15A interface.

Use the File menu in your web browser to save or print each report.

Use the File, Print Labels command to print labels for PalmPad remote controls. Specify the house code you want to use, or select All to print labels for all house codes.

## Finding Other Computers

To determine which X10 address ranges might be in use in your vicinity, click Tools, Find Other Computers. The X10 Code Usage–Historical window lists modules and macros you have added to your ActiveHome Pro system in green, activity from modules you have not yet added (or might belong to another home automation system nearby) in red, and ranges it might not be safe to use in yellow. See Figure 11.51 for an example.

**FIGURE 11.51**

X10 Address
Activity.

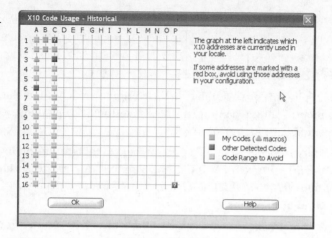

If you are using X10 or X10-compatible modules you have not yet added to your ActiveHome Pro configuration, they will show up as yellow or red blocks in this grid. After you have added all of your modules, switches and other devices to your configuration, this report will be useful in determining if you are receiving signals from another X10 installation.

## caution

If addresses in your preferred house code range(s) are being used by other systems, consider changing the house codes on your modules. If you do so, be sure to change the settings in ActiveHome Pro.

# Troubleshooting Computer Control of X10-Based Systems

If you're having problems with computer control of your X10 system, follow these guidelines to help solve the problem:

- Make sure that you are using only one method to control your system. Unplug mini-timers and don't let other family members fiddle around with remotes while you configure your system.

- If you switch home automation programs and you use an interface with a built-in timer and memory, clear the interface's onboard memory with its reset button. This will prevent the interface from running its existing program, which might interfere with new configurations you create.

- If some events don't work correctly, double-check your house and unit code settings for your devices and for any scenes you have created.

- Make sure that you select the correct device type for your module. For example, if you select a generic lamp module for a two-way module with scene capability, you won't be able to configure the module's advanced features with your program unless you program the module with a Maxi Controller and set up your program to control the module with the scene address rather than its physical address.

■ Check for program updates frequently.

■ If you are unable to send home automation commands with your selected controller, make sure that you are using a working USB or serial (COM) port. Try a different type of device with the selected port. If nothing works with the port you are using, the port is disabled or defective. See your computer's instruction manual to learn how to enable a disabled port or contact the vendor for help.

■ If you are using a serial interface controller, make sure that you have properly identified the port in the setup procedure for your program.

   ■ Use the reset button or reset command in your home automation program to clear the interface's memory and download fresh configuration and programming information.

   ■ If the module uses batteries, check battery condition and the battery terminals. Replace leaky or corroded batteries immediately to avoid damaging your module.

# THE ABSOLUTE MINIMUM

■ To control your home automation system with your home computer, you need a controller module that is compatible with your system and software compatible with your system and your controller.

■ Although serial port controllers for X10 are still available, you're better off using the USB port for your controller.

■ Before you purchase a controller for your PC, make sure that the software included with the controller has the features you want or that you can use third-party software with the features you want with that controller.

■ You must install the software provided with the controller before you connect the controller to your PC.

■ Smarthome Manager controls X10 devices using four icons: Locations, All Devices, Event Triggered Action, and Time Triggered Action.

■ Smarthome Manager can control a wide variety of standard X10 devices, and it has specific support for Smarthome's own LampLinc and SwitchLinc modules.

■ You can control an X10 module interactively with Smarthome Manager.

*continues*

- A timed action can contain many steps, including triggering of multiple devices and delays between each step.

- An event-triggered action can be triggered by one or more conditions; the full version of Smarthome Manager supports more conditions than the Essential version.

- Smarthome Manager can download its program to a controller with onboard memory and timer, enabling you to control your home when your computer is turned off or not present.

- Use the Advanced Controller option in the Tools menu to monitor X10 commands or to send commands to a specified device.

- Use the SwitchLinc/LampLinc dialog to make creating scenes and controlling other advanced options for these devices easier.

- HomeSeer works with X10, Z-Wave, and most other popular home automation products through the use of standard or optional extra-cost plugin modules.

- HomeSeer supports voice commands as well as standard types of event triggers for X10 and other devices.

- HomeSeer uses a single wizard to set up time- or conditional-triggered events.

- HomeSeer events can include program launches, email notifications, and computer-generated speech as well as triggering X10 or other home automation devices.

- HomeSeer's support for VBScript and other scripting languages enables you to customize the program to perform many different types of home automation and computer control tasks.

- ActiveHome Professional uses a single USB interface (the CM15A) to provide both computer control and RF remote control of your X10 home automation system.

- ActiveHome Professional uses a visual drag-and-drop interface to set up modules and macros.

- ActiveHome Professional can control X10 modules interactively.

- The Lifestyle Mode enables ActiveHome Professional to play back the last 24 hours of X10 commands sent by the program as an alternative to creating timers and macros.

- Add the optional SmartMacros plug-in to add conditional logic to macros.

- Problems with computer control of home automation can be caused by configuration problems with your computer's hardware, conflicts between controllers, or incorrect configuration of your X10 devices or your controller.

12

# ACCESSING X10 HOME CONTROL VIA YOUR HOME NETWORK AND THE INTERNET

If you use a home computer to control your X10-based home automation system (as discussed in Chapter 11, "Accessing X10 Home Control via Your Home Computer"), it's natural to wonder whether you can control your home from another computer on the network or from another location via the Internet. As this chapter reveals, you can indeed use the power of a home network and the Internet to make *remote* home control a reality.

# Methods for Accessing Your Home Automation System Remotely

There are several methods you can use to control your X10 based home automation system via a home network or the Internet:

- Web server application running on your computer
- Remote access software
- Remote access service

Depending on the software and hardware you use for PC-based home control (refer to Chapter 11 for some typical examples), you might be able to choose between two or more of these solutions.

If you want to control your X10 home automation system from another computer in your home, you need to install some type of wired or wireless home network. If you want to use the Internet to manage your home automation system, you need to install an always-on network connection such as cable or DSL and connect your home computer(s) to it.

**caution**

To learn how to choose, install, configure, and secure your home network and broadband Internet connection, see my book Absolute *Beginner's Guide to Home Networking* (ISBN 078973205X, Que, 2005).

## Integrated Web Server

Some X10 home automation programs include an integrated web server to enable remote access. A web server provides a web-based interface with your home automation software, enabling you to view and edit settings from other computers on your home network or the Internet. To access the web server from another computer on your home network, enter the IP address of the computer running the web server. To access the web server from a remote computer, enter your home network's public IP address and the TCP port used by the web server or an alias you obtain from a dynamic DNS provider.

See the sidebar "Discovering Web-Enabled X10 PLC Software Solutions," later in this chapter, for a list of home automation programs with integrated web servers and their websites.

---

### DISCOVERING WEB-ENABLED X10 SOFTWARE SOLUTIONS

For more information, including free trial versions in some cases, visit these vendors' websites:

- All House Access—www.allhouseaccess.com
- Premise Home Control—www.premisesystems.com
- HomeSeer—www.homeseer.com
- Central Home Automation Director (CHAD)—www.improvingtomorrow.com
- Event Control System (ECS)—www.omnipotencesoftware.com
- HAL (Home Automated Living) series (HALbasic, HALdeluxe, HAL2000)—www.automatedliving.com
- Home Domination Home Automation Software—www.homedomination.com
- Meedio HouseBot—meedio.com/whatismeedio/housebot/
- PowerHome—www.power-home.com

You can find direct links to most of these vendors and many others from the Home Automation Software Directory at X-10 Ideas (www.x10ideas.com/software/XcDirectory.asp). Many of this products also support webcams and netcams. See the vendors' websites for details.

If you already have HomeControl Assistant 5 Plus or Home Control Assistant 5 Pro, you can use the HCAWeb plug-in from Net Endeavors, Inc to add a web server. Download a trial version or buy it from www.homecontrolassistant.info.

Add Web-Link II to make Home Automation Inc's HAI Omni home automation products web-enabled. Learn more at www.homeauto.com.

---

## Remote Access Software and Services

If your preferred home automation software does not include or cannot be upgraded to provide built-in web access, you still have remote access options. You can use remote access software or remote access services from various vendors to create a connection between the home PC and a remote PC. Remote access software programs such as PC Anywhere (Symantec) or LapLink Gold are difficult for nonprofessionals to use and require you to install complex client and server software. On the other hand, remote access services offer web-based access with minimal configuration of the server and an easy-to-use client. Some remote access services support remote connections from PDAs, smart phone devices, and PCs running a non-Windows operating system, such as Mac OS or Linux.

# Selecting the Right Home Networking/Web Access Solution

As you learned in previous sections, you can choose from several methods for remote network or Web access to your X10 home automation system. Which one is right for you? Consider these issues when you select a home networking/Web access solution:

- **Does the vendor of your current hardware/software offer a software or service upgrade to provide web-based access?**—If so, this can be the least expensive choice, especially if your home computer has a static IP address. It's also the simplest because you don't need to install anything on the client PC you will use to access your home automation software remotely. All you need is a working Internet connection.

- **If you cannot upgrade your current software, do you need to control your X10 home automation system from more than one PC?**—If so, consider remote access services. As a bonus, remote access services, unlike a web server application, enable you to run all the programs on your home PC from a remote PC.

**caution**

Although web server support might be built into your X10 home automation software, it might not be a totally free upgrade.

If you're lucky enough to have a static (never-changing) IP address and only one computer connected to your broadband Internet connection, connecting to your web server remotely is as easy as entering the IP address of your home computer. However, if your ISP provides you with a dynamic (changing) IP address, you need to use a dynamic DNS service that can track the changes in your IP address and enable you to connect using an alias. And if your home computer is on a home network, you need to reconfigure your router or gateway to send traffic to the computer that runs your home automation software. See the "Using an Integrated Web Server" section later in this chapter for details.

Table 12.1 helps provide a visual checklist to help you make the right choice.

**TABLE 12.1**  Moving to Network or Web-Based X10 Home Automation Control

|  | Built-in Web Server Software | Web Server Upgrade | Online Service Upgrade | Remote Access Service | Remote Access Software |
|---|---|---|---|---|---|
| Works with any X10 controller and software | No | No | No | Yes | Yes |
| Free solution | 2 | No, 2 | No | 1 | 2 |
| One-time cost solution | — | Yes, 2 | No | No | 2 |
| Monthly, yearly subscription | No | No | Yes | 1 | No |
| Works with any remote PC with Web connection | Yes | Yes | Yes | Yes | No |

1. *Some vendors offer free basic remote access services. Advanced features such as file transfer and synchronization (which are not required for home automation remote control but are useful for other types of remote work) require a paid subscription.*

2. *Requires the user to use a static IP address to enable remote computers to access the web server or to subscribe to a dynamic DNS (DDNS) service to enable the web server to be accessed when the PC or home network uses a dynamic IP address (typical with almost all home broadband Internet access types).*

# Configuring Your Home Automation System for Remote Access

To get ready for remote access to your home automation software, you might need to

- Enable the web server feature in your home automation software
- Upgrade your home automation software to a version containing a web server
- Subscribe to a service provided by your home automation software vendor to make your system network/Web-enabled
- Install a hardware device to make your system network/Web-enabled
- Install remote access software
- Subscribe to a remote-access service

## Upgrading Software

If you need to upgrade your X10 home automation software to add web server capabilities, contact your vendor for upgrade details. Generally, you will need to

1. Pay an upgrade fee to move to a more sophisticated version
2. Download the upgrade
3. Install the upgrade

If you are using a noncurrent version of a home automation program, you might still be able to upgrade to a current version with a built-in web server. However, in most cases, a version/feature upgrade is more expensive than a feature upgrade in the same version.

## Using an Integrated Web Server

X10 home automation software that contains a web server (either built-in or as an upgrade) will generally have a menu option for starting and configuring the web server. HomeSeer, the example we'll look at in the following sections, enables you to start a web server either at startup or from its View menu.

### Enabling and Configuring the Web Server in HomeSeer

To start the web server from the HomeSeer Assistant Wizard, select Enable and Set Up the Web Server and View My Web Page; click Next to continue. Click Next on each of the next two dialogs until your default web browser opens and displays the HomeSeer Web Control dialog (see Figure 12.1).

**FIGURE 12.1**

The HomeSeer Web Control web server.

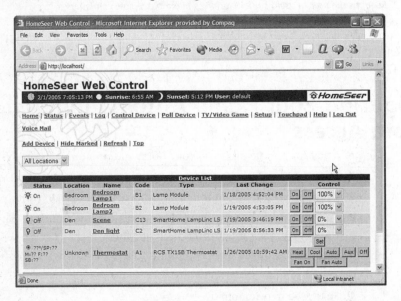

Users who log in to the web server will see a similar display. To close the configuration dialog and leave the web server running, click Finish on the Setup Web Server dialog shown in Figure 12.2. Before closing this dialog, be sure to note the IP address listed; you'll need it to log in to this computer from another computer on your home network.

Every time you start HomeSeer or another home automation program that includes a web server, make sure that you enable the web server. To keep it running for remote access, don't shut down your home automation program or computer.

**FIGURE 12.2**

Completing the HomeSeer web server setup. Take note of the IP address listed so that you can access the web server.

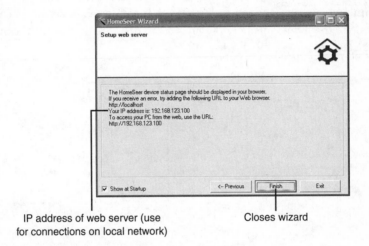

IP address of web server (use
for connections on local network)

Closes wizard

## Logging On to a Home Automation Web Server

To log on to the web server from another computer on your home network, enter the IP address of the computer running the web server into the web browser's address window on the remote computer. For example, if the computer hosting the web server is using an IP address of 172.16.0.100, open your preferred web browser, enter **http://172.16.0.100** into the address bar, and press the Enter key to open the web server interface to your home automation software.

As Figure 12.2 shows, HomeSeer displays this information in its Web Server Setup Wizard. If your home automation program's web server does not display the IP address of your PC, you can use the ipconfig command-line program or the Network Connections dialog, which shows your computer's local area connection, to determine your IP address in Windows XP or Windows 2000. See Figure 12.3 for examples of both methods. Note that the actual IP address on your computer will be different. The Winipcfg program provides similar information for Windows 9x/Me.

To log on to a web server from a remote computer not located on your home network, you normally cannot use the actual IP address of the computer on the home network. Here's why: On a home network, private IP addresses (addresses in the ranges 192.168.xxx.xxx or 172.16.xxx.xxx–172.31.xxx.xxx) are used; the 192.168.xxx.xxx network address range is the most common one. These addresses cannot be used on a public network. To connect to a public network, the *router* (the device used to connect a home network to a broadband Internet access device such as a cable or DSL modem) translates private IP addresses into a single public IP address and routes traffic between the computers on the home network and the Internet. Your home network's private IP addresses are never seen by the Internet. Even if the computer running your home automation software is connected directly to a cable or DSL modem, the modem usually provides a private IP address to your computer to help protect it against online hackers.

**FIGURE 12.3**

Using ipconfig or Network Connections to determine your web server's IP address.

Local Area Connection in use by web server

Network Connections

ipconfig command

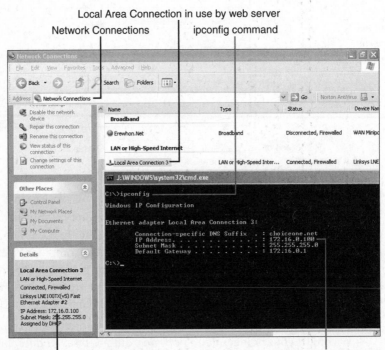

IP address of web server as listed by Network Connections

IP address of web server as listed by IPconfig.

Given this information, how can you log on to your web server from your office, a vacation home, or another remote location? You need to know the public IP address used by your home network or home computer. A no-cost way to learn this information is to use the WhatIsMyIP.com website (www.whatismyip.com) or the Current IP Check page provided by DynDNS.org (checkip.dyndns.org/) to view current public IP address of the computer used to run your home automation system (see Figure 12.4). Use this IP address to log in to your web server remotely.

**FIGURE 12.4**

Open the WhatIsMyISP website from the computer running your web server to determine its current IP address.

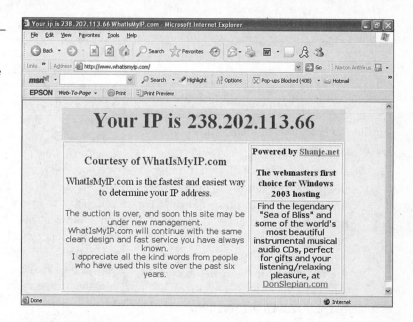

For example, if your home network or home computer's public IP address is 15.8.92.200, open an Internet connection on a remote computer, start your favorite web browser, enter **http://15.8.92.200** and press the Enter key to view the web server interface to your home automation software.

Be sure to configure your web server to ask for usernames and passwords to prevent unauthorized users from logging on to your home automation system and altering settings.

## Handling Nonstandard TCP Port Configurations

TCP ports assigned by default to typical Internet processes, such as web browsers (TCP port 80), file transfer protocol (FTP) programs (TCP ports 20 and 21), SMTP (email) programs (TCP port 25) are often called *well-known port assignments*. These port assignments can be vulnerable to attack from remote hackers. Most web servers enable you to change the default TCP port 80 normally used for the web server to a user-selected port number to improve security. If your home automation program provides for a user-selected TCP port, it will usually be found in the program's configuration screens. Consult your program's documentation for details.

**WHICH TCP PORTS ARE NOT WELL KNOWN?**
To find out which TCP ports are not assigned to default processes, go to www.iss.net/security_center/advice/Exploits/Ports/default.htm. Unlisted port numbers are available for use.

If you change your web server's default TCP port to a different value, you must also make the following changes to your network configuration to enable continued connection to your web server:

- You must add the TCP port number to the IP address you use to access the web server on your home network. For example, if you choose TCP port 1000 and your web server is using IP address 172.16.0.100, you would enter the following into your web browser to log on to the web server:
  **http://172.16.0.100:1000**

- When you access the web server from a remote location via the Internet, use the public IP address followed by the TCP port number. For example, if your home computer or home network uses a public IP address of 15.8.92.200 and your web server uses TCP port 1000, start the Internet connection on the remote PC and enter **http://15.8.92.200:1000**.

- You must also configure your router or wireless access point to allow traffic through the TCP port number you use. This is called *port forwarding*. See Figure 12.5 for a typical example on a Linksys router.

**caution**

Most residential broadband Internet services use dynamic IP addresses. A dynamic IP address can change. Consequently, you should not assume that the public IP address you have today will be the same tomorrow. Sure, you could check your public IP address before heading out to work everyday so that you can control your home automation system from work, but when you go on a vacation or business trip, the address might change before you get back. To learn how to connect with your web server no matter what its public IP address is, see the "Dealing with Dynamic IP Addresses in Your Internet Connection" section later in this chapter.

## Dealing with Dynamic IP Addresses on Your Home Network

If the computer running your home automation software is on a home network, accessing it remotely can be tricky. Here's why: Most home networks shield users from the complexities of setting up an IP address by using server-assigned IP addresses. The IP addresses used to identify computers and devices on a home network are provided by a dynamic host configuration protocol *(DHCP)* server built into a router or gateway. For typical home network and Internet access, this works very nicely. The problem for a computer running a web server (such as a computer running home automation software with web access enabled) is that the computer with the web server might be assigned to one IP address today and a different IP address tomorrow because of the order in which computers and other devices that use IP addresses are turned on and connect to the network.

**FIGURE 12.5**

Forwarding traffic for TCP port 1000 to the computer using private IP address 172.16.0.100.

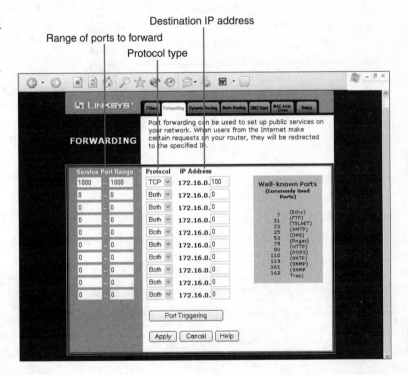

Destination IP address

Range of ports to forward

Protocol type

To enable port forwarding (refer to Figure 12.5) to send traffic to the correct IP address every time, you should configure the computer with the web server to use a fixed IP address.

## Fixed IP Address Configuration

To configure the computer running home automation software with web access to have a fixed IP address, you need to determine the following:

- **IP address and subnet mask**—Use an IP address in the same range as the rest of your network. It must *not* overlap the IP address range used by your router's DHCP server or the router's LAN address. Check the router's DHCP configuration to see allowable address ranges.

- **Default gateway**—This is the LAN address of your router.

- **DNS servers**—These are the IP addresses of the servers that translate hostnames such as www.erewhon.net into IP addresses.

## Determining Available IP Addresses

To determine what IP address to use, reopen your router's DHCP configuration screen and note the IP address range it provides. Use a nonconflicting address in the same range. For example, if the router uses 192.168.123.254 for its LAN address and provides IP addresses from 192.168.123.100 to 192.168.123.105 to clients, any IP address from 192.168.123.0 through 192.168.0.99 and from 192.168.123.106 through 192.168.123.253 would be acceptable. Figure 12.6 illustrates the range of in-use IP addresses as configured on a typical home network using a U.S. Robotics router.

**tip**

You'll probably want to use DHCP for most network clients. So, to leave room, make sure that the IP addresses that you assign are not directly after or directly before the IP addresses provided by the router. Assign the computer running a web server an IP address about 10 addresses before the first IP address provided by the router or after the last IP address provided by the router.

**FIGURE 12.6**

This router is configured to assign IP addresses using DHCP for only six stations (192.168.123.100–105), leaving other addresses in the 192.168.123.xxx range available for use.

First IP address provided by DHCP to other computers

IP address used by router

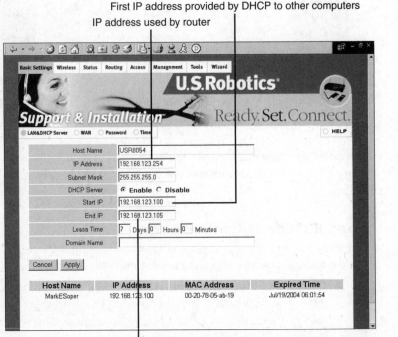

Last IP address provided by DHCP to other computers

The easiest way to get the rest of the information you need is to go to any computer that is working correctly on the network and use the ipconfig (Windows XP, Windows 2000) utility to display network information (see Figure 12.7).

**FIGURE 12.7**

Using ipconfig to determine the subnet mask, default gateway, and DNS server addresses to use for manual IP address configuration.

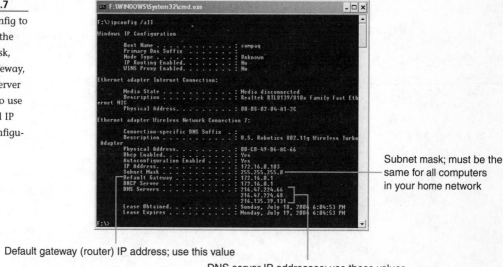

Subnet mask; must be the same for all computers in your home network

Default gateway (router) IP address; use this value

DNS server IP addresses; use these values

Use Tables 12.2 and 12.3 to list the information you need for any manual IP addresses you decide to use on your network.

## TABLE 12.2   Available IP Address Configuration Worksheet

| IP Address Used by (LAN Use for Default address; Gateway in Table 12.3) | IP Addresses Used by DHCP Server in Router | Available IP Addresses Range #1 | Available IP Router Addresses Range #2 |
| --- | --- | --- | --- |
| — | — | — | — |

## TABLE 12.3   Manual IP Address Configuration Information

| Device Description | Available IP Address (from Table 12.2) | Subnet (from ipconfig or Winipcfg) | Default Gateway (Router LAN Address from Table 12.2) | DNS Servers (from ipconfig or Winipcfg) |
| --- | --- | --- | --- | --- |
| — | — | — | — | — |

## Configuring a Windows XP/2000 Computer to Use a Manual IP Address

To configure a manual IP address on a computer running Windows XP or Windows 2000:

1. Right-click My Network Places and select Properties.

2. Right-click the connection you are configuring and select Properties (see Figure 12.8).

**FIGURE 12.8**

Selecting a network connection in Windows XP.

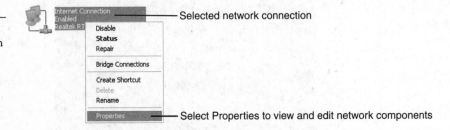

— Selected network connection

— Select Properties to view and edit network components

3. Scroll through the list of network components to Internet Protocol (TCP/IP) and select it.

4. Click Properties (see Figure 12.9).

**FIGURE 12.9**

Selecting TCP/IP for configuration in Windows XP.

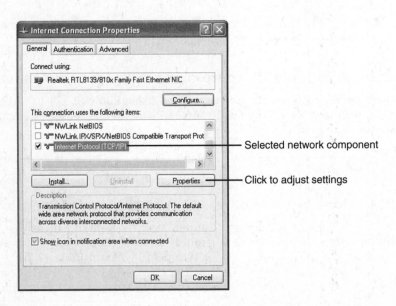

— Selected network component

— Click to adjust settings

By default, Windows 2000 and XP are configured to obtain an IP address automatically (see Figure 12.10). To change this configuration, click Use the Following IP Address and enter the information requested from your worksheet (see Table 12.3):

- IP address
- Subnet mask
- Default gateway

To add the DNS server information, click Use the Following DNS Server Addresses and enter the DNS servers' addresses from Table 12.3.

Figure 12.10 shows a typical configuration before making changes, and Figure 12.11 shows the same system after adding configuration information.

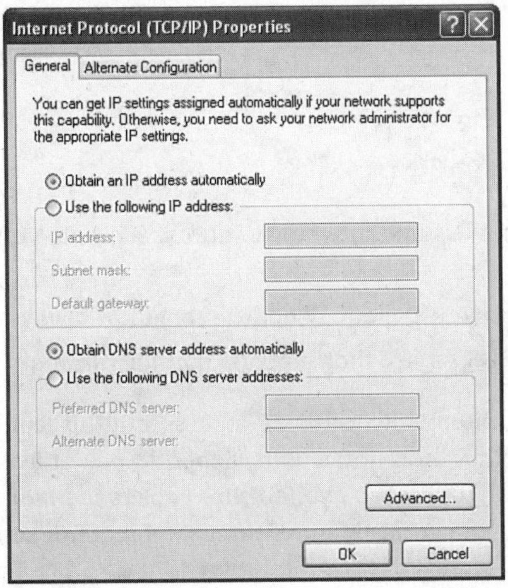

**FIGURE 12.10**

Windows XP
TCP/IP connection using
default server-assigned IP and
DNS settings.

After you've clicked OK, you might need to reboot your computer before the settings will take effect.

## Dealing with Dynamic IP Addresses in Your Internet Connection

Just as computers on a home network receive IP addresses from a range of possible addresses provided by a DHCP server, most home broadband Internet connections use a similar type of dynamic IP address provided by the cable or DSL modem. Although you can use a program to see the current public IP address of your home computer or home network (refer to Figure 12.3), the IP address might not stay the same over time. As with any other type of Internet activity, if you enter the wrong IP address into your web browser, you will end up on a different website or resource than you expected or not find any resource at all to view.

**FIGURE 12.11**

Configuring TCP/IP with user-assigned IP information in Windows XP.

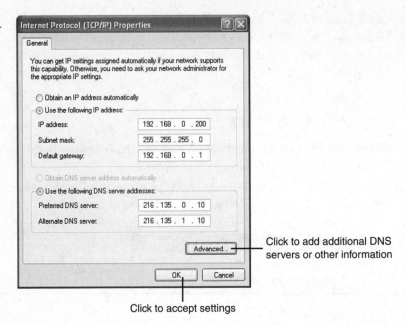

Click to add additional DNS servers or other information

Click to accept settings

There are two ways to make sure that you can always log in to your web server from a remote location:

- Ask your ISP to provide a static IP address (one that always stays the same)
- Use a dynamic DNS service that supports port forwarding

Many broadband ISPs can provide a static IP address, but this feature is usually standard for business rather than home users. Expect to pay at least $5 more/month for a static IP address if available for your residential service. With a static IP address, you no longer need to use WhatIsMyIP.com or similar sites to determine the public IP address of your web server.

For many users, a dynamic DNS service with port forwarding support is a better deal. How does dynamic DNS work? Dynamic DNS servers provide an always-working link between the changing IP address of your home automation or other web server and an alias provided by the dynamic DNS provider. Instead of entering the *IP address:TCP port number* to access the web server, you enter the alias provided by the dynamic DNS service. Dynamic DNS routes the request for the web server through the Internet and the router or gateway on your home network to the computer on your home network that is running the web server. If you don't want to add the TCP port used by your web server to the URL you use to access your home automation system's web server, use the optional port forwarding services offered by most dynamic DNS service providers. Figure 12.12 illustrates remote access using a dynamic DNS service that supports port forwarding.

**FIGURE 12.12**

Using a dynamic DNS service that supports port forwarding to connect a remote user to the computer on the home network with a web server running X10 home automation software.

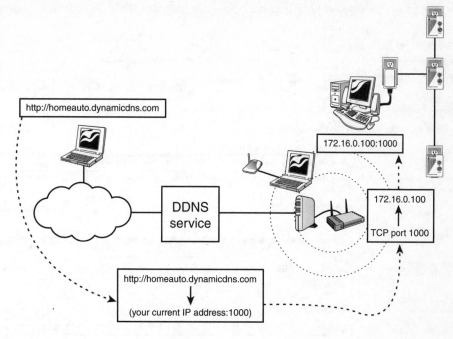

Keep in mind that you must configure your router to forward TCP port requests to the IP address used by your home automation program's web server as discussed in the "Dealing with Dynamic IP Addresses on Your Home Network" section earlier in this chapter.

### FINDING A DYNAMIC DNS SERVICE

Some of the leading dynamic DNS services are

- **No-IP**—www.no-ip.com
- **Dynamic Network Services, Inc**—www.dyndns.org
- **TZO DNS**—www.tzo.com

Depending on the vendor and options selected, you can get a basic dynamic DNS alias free of charge. A free or low-end commercial dynamic DNS alias is sufficient for use with a home automation web server.

TZO provides a good overview of using DNS services with a home automation system at www.tzo.org/MainPageSupport/HowToPage/SOLUTIONS-HOMEAUTOMATION.HTML

## Using the Web Server to Control Your Home Automation System

When you log on to your web server, regardless of whether you're using another computer on your home network or remotely via the Internet, you can access most of the features of your home automation program through your web browser, as shown in Figure 12.13.

**FIGURE 12.13**

The HomeSeer web server home page.

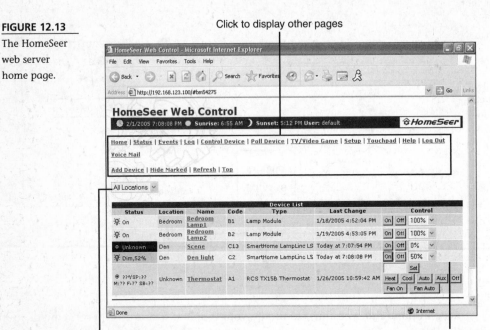

Click to display other pages

Click to select a particular location

Module controls

HomeSeer's web server, shown in Figure 12.13, shows all the devices in your home automation system in all rooms by default. Click All Locations and select a particular location to see only the devices in that location.

You can run events, view a log of activities, or control a particular device interactively through a typical web server. If your home automation system includes web cameras, you can also view video they capture.

## Using Remote Access Software and Services

If your home automation software does not include a built-in web server, you can use remote access services or remote access software to control your computer remotely. Remote access enables you to perform the following tasks remotely:

■ Control any program on your PC, not just those that are specifically web-enabled

■ Run maintenance applications such as defragmenting, disk checking, and antivirus programs

Some also support features such as file transfer between home and remote computers or file synchronization.

There are two ways to add remote access to your home computer:

- Purchase and install remote access software
- Sign up for a remote access service

Both types of remote access require you to install a host program on your home computer. The host program receives the connection from a remote PC and enables the remote PC to control your home computer. Remote access software programs such as PC Anywhere (www.symantec.com) and LapLink Gold 12 (www.laplink.com) are designed primarily for corporate networking. They are too expensive and complex for most home users, and require that you use a client PC running their client software. For most home users, remote access services are a better choice.

**FREE REMOTE ACCESS SERVER INSIDE!**

If you use Windows XP Professional (not Home Edition) on the home computer that runs your home automation program, you can install the Remote Desktop Web Connection component to enable remote web access from another Windows-based PC. Get a step-by-step tutorial from dynamic DNS vendor TZO at www.tzo.org/MainPageSupport/HowToPage/HowToXPRemoteDesktop.html.

Note that if you have a dynamic IP address, you will have to sign up for a dynamic DNS service to enable remote computers to connect with your PC.

## Remote Access Services

Like a traditional remote-access program, a remote access service requires you to install a host program on your home computer. However, you don't need to worry about router configurations or IP addresses to use a remote access service. Instead, a secure server operated by the remote access provider tracks changes in your home computer's IP address and provides a secure connection between your home computer and any remote location with Internet access.

The basic process of configuring a remote access service works like this:

1. Download and install the server application on your home computer.
2. Set up the credentials required (password or username/password) in the server's configuration program.
3. If you use a software firewall, permit the server application to access the Internet.
4. Leave the home computer that is connected to your home automation system and your broadband Internet connection (cable or DSL) running.

To access your home computer remotely

1. Start up an Internet connection on a remote computer.

2. Connect to the remote access provider's secure login site.

3. Log in to the service.

4. Select your PC.

5. Download a small client when prompted.

6. Log in to your PC with the credentials you provided when you set up the service.

Figure 12.14 shows a remote connection to my home computer made with LogMeIn Pro, which also offers a free basic remote control version (LogMeIn).

**caution**

If you use firewall software such as Zone Alarm or Norton Internet Security, the first time you run the server component of a remote access program or service, the firewall program will ask you if it's okay to allow the server to access the Internet. To allow the server to work, be sure to approve access and to remember your answer. Some servers use more than one program, so you might need to grant access to more than one program.

**FIGURE 12.14**
Operating
Smarthome
Manager
through a
remote connec-
tion made with
LogMeIn Pro.

Click to switch remote desktop to full-screen mode

Remote desktop

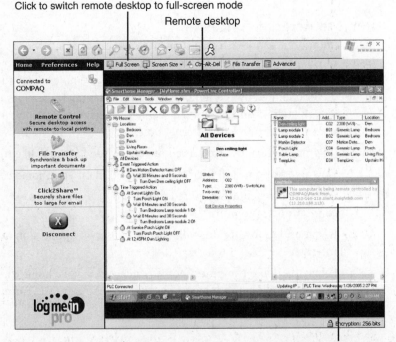

IP address of remote client

Some of these remote access services also enable you to control one PC on your home network from another PC. Try it to see if it works! Some leading vendors (many of which offer free trials or free limited versions) include

- **GoToMyPC**—I use this for remote access of my office PCs from home; www.gotomypc.com

- **I'm in Touch**—Works with PCs, PDAs, and BlackBerry devices; www.01com.com

- **Access-Remote-PC.com**—The companion RPC Service helps handle dynamic IP addresses; www.access-remote-pc.com

- **LogMeIn and LogMeIn Pro**—Pro offers file transfer and synchronization; https://secure.logmein.com

- **RealVNC**—Works with Mac OS, Linux, Windows; www.realvnc.com

- **WebExPC**—From the developers of WebEx; www.mywebexpc.com

- **LapLink Everywhere 3/LapLink Secure VNC**—Works with any Java-enabled browser; www.laplink.com

If you are considering a remote access service, keep the following issues in mind:

- **What operating systems are supported on the server side (the computer you use to run your home automation system)?**—Most remote access services support Windows, but if you use Mac OS or Linux, make sure that you choose a remote access service that supports your operating system.

- **What operating systems are supported on the client (remote computer) side?**—If you travel frequently and don't always use your own office or laptop computer, look for remote access services that support any web browser that uses Java. Some support only Windows clients or only Internet Explorer.

- **Cost per month or per year**—Although a few vendors offer free remote access solutions, most cost anywhere from $100–$150/year. You can most easily cost-justify this if you need the additional features provided with a paid subscription service, such as file transfer or file synchronization.

# Adding Webcams to Your Home Automation System

Some home automation systems that support web servers or use a hardware module can support webcams. Webcams, unlike the video security cameras discussed in Chapter 9, "Using X10 to Provide Security," are designed to connect to a PC's USB port or to an ethernet port on a router.

Webcams connected to a PC's USB port are controlled through the PC hosting them. Depending on the home automation software you use, you might need to add a plugin (sometimes at extra cost) to permit webcam support. Figure 12.15 shows a typical USB webcam, the Logitech QuickCam Pro 4000.

**FIGURE 12.15**

The Logitech Quick Cam Pro 4000 is a USB-based webcam that connects to the USB port on a home computer. Image courtesy of Logitech.

As an alternative to webcams, you can use a video capture card or USB video adapter to connect X10-compatible security cameras. X10's USB Video Adapter VA11 (www.x10.com/products/x10_va11a.htm) enables you to control a security camera with remote viewing software such as MultiView/WebView, Xray Vision, or PanTiltPro.

Webcams connected to an ethernet port or via wireless ethernet (Wi-Fi) are known as IP webcams or netcams (see Figure 12.16). These cameras often contain their own web servers for remote access.

Before you purchase a webcam for use with your X10 security system, check with the vendor to determine which types of cameras are supported and how. Many of the vendors listed in the "Discovering Web-Enabled X10 Software Solutions" sidebar earlier in this chapter offer support for USB or IP-based webcams. If the vendor has experience with particular models, those models (if available) are the best choice. Even if you want to use multiple cameras as part of your remote security setup, I recommend you try one camera first before you expand your setup.

**FIGURE 12.16**

The Logitech
WVC54G's built-
in web server
enables control
from other com-
puters on the
home network or
remotely on the
Internet. Photo
courtesy of Cisco
Systems Inc.

# Troubleshooting Home Network and Broadband Access to Your X10 System

When you add Internet access and home networks to an X10-compatible home automation system, you add a lot of complexity as well as a lot of versatility. Use the following sections to help you solve remote access problems.

## Home Automation Software with Integrated Web Server

If you use the integrated web server built in to your home automation software for remote access but you're unable to access it, check the following:

- **Do you know the correct address and TCP port to specify?**—To access the web server from another station on your home network, provide the web server's actual IP address and TCP port (if necessary). To access the web server from a remote location on the Internet, use the public IP address or a dynamic DNS alias.

- **Can you access the web server from your home network, but not the Internet?**—If you can, you need to configure your router to forward the appropriate TCP ports monitored by the web server to the IP address used by your web server.

- **Are you using dynamic DNS to access the web server remotely?**— Make sure that you have registered the correct name. You must specify the name you selected at registration. Contact the vendor for help.

- **Have you correctly specified usernames and passwords in the web server configuration?**—Recheck your user setup.

## Remote Access Software and Services

If you use remote access software or a remote access service to connect to your computer remotely, check the following if you're having problems:

- **Have you correctly installed the server application on the computer running your home automation software?**—Check settings, download any available patches or updates, and reinstall if necessary.

- **Have you configured your router properly?**—If your remote access software requires port forwarding or other nonstandard router settings, make sure that these settings are correct. You might also need to set up your host PC with a static IP address in some cases.

- **Where does the server get its list of allowable users from?**—Some programs and services use the computer's default users, but others might require you to specify usernames and passwords. If you use Windows XP on your computer but do not log in with a username, you might need to create a user and use that name and password to log in remotely with some programs and services.

- **Is your client supported?**—If you can log in from some remote PCs but not others, some PCs might not be using a supported web browser, might not have Java installed, or might not be running a supported operating system. If you plan to use unfamiliar computers in cybercafés, libraries, or other public locations to access your home remotely, make sure that you carry a list of client requirements for your remote access solution and make sure that the client PC meets those requirements.

- **Is your client software properly installed?**—Make sure that your remote client is installed and properly configured. If you use a remote access service that uses a download-on-demand client, watch out for security settings that might block pop-ups or prevent downloaded applications from being run. If you plan to use public-access computers to remotely control your home computer, you should consider remote access services that offer client software that does not need to be downloaded to run, such as GoToMyPC's universal viewer client.

# THE ABSOLUTE MINIMUM

- Some home automation software includes a web server, enabling you to use a standard web browser to access the home automation program via the home network or the Internet.

- Remote access services enable you to run any program on your PC remotely, but are easier to configure and use than classic remote access programs.

- For any remote access solution, you have to leave your computer running at all times and have it connected to an always-on broadband Internet service such as cable or DSL.

- To access a web server from your home network, you enter the IP address of the computer hosting the web server into the address bar of a web browser on any computer on the network. You might also need to add the TCP port used by the web server to the IP address.

- Most home networks use DHCP-assigned IP addresses, meaning that the IP address used by the computer running your home automation software might change. To enable you to access your home automation system remotely, you should assign the computer running your home automation software a static (fixed) IP address.

- To access the web server from the Internet, you must use the public IP address used by your Internet connection, which is not the same as the private IP address used on your home network.

- Most cable and DSL services for home use dynamic IP addresses, which can change from time to time. To enable you to access your home automation PC remotely at all times, you should get a static IP address from your broadband ISP or subscribe to a dynamic DNS service.

- With a web server or some types of remote access software, you might have to configure your router to forward traffic to the IP address used by your home automation computer.

- A dynamic DNS service tracks changes to your broadband Internet IP address to enable correct routing of remote access requests to your home computer.

- Remote access services such as GoToMyPC, LogMeIn, and others represent a simpler-to-use alternative to traditional remote access software programs.

- Depending on the type of home automation software you use, you might be able to use USB webcams, netcams with their own IP addresses, or adapters that convert standard security cameras into webcams to provide remote video.

- Troubleshooting problems with remote access to home automation systems might involve checking router settings, software settings, user settings, and settings on the remote (client) PC and browser.

# PART V

# APPENDICES

# A

# Integrating X10 with Other Home Control Systems

If you decide it's time to move to another home automation system, will it work with X10? Which home automation brands are made by, or work with, X10? Get the answers here.

# Methods for Integrating X10 with Third-Party Home Control Systems

As you have learned in other parts of this book, X10 is a very powerful, very flexible home automation standard. However, you might decide at some point to move beyond what do-it-yourself X10 can do. Fortunately, many different home automation systems can be interconnected with your X10 system, enabling you to continue to use X10 modules to control existing features while you add additional automation through a commercial system.

As you learned in Chapter 11, "Accessing X10 Home Control via Your Home Computer," you can use your PC to control your X10 home automation system. Many third-party vendors' home automation control software can also send commands to X10 and X10-compatible modules. Depending on the system, you might need to use a separate hardware interface to bridge your X10 and third-party systems or the third-party system might feature built-in X10 support.

Some third-party home automation systems interface with X10 through a hardware controller that can work independently of a PC.

The following sections discuss how you can interconnect leading third-party home control systems with your existing X10 system, and what aliases are used by various vendors for their X10 products.

# Integrating HAI with X10

HAI (Home Automation, Inc.) has been developing home automation and security products since 1985. It offers three whole-house product lines:

- OmniLT
- Omni II
- Omni Pro II

The heart of each system is a hardware controller that supports multiple thermostats, multiple scenes, lighting controls, security, and consoles. OmniLT is designed for homes up to 2000 square feet, whereas Omni II and Omni Pro II are designed for larger homes and offer support for more devices and greater levels of programmability.

All three Omni-series controllers support a two-way X10 interface, enabling the controller to respond to X10 commands. For example, if you have already programmed your X10 system to create a scene (dimmed lights, opened window shades, and so forth), you can use an Omni controller to detect the command and make adjustments to temperature, ventilation, and so on. Most Omni controller kits include the two-way X10 controller (TW523), or you can add one separately.

In addition to supporting X10 signaling, Omni-series controllers can also improve the reliability of your X10 home automation system:

- The Dual X10 Transmitter Kit (#10A09-1) includes a TW523 controller, a 25-foot signal cable, and an adapter enabling you to plug two TW523 controllers into separate outlets on separate signal phases of your house wiring to improve signal reliability. (See Appendix B, "Troubleshooting X10," for more information on signal phases.)

- The Split X10 Signal Kit (#10A09-2) includes a TW523 controller, a 25-foot signal cable, and a signal splitter enabling one TW523 to transmit X10 signals and the other to receive X10 signals.

Both kits assume that your Omni-series system already includes a TW523 controller. If not, order #10A09-7 from your dealer.

HAI products can be installed by HAI dealers, and can be purchased through various suppliers.

---

**HAI ONLINE**

For more information, see the HAI website at www.homeauto.com.

---

# Integrating Xanboo with X10

Xanboo is an Internet-based home monitoring system. Xanboo uses a hardware controller to receive information from cameras and sensors and make it available for remote access. Xanboo can notify you by email, pager, or text messaging when its water, temperature, motion, sound, door/window sensors, or cameras are triggered.

Xanboo is designed to use an always-on broadband Internet connection such as a cable or DSL modem to enable you to receive notifications remotely. You monitor and control your system by logging in to a secure account at Xanboo.com.

Xanboo software version 1.02 can control X10 lamp and appliance modules if you have a CM11A Active Home, CM17A Firecracker, or another supported X10-computer interface connected to the computer running Xanboo software. Other X10 control software should be disabled; otherwise, Xanboo will not be able to control your X10 system.

---

**XANBOO ONLINE**

For more information, see the Xanboo website at www.xanboo.com. Xanboo technology is now incorporated into Motorola's new Home Monitoring and Control System (see the website at broadband.motorola.com/consumers/home_monitoring.asp), which is not X10-compatible.

---

# Integrating Leviton DHC with X10

Decora Home Controls (DHC) is Leviton's brand of home control products. DHC products include interior and exterior lighting control, appliance and motor controls useful for automating pool maintenance, dimmer switches, AC electrical outlets, circuit-breaker–mounted programmable control panels, and more.

Although it's not obvious from Leviton's website, DHC products use the X10 protocol, enabling them to work with standard one-way and two-way X10 devices without additional hardware. Leviton has improved on generic X10 by incorporating an improved form of automatic gain control, called *Intellisense,* into its DHC receivers. Intellisense is designed to prevent electrical interference.

Most Leviton DHC receivers use the standard X10 house and unit code dials (and are actually manufactured by X10 for Leviton), but a few are programmed through a DHC or other X10-compatible controller.

---

**LEVITON DHC ONLINE**

To learn more about the technical features of Leviton DHC devices as well as valuable advice in planning and troubleshooting your X10-compatible home automation systems from any vendor, download the DHC tech manual from the Leviton website (www.leviton .com/dhc). The DHC tech manual was written by this book's technical editor, Dave Rye.

You will need the free Abobe Reader software (www.adobe.com) to view the tech manual.

---

# Integrating Z-Wave with X10

Z-Wave, developed by Zensys, is a wireless home automation system which is designed for the do-it-yourself home automation fan. Each Z-Wave module supports receiving and transmitting of Z-Wave signals, creating a mesh network so that range issues are not a problem. Z-Wave modules, sold under the brand names Sylvania Z-Wave, HomePro RF, and others, support lamps, appliances, and computer interfacing.

To integrate Z-Wave with X10, connect your home computer to a Z-Wave computer interface module and an X10 computer interface module and use HomeSeer Technologies' HomeSeer software to control both Z-Wave and X10 devices via your home network or Internet connection. Note that HomeSeerSE (bundled with some Z-Wave kits) does *not* support X10—you must use the full version of HomeSeer software.

**HOMESEER AND Z-WAVE ONLINE**

To learn more about HomeSeer software, visit the HomeSeer Technologies website at www.homeseer.com. HomeSeer is also discussed in Chapters 11 and 12, "Accessing X10 Home Control via Your Home Network and the Internet." To learn more about Z-Wave, visit the Zensys website at www.zen-sys.com.

# Integrating Home Automated Living with X10

Home Automated Living (HAL) is a series of home-control systems that enable you to control your home via voice commands through a telephone at home or remotely. All HAL systems (HALbasic, HALdeluxe, and HAL2000) work with a broad range of X10 and X10-compatible devices, including modules, computer interfaces, and specialty controllers. HAL also supports many non-X10 home automation systems and devices, enabling you to create a mix-and-match home automation system if you prefer.

**HAL, X10, AND YOU**

To learn more about HAL, visit the Home Automated Technology website at www. automatedliving.com. For a list of X10 and X10-compatible devices supported by HAL systems, see www.automatedliving.com/products_interfaces.html.

# Integrating JDS Stargate with X10

JDS Technologies' Stargate is an integrated home automation system with support for lighting, HVAC, security, home theater systems, pools, and other home systems. It features interactive voice response, and telephone and computer-based control. Stargate features built-in support for X10 hardware, and also supports RS-232 interfaces to computers and RS-485 interfaces for keypads, thermostats, and other components.

Stargate's X10 support features include

■ X10 module control via touch-tone telephone

■ Customized mapping of touch-tone codes to X10 codes

■ Customized definition of X10 modules

■ Powerful scripting language

**STARGATE ONLINE**

Learn more about Stargate from the JDS Technologies website at www.jdstechnologies.com.

# Integrating Lightolier Controls Compose with X10

Lightolier Controls' Compose line of lighting controls uses intelligent switches in conjunction with a firewall connected to the circuit breaker panel. The firewall device helps to reduce line noise and provide additional reliability in operation.

Compose is compatible with standard X10 signaling. The Compose PLC Technical Guide (available in Adobe Reader/Acrobat PDF format on the Lightolier Controls website) provides information about translating X10 commands into Compose commands.

### LIGHTOLIER CONTROLS ONLINE

Learn more about Compose from the Lightolier Controls website at www.lolcontrols.com.

# Integrating Applied Digital, Inc. Controllers with X10

Applied Digital, Inc. manufactures a touch-screen home automation controller (Leopard II) and a standalone/PC-based home automation controller (Ocelot). Both products are designed to work with X10 and X10-compatible modules.

### LEOPARD II AND OCELOT ONLINE

Learn more about Leopard II and Ocelot controllers from the Applied Digital, Inc. website at www.appdig.com.

# Integrating HomeLink with X10

Johnson Controls' HomeLink system is a vehicle-mounted interface to existing garage-door opening and home automation systems including X10, the X10-compatible Black & Decker freewire, and others. HomeLink is installed at the factory, or with some makes of cars, as a dealer option.

To use HomeLink to control your X10 or X10-compatible system, you need to purchase the HomeLink Vehicle Interface. This is a wireless receiver that plugs into an AC electrical outlet in your home and relays signals from HomeLink to your lighting or appliance modules.

### HOMELINK ONLINE

Learn more about HomeLink and vehicles that can be ordered or retrofitted with HomeLink from the HomeLink website at www.homelink.com.

# Brand Names for X10-Compatible Equipment

When you're shopping for X10-compatible modules, receivers, and transmitters, the wide variety of vendors and brand names can make it difficult to determine whether a particular product is X10 compatible. Table A.1 lists some of the major brand names used by different companies for their current or recent X10-compatible products, listed in alphabetical order by company.

**TABLE A.1** Brand Names Used for X10-Compatible Equipment

| Brand Name | Vendor | Website |
| --- | --- | --- |
| freewire | Black & Decker | www.blackanddecker.com/freewire* |
| Home Director | IBM | www.ibm.com/homedirector |
| DHC (Decora Home Controls) | Leviton | www.leviton.com |
| SceneMaster | Powerline Control Systems | www.pcslighting.com |
| Plug 'n Power | Radio Shack | www.radioshack.com |
| LampLinc, SwitchLinc, ApplianceLinc | Smarthome | www.smarthome.com |
| X10 Powerhouse, X10 Activehome, X10PRO | X10.com, X10 (USA), Inc., X10 PRO | www.x10.com www.x10pro.com |

*\* Refer to Chapters 4 and 5 for more information about freewire.*

---

**WHO IS (AND WAS) WHO IN X10**

A more complete list of X10 and X10-compatible vendors, including many that are no longer selling or supporting X10 products, is available from the ActiveHome Professional website at www.activehomepro.com/compatibility.html.

---

## IN THIS APPENDIX

- Typical Causes for Problems with X10

- Diagnosing and Solving Problems with X10 PLC Signals

- Solving Problems with X10 Wireless Transceivers and Remotes

**B**

# TROUBLESHOOTING X10

Whether you're having problems with an X10 installation, range problems with X10 transceivers, or you're tired of installing multiple transceivers for different house codes, you've come to the right place for help.

# Typical Causes for Problems with X10

X10 is a power line carrier *(PLC)* automation system. Because X10 uses power lines to carry signals, issues involving power lines could cause problems with X10. Some issues you might encounter include

- House wiring usually involves a single 240-volt AC service that has been split into two 120-volt AC phases (a system known as *single split-phase*). If an X10 controller or transceiver is plugged into wiring connected to one phase, and some of the receivers are plugged into wiring connected to another phase, the controller or transceiver's signals might not reliably reach some receivers.

- House wiring can be electrically noisy. Interference caused by loose outlets or switches, refrigerators, or vacuum cleaners can disrupt X10 signals.

- X10 transmitters such as transceivers and two-way light switches and appliance modules can absorb X10 signals. If too much of the X10 signal is absorbed before it reaches the destination module, the module might not receive the signal.

- X10 power line signals can travel between homes and apartments, so the X10 modules in your location might be triggered by signals from elsewhere.

Other issues with your X10 installation might include

- By default, virtually all X10 modules, switches, transceivers, remotes, and tabletop controllers are set to house code A. If you don't change your house code to a different value, it's possible that your transceiver might pick up signals from a nearby home or apartment that also uses X10 home automation. Although a few X10-compatible systems such as Black & Decker freewire and HomeAuto feature transceivers with security codes, standard X10 and X10-compatible transceivers do not use security codes.

- If you have a large home (more than 2,500 square feet) or a home with brick or concrete walls, you might have problems sending or receiving X10 signals with conventional transceivers and remotes.

- With only 16 unit codes per house code, it's likely that you'll need to use two or more house codes for a large-scale automation project. If you use conventional tabletop controllers or transceivers, you must use a separate unit for each house code you want to control or else turn the house code dial every time you want to control devices on another house code. This can create confusion and inconvenience.

- If you are working with a module in a remote part of your home, or you are controlling your home via an Internet connection, conventional X10 modules do not provide feedback of status or problems. You might not know whether your signal reached the module.

If any of these issues are problems for you, this appendix can help.

# Diagnosing and Solving Problems with X10 PLC Signals

X10 is a PLC technology. Even if you use a wireless transceiver and remote control to run your X10 system, the transceiver sends signals via your home's AC wiring to the module you want to operate. The following sections discuss various tools and devices you can use to diagnose and solve problems with the reliable transmission of X10 PLC signals in your home.

## Solving Wiring Phase Problems with X10

Homes in North America are typically wired with two 120-volt AC lines split from an incoming 240-volt AC service. This is known as *single split-phase* or *two-phase wiring*. Some AC outlets are wired to one phase and some to another. Although normal electrical outlets in your home use 120-volt AC power, you probably also have one or more 240-volt AC outlets for an electric range, a clothes dryer, or a high-powered window air conditioner.

In a typical home automation installation, some X10 or X10-compatible modules, transceivers, and desktop controllers are likely to be plugged into one phase and some into the other. If the two 120-volt AC lines are not coupled correctly, signals sent from a controller or transceiver on one phase might not be received correctly by modules on the other phase (see Figure B.1).

If X10 modules work erratically when you are not using a 240-volt appliance such as an electric range or clothes dryer, but work very well when you are cooking or drying clothes, you have a problem with phase coupling.

At one time, phase coupling problems required installation of a phase coupler (also referred to as a *signal bridge*) into your electrical panel. Hardwired phase couplers are still available. However, you can now use a plug-in phase coupler instead if you have a suitable 240-volt electric outlet. A plug-in phase coupler connects to a 240-volt electric clothes dryer outlet to provide a reliable connection between the two 120-volt phases (see Figure B.2). Use the pass-through outlet on the front of the phase coupler (see Figure B.3) for your electric dryer.

Phase couplers are available in passive models (recommended for houses up to 3,000 square feet) and active models that also act as signal boosters and repeaters (for larger homes). Table B.1 lists plug-in phase couplers, and Table B.2 (in the next section) lists active phase couplers and other types of signal boosters.

**FIGURE B.1**

The signal from a transceiver on phase 2 might not reach a module on phase 1 if the phases are not properly coupled.

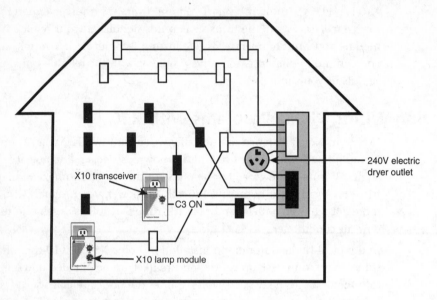

- ▯ Electric outlets on Phase 1
- ▮ Electric outlets on Phase2

X10 transceiver

C3 ON

240V electric dryer outlet

X10 lamp module

**FIGURE B.2**

Using a plug-in phase coupler helps signals from a transceiver on one phase to reach a module on another phase.

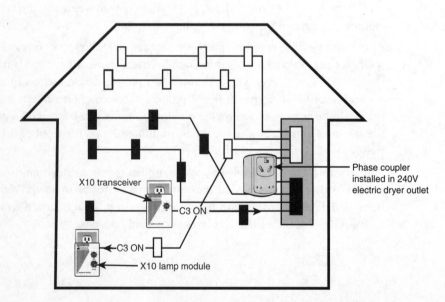

- ▯ Electric outlets on Phase 1
- ▮ Electric outlets on Phase 2

X10 transceiver

C3 ON

C3 ON

X10 lamp module

Phase coupler installed in 240V electric dryer outlet

**TABLE B.1**   X10-Compatible Plug-in Phase Couplers

| Vendor | Model# | Connector Type | Repeater/Booster |
|--------|--------|----------------|------------------|
| Smarthome | 4816A2 | Four-pin plug-in | No |
| | 4826B | Three-pin plug-in | Yes |
| | 4826A | Four-pin plug-in | Yes |
| | 4816A | Hardwired | No |

Figure B.3 compares plug-in signal couplers.

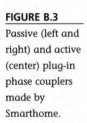

**FIGURE B.3**

Passive (left and right) and active (center) plug-in phase couplers made by Smarthome.

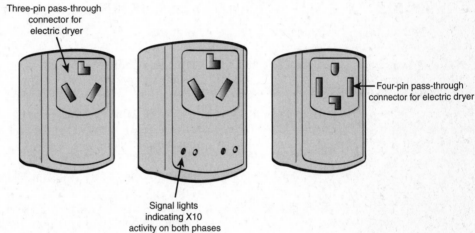

Three-pin pass-through connector for electric dryer

Four-pin pass-through connector for electric dryer

Signal lights indicating X10 activity on both phases

## Using Signal Boosters

Although passive signal couplers can significantly improve X10 reliability, they might not solve every problem associated with X10 signals. Every X10 transceiver and controller, and two-way switches or modules in use absorb some of the X10 signals being transmitted through house wiring. In addition, many other types of electronic equipment can cause interference with X10 signals (see the "Using Noise Filters" section later in this appendix for details).

If X10 signals are too weak for reliable operation in some parts of the home and a passive signal coupler has already been installed, consider adding a signal booster (amplifier) to your X10 home automation system. Signal boosters are designed to detect X10 signals as low as 100mV and boost them to 5V AC (120-volt systems).

Signal boosters are available in plug-in modules for use in 120-volt AC electrical outlets that are not used by other X10 modules, transceivers, or controllers. They're also available in hardwired devices (these also include phase coupling) and are sometimes incorporated into switches.

Some signal boosters are designed to be the only signal booster in use, whereas others are designed for very large (4,000 square feet and more) homes where another signal booster might already be in use. Signal boosters designed for use in addition to another booster can be configured to ignore already-boosted signals.

If want to use X10 to control modules in an apartment or a commercial building, these structures typically use three-phase wiring. To boost signal strength in a three-phase installation, you must use a signal booster that supports three-phase service (see Table B.2). Table B.2 lists some of the signal boosters and active phase couplers available in the United States.

## TABLE B.2  X10 Signal Boosters and Active Phase Couplers

| Vendor | Model# | Features | Service Type | How Installed |
|---|---|---|---|---|
| Advanced Control Technologies Inc. | HomePro CR230 | Provides signal coupling | Two-phase | Hardwired |
| | HomePro CR234 | Can work with other signal boosters; provides signal coupling | Two-phase | Hardwired |
| | HomePro CR134 | Can work with other signal boosters; provides signal coupling | Three-phase | Hardwired |
| Smarthome | BoosterLinc 4827 | Can work with other signal boosters; includes X10 test signal generator | Either | Grounded AC outlet |
| | ToggleLinc two-way wall switch 23890 (dimmer), 23893 series | Incorporates BoosterLinc signal booster (can be disabled) | Two-phase | Three-wire light switch wall box |
| X10 Pro | XPCR | Provides signal coupling | Either | Hardwired |
| Leviton | HCA02 | Provides signal coupling; includes X10 test signal generator | Two-phase | Hardwired |

Figure B.4 shows an installed Leviton HCA02 hardwired signal coupler. Installation is similar for other hardwired active and passive signal couplers.

**FIGURE B.4**

How the Leviton HCA02 hardwired active signal coupler (left) is connected to the electrical panel (right).

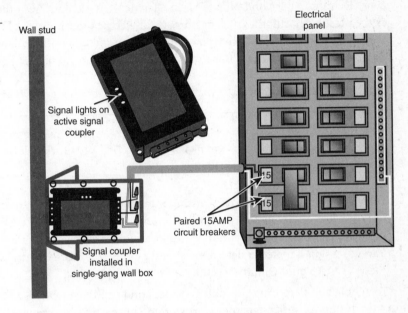

Wall stud

Electrical panel

Signal lights on active signal coupler

Paired 15AMP circuit breakers

Signal coupler installed in single-gang wall box

Figure B.5 illustrates the devices listed in Table B.2.

**FIGURE B.5**

Hardwired coupler-repeaters from HomePro (upper left), Leviton (lower left), and X10 Pro (lower right) compared to a BoosterLinc plug-in signal booster (upper right). Drawing not to scale.

POWER
READY
RECEIVE
TRANSMIT
ERROR

# Using Noise Filters

If your X10 home automation system was working well until you brought home a new electronic device and plugged it in, electrical interference from the new device is the most likely culprit. From rechargers for electric toothbrushes and other battery-powered devices to computer monitors, many different types of electronic devices can interfere with X10 signals, even when the device is turned off.

**TRACKING DOWN SIGNAL SUCKERS**

To learn more about the devices most likely to cause interference (known fondly as *signal suckers*), read "Using Large Quantities of SwitchLinc 2-Way Wall Switches in a Home," at www.smarthome.com/solution45.html and "How to Find X10 'Black Holes' in Your Home" at www.smarthome.com/solution18.html.

To determine which devices are causing interference, unplug each device, and then retry sending X10 commands. When you unplug the devices that were causing interference, your X10 performance will become noticeably more reliable. You can also use a signal meter to determine signal quality. For more information, see the "Testing X10 Signal Quality" section later in this appendix.

To enable you to reconnect problem devices and still have reliable X10 performance, install AC line filters that start working at the 100kHz frequency and connect the problem devices to the line filters. Surge suppressors with noise filtration starting at 100kHz or lower (not higher) can also be used. Table B.3 lists some of the common plug-in and wired-in line filters that can be used with X10.

**TABLE B.3**   Line Filters for Use with X10 Systems

| Vendor | Model# | Max Electrical Load | How Installed |
|---|---|---|---|
| Advanced Control Technology, Inc. | HomePro AF100 | 5 amp | Plug-in (three-wire AC outlet) |
| | HomePro AF120 | 15 amp | Plug-in (three-wire AC outlet) |
| Leviton | 6288 | 5 amp | Plug-in (three-wire AC outlet) |
| | 6287[1] | 5 amp | Hardwired |
| | 6289[2] | — | Hardwired |
| Smarthome | 1626 | 5 amp | Plug-in (three-wire AC outlet) |
| X10 Pro | XPF[3] | 20 amp | Hardwired |
| X10 Pro | XPPF | 5 amp | Plug-in |

[1] *Designed to handle electrical noise problems caused by low-voltage, HID (high-pressure discharge) and fluorescent lighting, and small electrical motors.*

[2] *Designed for higher-amp devices than Leviton 6287.*

[3] *Designed for use with large appliances such as refrigerators, hot tubs, and so forth.*

## Blocking X10 Power Line Signals from Entering Your Home

X10 power line signals can travel from house to house via the electrical service connections. If X10 modules in your home are turning on and off when they should not, it's possible that X10 signals from a nearby location have entered your electrical wiring.

To stop X10 signals from another home from entering your home wiring, ask a professional electrician to install a passive blocking filter such as the X10 Pro PZZ01 or the similar Leviton 6284. Passive blocking filters must be installed over the neutral wire where the electric service enters your building.

These devices also prevent X10 signals from leaking from your home via the electrical panel and provide passive signal coupling.

You should also consider using a house code other than A for your home automation system. Almost all X10 and X10-compatible modules are set to house code A by default. Some users might not select a different house code, and if you and a neighbor both use wireless transceivers set to house code A, you might accidentally control each others' modules. Use other house codes than A, and you substantially reduce the odds of AC or wireless signals from other X10 users' interfering with your installation.

## Testing X10 Signal Quality

If you're planning to use X10 for a large-scale automation project (such as several rooms or your entire home), you might want to consider adding an X10 signal tester to your toolkit. And, if you're already in the midst of X10 automation that's not always working as well as you'd like, testing X10 signal quality can help you determine what the best solutions are.

Although many X10 signal testers are priced at more than $200, making them more suitable for use by professional installers, some testers are available for $100 or less. Smarthome's TesterLinc (#4819) works with the Smarthome PowerLinc II (#1132B) to determine signal addresses received, signal quality, and line noise. Elk Products' ESM1 Signal Meter indicates with a green LED whether a valid X10 signal has been received and also indicates the strength of the X10 signal. It is best used with a plug-in X10 controller that can send a continuous stream of signals such as an X10 Powerhouse Powerflash Interface (PF284) when set to mode 2. Figure B.6 illustrates the ESM1 receiving a good-quality X10 signal.

**FIGURE B.6**

The Elk ESM1 Signal Meter is receiving a valid X10 signal of about 2.5 volts.

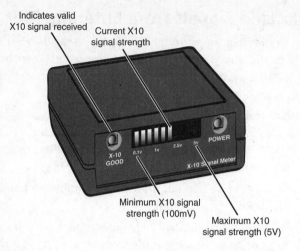

Indicates valid X10 signal received

Current X10 signal strength

X-10 GOOD   0.1v   1v   2.5v   5v   POWER

X-10 Signal Meter

Minimum X10 signal strength (100mV)

Maximum X10 signal strength (5V)

If you are a professional X10 installer, you might prefer to use one of the professional-level X10 signal testers shown in Table B.4.

## TABLE B.4   Professional X10 Signal Testers

| Vendor | Model# | Features |
|---|---|---|
| Advanced Control Technologies, Inc. | AT004 | Transmits and receives X10 standard and extended signals, displays noise and signal level, logs test results for up to 24 hours, and more. Can be connected to AC outlet or electrical panel. |
| Leviton | 6385 Signal Strength Transmitter | Transmitter sends P1 house/unit code combination to indicator; indicator displays signal strength, noise level detected where connected. |
| | 6386 Signal Strength Indicator | The Leviton HCA02 signal coupler can be used in place of 6385 as a source for signals. |
| Marrick Limited, Inc. | LynX-TOOLS | Bundles LynX-10 PLC X10- vcompatible PC-based transceiver with LynX-View software and other utilities to monitor signals, noise, and X10 packets. Supports Lightolier Compose codes. |
| Monterey Instruments | Powerline Signal Analyzer | Provides bit-level examination of X10 signal packets, signal strength, preset dim, extended data, command log option; identifies specific X10 error codes, and more. |
| X10 Pro | XPTT | Transmitter sends P1 house/unit code combination to indicator; indicator displays signal strength, noise level detected where connected (same as Leviton #6385) |
| | XPTR | Indicates signal strength; plugs into AC outlet (same as Leviton #6386) |

**X10 SIGNAL ANALYZERS ONLINE**

See the following websites for more information about the signal analyzers listed in this section:

- Advanced Control Technologies, Inc. at www.act-solutions.com
- Leviton at www.leviton.com/dhc
- Merrick Limited, Inc. at www.merrickltd.com
- Smarthome at www.smarthome.com

# Solving Problems with X10 Wireless Transceivers and Remotes

Most X10 and X10-compatible starter kits include a wireless transceiver and remote control. However, unlike IR remotes that are used a few feet away from the receiver built into a TV, VCR, boom box, or DVD player, X10 remotes use radio-frequency signals that might be transmitted from several rooms away or from outside. Making sure that wireless X10 signals are to the transceiver from the remote can be a challenge. The following sections will help you meet that challenge.

## Adding Wireless Signal Repeaters for Greater Range

If you sometimes find yourself walking toward an X10 transceiver in another room to get your X10 remote to turn on the lights or the radio, you should consider a wireless signal repeater. Wireless signal repeaters retransmit wireless signals from X10 or X10-compatible remotes for more reliable reception by X10 or X10-compatible wireless transceivers.

Up to four SR371 wireless repeaters from X10 (USA) can be used in a single location, providing coverage for up to 80,000 square feet. A single SR371 can be used with an X10 security console. In practice, a single repeater boosts the connection range by about 100 feet. If more than one repeater is used, adjust the four-position dial (A-B-C-D) on each repeater to a unique setting. Figure B.7 shows an SR371 wireless repeater (also known as the *X10 Pro PSX01*) .

## Upgrading to All-House-Code Transceivers

If you use more than one house code in your X10 home automation system and you use wireless transceivers and remotes, you have a problem. Standard wireless transceivers support only one house code. Therefore, you have to install an additional transceiver for each additional house code you want to use.

**FIGURE B.7**

Use an X10 signal repeater such as the X10 Powerhouse SR371 to improve the reliability of your X10 wireless remotes and transceivers.

Additional transceivers can be hard to place in a central location, and can prevent you from using an electrical outlet in the way you prefer. As an alternative, consider using a single transceiver capable of receiving all house codes, such as the WGL & Associates V572 Whole House Transceiver, the Leviton HCPRF, or the X10 CM15A (which also provides PC-USB interfacing and is included as part of X10's Active Home Pro home automation system).

## V572 Whole House Transceiver

The WGL & Associates V572 Whole House Transceiver is available with a self-contained antenna (V572TW) or an external antenna for boosting range (V572A). The V572 must be connected to one of the following X10 or X10-compatible two-way modules for interfacing to AC power lines:

- X10's TW523 (or the similar X10 Pro PSC05); bundle available from many different vendors
- Smarthome's PowerLinc II (bundle available from Smarthome)

When used with the TW523/PSC05, the V572 must be connected to an AC power source. PowerLinc II provides power to the V572.

Because of the whip antenna used by the V572A, this unit could also be used as an alternative to repeaters. The vendor claims 150-foot range, but many users have had success at much longer ranges.

Figure B.8 shows a typical installation of the V572A.

---

**VISITING V572A ONLINE**

Learn more about the V572A from the WGL & Associates website: www.wgldesigns.com.

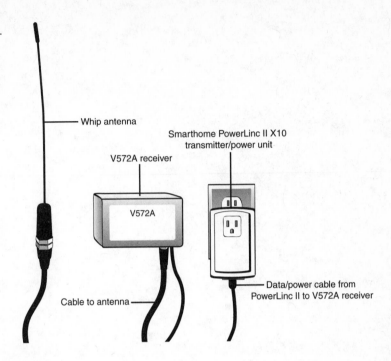

The WGL &
Associates
V572A receiving
power and X10
interfacing from
the Smarthome
PowerLinc II
module.

Whip antenna

Smarthome PowerLinc II X10
transmitter/power unit

V572A receiver

V572A

Data/power cable from
PowerLinc II to V572A receiver

Cable to antenna

## Leviton HCPRF

The Leviton DHC HCPRF plugs directly into an AC outlet. Its integrated two-prong
X10-compatible DHC transceiver is programmed with a transceiver or tabletop controller instead of with code wheels.

It accepts signals from any X10-compatible RF wireless remote, or you can use it with
an X10/IR universal remote such as the companion Leviton DHC HCCUR remote.

**CHECKING OUT LEVITON'S ALL-HOUSE-CODE SOLUTION**
Learn more at Leviton's DHC website: www.leviton.com/sections/prodinfo/decora/sheets/
dhcRemotes.htm.

## X10 CM15A

The X10 CM15A is the hardware component of X10's Active Home Professional
PC–based home automation system (refer to Chapter 11, "Accessing X10 Home
Control via Your Home Computer," for details), providing USB interfacing to your X10
home automation system. However, it can also be used as an all-house-code transceiver without a PC. It works as a direct replacement for X10's RR501 and TM751
transceivers. It also replaces the CM19A PC transceiver used to control wireless X10
cameras. For more information about the CM15A when used with Active Home Pro,
see Chapter 11.

# Index

## E

EagleEye (MS14A) motion sensors, 190

ECS (Event Control System) website, 299

Edit Module dialog (ActiveHome Pro), 279-281

Edit Shutdown Script option (HomeSeer Tools menu), 277

Edit Startup Script option (HomeSeer Tools menu), 277

electrical loads, appliance modules versus lamp modules, 95

electrical outlets, X10 control, 174-176

Elk ESM1 Signal Meter, 341

Enable Programming option (Smarthome Manager SwitchLinc/LampLinc dialog), 263

Enables All Events option (HomeSeer Tools menu), 277

ESM1 Signal Meter (Elk), 341

ethernet, 13-14, 23

ethernet switches, defining, 25

Event Properties dialog (HomeSeer), 272

Event Triggered Action dialog (Smarthome Manager), 257-258

event-triggered actions, creating in Smarthome Manager, 257-258

exterior lighting
  accent lighting, 176-177
  deck lights, X10 control, 167-169
  holiday lighting, 176-177
  incandescent lights, switches for, 168-169
  nonincandescent lights, switches for, 169
  patio lights, X10 control, 167-169
  photocell sensors, 169-172
  porch lights, X10 control, 166-169
  swimming pool lights, X10 control, 167-169
  troubleshooting, 178-179
  unique unit codes, 177

## F

fans, 161. *See also* whole-house fans

feature selection (automation budgeting strategies), 48

File Reports menu (ActiveHome Pro), 293

filters (pool/spa/hot tub), X10 control, 177-178

Find Other Computers option (ActiveHome Pro Tools menu), 293

FireCrack (CM17) serial ports, 248

floodlights, motion detectors, 203-205

fluorescent lights, 23, 87

free trial software websites, 52

freewire lighting control system (Black & Decker)
  Bulb Lamp Receiver, 72-73
  house/unit codes, setting, 97-98
  Indoor Remote, 71-74
  Lamp Receiver, 72
  Messenger Hub, 71-74
  Outdoor Lamp Receiver, 72-73
  website, 74

## G - H

garages, X10 control, 173-175

gateways, 23, 307

General option (HomeSeer Assistant Wizard), 269

Get Device Status option (HomeSeer Tools menu), 277

Get Time option (Smarthome Manager Tools menu), 260

GFCI electrical outlets versus X10 outlets, 176

GG-100 ethernet-based home automation controller (Global Cache) website, 14

glossary (home technology), 21-26

goal selection (automation budgeting strategies), 50

GoToMyPC remote access service website, 317

Grade 1 cable, defining, 22

Grade 2 cable, defining, 22

ground wire, defining, 23

grounded outlets, defining, 23

grounding appliance modules, 174

groups, defining, 23

HAI (Home Automation, Inc.), 299, 326-327

HAL (Home Automated Living), 230
  configuring, 232
  Device Wizard, 233-234
  macro creation, 234
  mode creation, 234
  PCI voice portal modems, 231
  rule creation, 234
  Setup Wizard, 232
  telephone settings, adjusting, 232
  version comparisons, 230
  voice recognition settings, adjusting, 233
  website, 299, 329
  X10 integration, 329
  X10 modules, 233-236

HAL2000, 230, 234

HALbasic, 230, 234

HALdeluxe, 13, 230, 234

Halloween lighting, automating, 54

halogen lights, lighting control systems, 87

Hardware Interfaces dialog (ActiveHome Pro), 289

HCA02 active phase couplers (Leviton), 338-339

hiring contractors (automation strategies), 53

holiday lighting, X10 control, 176-177

Home Automated Technology website, 329

home automation, product compatibility, 14

home automation methods
  all lights on/all units off controllers, 16
  computer controls, 19
  home network controls, 21

# P

## Y - Z